CW00400138

Latin American Economic Crises
Trade and Labour

This is IEA conference volume no. 136

Latin American Economic Crises

Trade and Labour

Edited by

Enrique Bour
Universidad de Buenos Aires, Argentina

Daniel Heymann
Universidad de Buenos Aires, Argentina

and

Fernando Navajas
Universidad de la Plata, Argentina

in association with the
International Economic Association

© International Economic Association 2004

All rights reserved. No reproduction, copy or transmission of this publication may be made without written permission.

No paragraph of this publication may be reproduced, copied or transmitted save with written permission or in accordance with the provisions of the Copyright, Designs and Patents Act 1988, or under the terms of any licence permitting limited copying issued by the Copyright Licensing Agency, 90 Tottenham Court Road, London W1T 4LP.

Any person who does any unauthorized act in relation to this publication may be liable to criminal prosecution and civil claims for damages.

The authors have asserted their rights to be identified as the authors of this work in accordance with the Copyright, Designs and Patents Act 1988.

First published 2004 by
PALGRAVE MACMILLAN
Houndmills, Basingstoke, Hampshire RG21 6XS and
175 Fifth Avenue, New York, N. Y. 10010
Companies and representatives throughout the world

PALGRAVE MACMILLAN is the global academic imprint of the Palgrave Macmillan division of St. Martin's Press, LLC and of Palgrave Macmillan Ltd. Macmillan® is a registered trademark in the United States, United Kingdom and other countries. Palgrave is a registered trademark in the European Union and other countries.

ISBN 0–333–99935–5

This book is printed on paper suitable for recycling and made from fully managed and sustained forest sources.

A catalogue record for this book is available from the British Library.

Library of Congress Cataloging-in-Publication Data
Latin America economic crises : trade and labour / edited by Enrique Bour,
    Daniel Heymann, Fernando Navajas.
        p. cm. – (International Economic Association publications)
    Includes bibliographical references and index.
    ISBN 0–333–99935–5 (cloth)
        1. Latin America–Economic conditions–1982–Congresses. 2. Financial
crises–Latin America–Congresses. 3. Latin America–Commerce–Congresses.
4. Labor market–Latin America–Congresses. 5. Income distribution–Latin
America–Congresses. I. Bour, Enrique. II. Heymann, Daniel. III. Navajas,
Fernando. IV. Series.
HC125.L3437 2003
338.5'42'098–dc21   2003045181

10   9   8   7   6   5   4   3   2   1
13 12 11 10 09 08 07 06 05 04

Printed and bound in Great Britain by
Antony Rowe Ltd, Chippenham and Eastbourne

Contents

The International Economic Association

A non-profit organization with purely scientific aims, the International Economic Association (IEA) was founded in 1950. It is a federation of some 60 national economic associations in all parts of the world. Its basic purpose is the development of economics as an intellectual discipline, recognizing a diversity of problems, systems and values in the world and taking note of methodological diversities.

The IEA has, since its creation, sought to fulfil that purpose by promoting mutual understanding among economists through the organization of scientific meetings and common research programmes, and by means of publications on problems of fundamental as well as current importance. Deriving from its long concern to assure professional contacts between East and West and North and South, the IEA pays special attention to issues of economies in systemic transition and in the course of development. During its 50 years of existence, it has organized more than 100 round-table conferences for specialists on topics ranging from fundamental theories to methods and tools of analysis and major problems of the present-day world. Participation in round tables is at the invitation of a specialist programme committee, but 12 triennial World Congresses have regularly attracted the participation of individual economists from all over the world.

The Association is governed by a Council, comprising representatives of all member associations, and by a 15-member Executive Committee which is elected by the Council. The Executive Committee (1999–2002) at the time of the Buenos Aires Congress was:

President: Professor Robert Solow, USA
Vice-President: Professor Vittorio Corbo, Chile
Treasurer: Professor Jacob Frenkel, Israel
Past President: Professor Jacques Drèze, Belgium
Other members: Professor Bina Agarwal, India
                     Professor Maria Augusztinovics, Hungary
                     Professor Eliana Cardoso, World Bank
                     Professor Gene Grossman, USA
                     Professor Seppo Honkapohja, Finland
                     Professor Valery Makarov, Russia
                     Professor Andreu Mas Colell, Spain

	Professor Mustapha Nabli, Tunisia
	Professor Adrian Pagan, Australia
	Professor Hans Werner Sinn, Germany
	Professor Kotaro Suzumura, Japan
Secretary-General:	Professor Jean-Paul Fitoussi, France
General Editor:	Professor Michael Kaser, UK

Sir Austin Robinson was an active Adviser on the publication of IEA Conference proceedings from 1954 until his final short illness in 1993.

The Association has also been fortunate in having secured many outstanding economists to serve as President:

Gottfried Haberler (1950–53), Howard S. Ellis (1953–56), Erik Lindahl (1956–59), E.A.G. Robinson (1959–62), Ugo Papi (1962–65), Paul A. Samuelson (1965–68), Erik Lundberg (1968–71), Fritz Machlup (1971–74), Edmund Malinvaud (1974–77), Shigeto Tsuru (1977–80), Victor L. Urquidi (1980–83), Kenneth J. Arrow (1983–86), Amartya Sen (1986–89), Anthony B. Atkinson (1989–92), Michael Bruno (1992–95) and Jacques Drèze (1995–99).

The activities of the Association are mainly funded from the subscriptions of members and grants from a number of organizations, including continuing support from UNESCO, through the International Social Science Council. Specific support from the latter was received for the Buenos Aires Congress under its Project R4/CAR.

Preface and Acknowledgements

The Twelfth World Congress of the International Economic Association (IEA) was held in Buenos Aires on 23–27 August 1999, at the invitation of the Asociación Argentina de Economa Política (AAEP). The IEA is deeply grateful to the AAEP for its willingness to host the congress, and above all for superbly handling the local arrangements. The 1,260 registered participants undoubtedly feel equally grateful.

The congress was dedicated to the memory of the late Michael Bruno, President of the IEA 1992–95, as a tribute to his valuable contributions to economics, and in particular to the IEA.

The Organizing Committee consisted of Enrique Bour, president, Rolf Mantel, vice-president, Victor Beker, executive secretary, Marcela Cristini, Maria Echart, Marcos Gallacher and Javier Ortiz. It is very sad that Rolf Mantel died prematurely in February 1999; he had been a productive researcher and an influential member of the Latin American scientific community. He was an exceptionally fine person. The IEA joins Mrs Mantel and Rolf's numerous friends in treasuring his memory.

Special thanks go to Enrique Bour, former AAEP President, who shouldered much responsibility as president of the Organising Committee. He showed exceptional dedication, ability and congeniality.

Financial support towards the local organization came first from Banco Central de la República Argentina, soon complemented by Banco de la Nacíon Argentina, Banco de la Provincia de Buenos Aires, Banco Hipotecario, Ministerio de Relaciones Exteriores, Comercio Internacional y Culto, Secretaría de Industria, Comercio y Miniera and Secretaría de Programacíon Económica y Regional. Their support is gratefully acknowledged.

The logistics of the congress were handled with competence by the staff of María Graziani y Asociados of Buenos Aires, and by IEA administrative assistants Marie David and Véronique de Labarre.

The scientific programme included two series of invited lectures, one on 'Macroeconomics' organized by Jacques Drèze (Université Catholique de Louvain) and one on 'Inequality' organized by Richard Freeman (Harvard University and London School of Economics). The rest of the programme comprised 310 contributed papers, selected from a still larger number of submissions by a 30-member Programme Committee ably and diligently chaired by David de la Croix (Université Catholique de Louvain). From these, 15 important papers dealing with Latin American issues constitute the present volume, edited by Enrique Bour, Daniel Heymann and Fernando Navajas. A major theme of this volume is the exploration of the causes of crises, and the alternative solutions adopted by different Latin American countries. The chapters dealing with Argentina provide an illuminating backdrop to the 2001 financial crisis and help to explain the difficulty of finding a solution that meets the aspirations both of the Argentine people and international institutions. The fifteen chapters are arranged in three Parts: Macroeconomic crises; Trade and Trade Agreements; and Labour and Income Distribution. Maureen Hadfield and Michael Kaser supervised the editorial process. The IEA expresses its gratitude to all participants in their efforts for both programme and publication.

Some hundred authors of invited papers, in particular authors from emerging countries, received travel grants to Buenos Aires. These grants were funded by the World Bank, the World Bank Institute, the Inter-American Development Bank, the Asian Development Bank and the European Investment Bank. Their support is gratefully acknowledged.

The main credit for the success of the congress goes to the authors of invited lectures and contributed papers. They supplied a rich intellectual material, incompletely but representatively covered in these three volumes.

List of Contributors

Professor Enrique Bour, Fundación de Investigaciones Económicas Latino Americanas (FIEL) and Universidad de Buenos Aires, Argentina.

Dr Guillermo A. Calvo, Inter-American Development Bank, Washington and University of Maryland, USA.

Professor Alessandro Cigno, Università di Firenze, Florence, Italy.

Professor Vittorio Corbo, Pontifica Universidad Católica de Chile, Santiago, Chile and Governor, Central Bank of Chile.

Professor Alfonso Ferreira, Universidade Federal de Minais Gerais and Centro de Pesquisa em Economía, Belo Horizonte, Brazil.

Professor Marcel Fratzscher, European Central Bank, Frankfurt am Main, Germany.

Dr Alicia García–Herrero, Banco Central de España, Madrid, Spain.

Professor Koichi Hamada, Yale University, New Haven, Connecticut, USA.

Professor Daniel Heymann, Universidad de Buenos Aires and La Plata, Argentina.

Professor Talan İşcan, Dalhousie University, Halifax, Nova Scotia, Canada.

Professor Adriana Kugler, Universitat Pompeu Fabra, Barcelona, Spain.

Professor Luis Miotti, Université de Paris 13, Paris, France.

Proessor Fernando Navajas, Fundación de Investigaciones Económicas Latino Americanas (FIEL), Buenos Aires and Universitá de la Plata, Argentina.

Dr Graciela Pinal, Universidad Nacional di Salta, Salta, Argentina.

Professor Carlos Quenan, CREDAL, Université de Paris 3, Paris, France.

Professor Ranjan Ray, University of Tasmania, Hobart, Australia.

Professor Hernán Rincón, Banco de la República, Bogotá, Colombia.

Professor Andreu Sansó, Universitat de Barcelona, Spain.

Professor T. N. Srinivasan, Yale University. New Haven, Connecticut, USA.

Professor Victor Urquidi, El Colegio di México, Mexico City.

Professor Carlos Winograd, Delta-Ens and Université de Paris-Evry, Paris, France.

Abbreviations and Acronyms

AA	absorption approach
ADF	augmented Dickey–Fuller (test)
ADM	anti-dumping measure
ALADI	Latin American Integration Association
BIS	Bank for International Settlements
BRM	Bickerdike, Robinson, Metzler (model)
CA	current account
CARICOM	Caribbean Community and Common Market
CARIFTA	Caribbean Free Trade Area
CBP	Central Bank of Paraguay
CBRA	Central Bank of Republica Argentina
CBV	Central Bank of Venezuela
CPI	consumer price index
CTP-Data	Comparative Trade Performances Data Base
DOTS	Direction of Trade Statistics
DP	Dickey and Pantula (procedure)
DSM	dispute settlement mechanism
ECLAC	UN Economic Commission for Latin America and the Caribbean (CEPAL in Spanish)
EMBI	emerging markets bonds index
ERP	effective rates of protection
ESI	economies of scale–intensive (goods)
EU	European Union
FOGADE	Deposit Guarantee Fund (Venezuela)
FIEL	Fundación de Investigaciones Económicas Latinoamericanas
GATT	General Agreement on Tariffs and Trade
GDP	gross domestic product
GSP	generalized system of preferences
HES	household expenditure survey
HIID	Harvard Institute of International Development
HOS	Hecksher–Ohlin–Samuelson
IDB	Inter-American Development Bank
IFS	*International Financial Statistics*
i.i.d.	independently and identically distributed
ILO	International Labour Organization

IMF	International Monetary Fund
INDEC	Instituto Nacional de Estadística y Censos (National Institute of Statistics and the Census)
INEGI	Instituto Nacional de Estadística, Geografía y Informatíca (Mexico)
ISS	import substituting strategies
LAFTA	Latin American Free Trade Area
LDC	less-developed countries
LLR	lender of last resort
LSMS	Living Standards Measurement Study
MA	monetary approach
Mercosur	South American Regional Organization
MFN	most-favoured nation
MFT	more-favourable treatment
ML	Marshall–Lerner
MTN	multilateral trade negotiations
NSC	no-shirking condition (Colombia)
NAFTA	North American Free Trade Agreement
NHS	National Household Survey (Colombia)
OECD	Organisation for Economic Co-operation and Development
PLSS	Peru Living Standards Measurement Survey
PTA	preferential trading agreement
R&D	research and development
RCA	revealed comparative advantage
RER	real exchange rate
REER	real effective exchange rate
ROME	Research Opportunity in Mathematics and Economics
ROW	rest of the world
SP	Schmidt–Phillips (test)
TL	Trade liberalization
TRIMS	trade-related investment measures
TRIPS	trade-related (aspects of) intellectual property rights
UNCTAD	United Nations Conference on Trade and Development
UR	Uruguay Round
WIPO	World Intellectual Property Organization
WTO	World Trade Organization

Introduction

Enrique Bour, Daniel Heymann and Fernando Navajas

This volume on Latin America focuses on studies of economic crises during the 1990s. While the authors completed their research before the 2001 crisis in Argentina, the analyses of macroeconomic issues provide an insight into how economies can break down and even degenerate into chaotic behaviour, while the chapters on Argentina help to provide an understanding of recent events there.

Macroeconomic crises

The five chapters in Part I concentrate on financial crises. Latin American economies have long experience of sudden breakdowns of currency pegs, widespread bank failures or abrupt declines in spending and output. Interest in studying crisis episodes surged recently as new crises generated new analytical problems for study. The authors use different approaches to analyse recent Latin American and Asian experience, and draw conclusions relevant to the management of large macroeconomic disturbances.

Koichi Hamada, in Chapter 1, first examines Asian crises and associates crisis events with misjudgments in economic calculations. He observes that in high-saving, high-investment Asian economies, a rapid growth generated highly optimistic expectations on the part of local agents and foreign lenders, and that 'disillusionment triggered the crisis in these overconfident economies'. Significantly, Hamada's argument does not depend on 'bad' current indicators before a crisis, but only on the perception of future prospects being revised downwards. Hamada cites real-estate investment in Asian cities based on unrealistic forecasts. He argues that the belief by market participants that they have been overoptimistic can trigger a sudden fall in the demand for a country's assets. Turning to Latin America, Hamada observes that, while in Asia most of the foreign debt was owed by the private sector, in Latin America it was owed by governments, and he highlights weaknesses in fiscal and monetary policies, which could precipitate a crisis.

Vittorio Corbo in Chapter 2 presents a broad overview of the response of Latin American economies to the shocks that hit the region in the late 1990s. Corbo identifies several disturbances which resulted in a sharp drop in export prices and tighter conditions of access to foreign financing. He argues that the policy reforms undertaken by many countries in the 1990s, including measures such as strengthening bank regulations after the 1994–5 crisis, helped these economies deal with shocks. They were also able to avoid imposing trade restrictions or expanding domestic demand to compensate for external shocks. His data show that in 1999, growth in the region had virtually stopped; indeed, growth in several countries (including Chile after over a decade of growth) contracted.

Corbo concentrates on monetary and exchange-rate systems. He discusses inflation targeting, which several countries defined as their preferred monetary framework, pointing out potential benefits and possible problems such as output or exchange-rate volatility. In discussing exchange-rate regimes, the advantages of floating are stressed, and he notes that the countries that suffered severe crises in the 1990s all operated some form of fixed exchange rate. However, Corbo observes that in practice 'strong path dependence is the rule' in the choice of system, given that the trade-offs would have different outcomes depending on past economic history.

In her study of three Latin American banking crises, Alicia García-Herrero (Chapter 3) suggests that the macroeconomic consequences of a crisis and the range of policy options may be influenced by features of the financial sector and the nature of the problems. García-Herrero identifies distortions in the behaviour of banks in a system without adequate supervision as a major cause of the Paraguay crisis. In Venezuela, inadequate regulation and control and a weak oil market caused macroeconomic tensions and a distrust of government policies. In Argentina, the author identifies the origin of the crisis in 1997 in the provincial banking sector. The situation was exacerbated by the effects of the Mexican shock on an economy with persistent current-account deficits and a worsening fiscal situation.

The remaining two chapters in this section are devoted to models of crises. In Chapter 4, Marcel Fratzscher presents a model of financial crises. He considers the hypothesis that currency crises result from self-fulfilling expectations driven by an external event. He proposes a model with multiple equilibria which do not result from government incentives (as in the case where, for example, expectations of a currency devaluation lead to high interest rates on debt, and induce the authorities to devalue rather than raise taxes). In Fratzscher's argument, initial government reserves are fixed, and fully available to defend a peg. The demand for foreign currencies originates from different sources: producers who buy imports and pay debt service; foreign creditors who choose whether to refinance or recall the debt. Then there is a set of speculators with limited resources, who attack the currency when they anticipate a devaluation. Multiple equilibria arise if the 'fundamental demand' for foreign currencies is such that reserves will not be exhausted when creditors refinance and speculators do not attack, but do not sustain a credit stop and/or a move by speculators.

The author uses regime-switching models to analyse empirically the transmission of the crises in Mexico (1994) and Thailand (1997). Fratzscher remarks that the assumption that changes in the intercept of a regression represent shifts due to beliefs unrelated to fundamentals ignores the possibility that those changes represent fundamentals unaccounted for, or expectations about fundamentals. In order to include variables that he interprets specifically as 'sunspots', the author uses dummies for crises occurring in other economies. This model of exchange-market pressure considers a number of fundamental explanatory variables (such as foreign debt and capital-flow indicators, trade balances, real exchange rates, reserves, credit expansion and the budget deficit). Fratzscher observes that in most cases a specification with three regimes is appropriate. He also finds that crisis dummies are significant, and argues that this provides evidence for sunspot phenomena, although contagion effects may arise from a variety of sources.

Guillermo Calvo's analysis (Chapter 5) is inspired by the contagion effects of the Russian crisis, which had strong repercussions in Latin America. The basic assumption is that prospective asset-holders face large fixed costs (relative to the funds they are prepared to invest in) in obtaining knowledge about the economy whose debt they consider buying. The argument does not specify if the costs result from a non-zero price of raw data, or from difficulties in interpreting information, which would imply that the 'model of the economy' is subject to learning. Calvo notes that fixed costs create economies of scale, and agents will be divided into two groups: those who will pay to be 'informed', and those who base decisions on the market price, and the inferences drawn from observing the actions of the informed investors.

Calvo considers the case where the demand for a country's assets by the informed group depends on the conditions of that economy and factors unrelated to those conditions (such as the liquidity position of the agents). The model assumes that the idiosyncratic factors are common to all informed agents (although the consequences of lifting that assumption are discussed). The 'non-informed' face a signal-extraction problem, and may react strongly to the behaviour of the influential segment of investors when there are no 'fundamental reasons' to do so. Since the uninformed agents will tend to follow more closely the actions of the informed the smaller the variance of the idiosyncratic factors, episodes with large contagion effects of this type would be relatively infrequent. However, Calvo argues that the resulting shocks may have a strong impact on the borrowing economy, especially if these are amplified by a fall in the productivity of capital as a consequence of the sudden contraction of international credit.

These chapters – a sample of a large and growing literature on crisis economics – indicate an active search for better analytical and practical solutions. This implies that analysts are engaged in learning about the origins and mechanisms of crises and in searching for appropriate policies to reduce their occurrence, and limit adverse macroeconomic consequences. It seems natural to assume that private agents have also been trying to learn from large disturbances. This observation is relevant to any discussion of how to represent expectations in economic models of those events.

Trade and trade agreements

In Chapter 6, T. N. Srinivasan argues strongly for free trade, and criticizes several points of the theory of international trade negotiations. Srinivasan argues against propositions that viewed a managed international market and discriminatory trade arrangements as a good way to close the 'foreign exchange gap' at GATT discussions. He considers that the attitudes of developing countries were driven by 'import-substitution ideology', which 'triply hurt them': first, through the costs of import substitution strategies; second, by allowing developed countries to get away with their own GATT-inconsistent barriers; and, third, by allowing industrialized countries to keep higher than average 'most-favoured-nation' tariffs on goods of export interest to developing countries. He concludes that had these countries adopted an outward-oriented development strategy, they could have achieved 'faster and better growth'.

From the perspective of developing countries, Srinivasan proposes a new agenda for the next round of trade negotiations under which intellectual property and related concerns would be negotiated at the World Intellectual Property Organization, not the World Trade Organization. The author argues for rapid negotiation on the movement of natural persons, the elimination of export subsidies by developed nations, and the removal of anti-dumping measures from the arsenal of permitted trade-policy instruments. Srinivasan also proposes the elimination of practices such as peaks in tariffs and the escalation in tariffs by stages, which restrict the exports of developing countries. The author suggests replacing GATT Article XXIV by extending preferences granted to a partner of a preferential trade agreement to all members of the World Trade Organization within a specified period. The proposals presented by Srinivasan also include abstaining from negotiating a multilateral agreement on investment for the present, and correcting flaws in the Dispute Settlement Mechanism.

Victor Urquidi (Chapter 7) disputes the notion that the whole of Latin America should seek economic integration. In a discussion that reviews the history of integration projects, he sees full economic integration between highly dissimilar countries as unrealistic in today's globalized economy. Instead, he recommends limited sub-regional agreements. Pointing to the trade-creation role of investment, he foresees clusters of suppliers emerging through sub-regional integration. Urquidi expects the development of horizontal integration more similar to existing arrangements among industries in industrialized countries. To enable the lesser economies to acquire the necessary skills, he recognizes the need for substantial long-term financing and technological and management support. This would constitute a new role for Mercosur and other international entities.

In Chapter 8, major shifts in the composition of external trade are analysed by Miotti, Quenan and Winograd with reference to Argentina and Mercosur. They reexamine the theories of comparative advantage, technological development and the dynamics of international markets, highlighting the pattern of capital goods, energy and labour. They view these theories as complementary. They identify successive phases of protection and trade liberalization, separated by crises which triggered regime shifts. The authors conclude that trade liberalization is not always accompanied by rapid export growth, as suggested by simple economic theory.

Conventional wisdom argues that nominal devaluations entail an improvement in the trade balance. Rincón (Chapter 9) tested this proposition for Colombia, using a model that incorporates the effects of income and money. He found that the behaviour of the exchange rate and the trade balance conforms to the traditional analysis of authors Bickerdike, Robinson, Metzler, Marshall and Lerner under the 'small-country' hypothesis. The econometric procedure is based on the analysis of multivariate cointegrated systems developed by Johansen and expanded by Johansen and Juselius. One conclusion is that besides varying with the exchange rate, the trade balance responds to decreases in the money stock and increases in income.

Although the experience of nominal devaluations has certainly been traumatic in Latin America, Talan İşcan, in Chapter 10, explores the potential benefits of these policy measures. A key parameter of trade models is the elasticity of substitution between the consumption of tradable and non-tradable goods. He finds that the reallocation of factors between sectors has been one of the more important consequences of real devaluations in Mexico. Using cross-section and time series for Mexico, the extent to which the real exchange rates and the terms of trade have been conducive to reallocation in the Mexican production sector are examined and a pattern of diverse behaviour is revealed. However, the analysis finds significant sectoral output effects of terms-of-trade shocks and real-exchange movements. Improvements in Mexican terms of trade tend to be associated with a relative expansion in the output of non-traded goods, while depreciation of the Mexican peso correlates with contractions in that sector. The author concludes that, in Mexico, the elasticity of substitution in consumption between traded and non-traded goods seems to be lower than 1. As to the effects of real exchange-rate movements, Iscan notes that the response of a dynamic output regression model using a random coefficient regression technique suggests that relative price effects on sectoral output were highly significant. The short-run contractionary effects of currency devaluations appeared to be temporary. The author concludes that devaluations in Mexico increased the trade balance by changing relative prices.

Afonso Ferreira and Andreu Sansó (Chapter 11) produce evidence that exchange-rate variations were not substantially reflected in the selling prices of Brazilian exported goods, and argue that this limited the success of the exchange-rate policy. They analyse the 'exchange pass-through' coefficient in the equation of external prices of Brazilian manufactured goods; that is, the coefficient which relates a variation of the exchange rate to a variation of the foreign currency price. They calculate its range between 10 per cent and 27 per cent. They argue that the reason for this relatively small coefficient is that to preserve market share, exporters maintain prices in foreign currencies when exchange rates are perceived as transitory. They suggest that the coefficient depends on the behaviour of the exchange rate itself, with periods of exchange-rate instability being reflected in low pass-through coefficients. More generally, their results validate the 'small country' hypothesis for Brazil, implying that in times of domestic currency appreciation, exporters' profit margins tend to be squeezed, possibly to the point of eliminating all incentive to sell abroad.

Employment and income distribution

The final section deals with labour issues and income distribution. These topics have been at the top of the policy and research agenda during the 1990s, particularly in Latin America. Deregulation of domestic markets, trade liberalization, large-scale privatizations and labour-market reforms are major examples of policies which changed the configuration and the behaviour of Latin American economies. However, with few exceptions, well-designed policies to deal with social problems have lagged behind. The analysis of changes in employment and income distribution and the evaluation of relevant policies are ongoing processes. The chapters by Adriana Kugler and Fernando Navajas discuss matters relating to structural reform and macro-policy. Those by Ranjan Ray and Alessandro Cigno and Graciela Pinal look, respectively, at household allocation and labour participation, and the impact on children.

Chapter 12 by Adriana Kugler contributes to the literature on job security regulations on labour-market performance. She studies empirically the effects of a major Colombian labour reform. The relaxation of job security regulations often recommended in Latin America and elsewhere to improve the quality of employment and reduce unemployment has been controversial. The theoretical analysis of the net effects of hiring and firing on employment and unemployment during the 1990s produced ambiguous qualitative results, which were not resolved by empirical testing. Kugler tries to improve on previous testing methods by avoiding the selection-bias problems that may have influenced the econometric results of pooled time-series and cross-section data models. She develops a model to explain how job security provisions induce selection bias and tackles the compositional changes between formal and informal workers – a relevant dimension in Latin American economies – on grouping estimates. The empirical testing focuses on the Colombian Labour-market Reform Act of 1990 using National Household Survey data. The results show that after controlling for compositional change, the relaxation of job security regulations appear to contribute to reducing unemployment. Kugler concludes that labour reform in Colombia induced efficiency gains through greater mobility, and welfare gains from lower unemployment and the formalization of the economy.

In Latin America, Argentina was one of the more prominent economic reformers during the 1990s. As a result, major changes took place in the organization of economic activities and government participation in public services. Fernando Navajas (Chapter 13) extends the methodology used by Newbery for Hungary and the UK, to evaluate the distributional effects of relative price changes after a decade of structural reform. The model is developed from the theory and measurement of marginal tax reform, and relies on the concept of the distributional characteristics of goods. Using data from household expenditure surveys and the price movements of detailed items in the consumer price index, the chapter evaluates the overall welfare change for different degrees of inequality-aversion. It also attempts to decompose the causes of the observed aggregate changes in welfare. The main finding is that, in Argentina, reforms induced relative price changes leading to social welfare gains and positive distributional effects. This is explained by the reduction in the relative price of goods with high distributional characteristics such as clothing, food, durable goods and to a lesser degree some public services. Thus, despite an increase in income inequality, arising from higher unemployment or larger wage dispersion, price changes associated with reforms did not themselves harm the poor. Positive distributional impacts can be attributed to measures such as trade reform and retail competition. Results were less clear for privatizations, because of increases in public-sector prices in recent years. However, other aspects of the distributional effects of privatization, such as changes in the access of the poor to public infrastructure services, were positive.

In Chapter 14, Alessandro Cigno and Graciela Pinal extend an earlier model by Cigno on the interaction between child mortality and fertility decisions, to calculate the effects of the prices of child-specific goods. In this model, household allocation under uncertainty about children's survival jointly determine fertility and infant mortality. According to their hypothesis of endogenous survival probability, parents know the effects of their resource-spending and fertility decisions on child survival probabilities, and react to changes in the observed aggregate survival rate on which they base their expectations. The marginal benefits of resources spent on children, as perceived by their parents, are increased by public spending programmes that raise the aggregate survival rate, and by any fall in the price of child-specific goods. Thus, complementarity between public and private spending reinforces the social productivity of public expenditure in sanitation, preventive medicine and subsidies to child-specific goods. The authors test the positive implications of the model on time-series data collected from the province of Salta, in northern Argentina, during the last quarter of the twentieth century. They find that fertility decisions are negatively affected by the observed survival rate and positively affected by the price of child-specific goods in a way consistent with the predictions of their model.

The interaction of poverty and child labour has generated much interest in research and policy-oriented debate. In particular, given the undesirable consequences of child labour, child labour and the identification of factors that affect child employment have become an area of study. A common theme in the development literature, although it seems to apply specifically to rural areas, is the hypothesis that child-labour participation rises in response to temporary income short-falls in the presence of credit rationing. In more general terms, this analysis looks for links between household income, poverty and child labour. Empirical testing of these factors has increased in recent years.

In the final chapter, Ranjan Ray contributes to this study using the Peru Living Standards Measurement Survey for 1994, obtained from the World Bank Living Standards Measurement Study. Using probit and tobit estimation procedures, he tests the determinants of child-labour participation and child-labour hours, taking into account the interaction with participation in schooling, and the effects of adult male and female wages. In contrast to findings for other developing economies, such as Pakistan, the main result is that the case of Peru does not support any relation between poverty and child labour, but suggests an interaction with school provision. The effects of male and female wages on child-labour participation differ widely, but the gender channel of interaction and the magnitude of the coefficients (which are different from those obtained for Ghana) lead to ambivalent conclusions.

Part I
Macroeconomic Crises

1

A Comparison of Currency Crises Between Asia and Latin America

*Koichi Hamada**

* I am indebted to Yoshiko Inoue for assistance under the ROME (Research Opportunity in Mathematics and Economics) project at Yale and to Carlyn Beaulin for improving the English.

Within a month of inviting me to contribute to the XIIth IEA Congress Rolf Mantel departed from us forever. In the early 1960s when I came to Yale from Japan, I met many impressive graduate students. Yet Rolf's was the most brilliant, analytical mind. He was truly a star in the econometric class of John Hooper and the mathematical economics class of Herbert Scarf. Intellectually challenging problems presented no difficulty for Rolf. Ann Maria, his gracious and brilliant wife, was also in our class, and we all admired his talents, and his calm, thoughtful attitude towards economics. In his letter of invitation, Rolf referred to the problem of endogenous rates of time preference – a topic in which I also am interested. We promised, in vain, to discuss the question in Buenos Aires. The question of the variable time preference for developing nations indicated the intersection of his deep analytical insight of this non-concave optimization problem on the one hand, and his human concern with people in developing nations who struggle to save for the future on the other. May his soul rest in peace!

1 Introduction

To quote Alexander Pope, 'To err is human' and economic calculations are no exception. Economic agents try to optimize, but due to imperfect and incomplete information and limited processing capacity, their activities are subject to error. Since market participants often regard the market as divine, they tend to expect the market to forgive their errors.

At best, the market only corrects errors, although not instantaneously. And correction is painful.

Before the collapse of a national currency, a string of errors will have been committed both by lenders and borrowers – at least two parties need to agree to a potentially delinquent loan. The market is supposed to correct errors by giving economic agents appropriate signals (Hayek, 1949), but more often sustains incorrect beliefs and magnifies errors, as observed in financial and currency market bubbles. When the market corrects such errors, the bubble collapses, currencies are revalued, leading as shown by Radelet and Sachs (1998) to a reversal of fund flows and the difficult process of retrieval, readjustment and re-construction. There are numerous studies of the causes of financial collapse, so I shall concentrate on the adjustment process.

My analytical framework is the 'portfolio' or 'assets' approach to the balance of payments. Introduced by Kouri (1976), Branson and Henderson (1985) and others, this took account of imperfect substi-tutability of international assets, and incorporated country risk into the analysis. It was criticized because it failed to fully explain exchange-rate movements and the degree of effectiveness of sterilized interventions. I maintain that this approach is a proper explanatory tool of currency crises, the recovery process and the evaluation of the effects of alternative coping strategies.

What the portfolio approach captures is the interaction between the adjustment in the flow dimension and the stock (assets) dimension. For example, the flow dimension is captured by current-account bal-ances and government budgets, whereas the stock dimension is cap-tured by asset-holding behaviour and the movement between foreign and domestic-held stocks. When the International Monetary Fund (IMF) recommends budget tightening, it adjusts the flow dimension; when it recommends raising interest rates, it adjusts the stock dimen-sion. This distinction is often crucial.

In 1995, the IMF *World Economic Outlook*, as shown in Table 1.1, compared Asian and Latin American performance before and after the Asian currency crisis. Asian countries were generally higher saving, their government budgets more balanced, and their monetary authori-ties more disciplined. Real gross domestic product (GDP) growth rates were higher in Asia and inflation rates lower. Indeed, these high-saving/high-investment economies flourished so well that the pitfalls were hidden. Fuelled by overoptimistic expectations, Asian countries were vulnerable to any change in expectations, and disillusionment triggered the crisis in overconfident Asian economies. The simple ana-

Table 1.1 Macroeconomic indicators for selected developing countries
(per cent of GDP)

	Asia		Latin America	
	1983–89	1990–94	1983–89	1990–94
Real GDP	6.2	5.5	3.1	3.5
Consumer prices	6.9	8.4	193.7	222.5
Money growth	20.0	18.1	200.5	258.1
Private consumption	62.8	58.5	64.4	68.0
Private saving	16.8	22.4	18.6	13.5
Fiscal balance	−4.8	−2.8	−5.6	0.1
Current account balance	−1.9	−2.7	−0.9	−2.4
Real effective exchange rate	−6.3	−3.0	0.8	4.3
Total net capital inflow	2.0	4.1	−1.7	1.4
Change in reserves	0.4	1.9	0.3	1.2
Total saving	24.0	28.0	19.2	18.6
Total investment	25.9	30.7	20.1	20.0

Notes: Asia includes India, Indonesia, Korea, Malaysia, the Philippines, Thailand; Latin America includes Argentina, Brazil, Chile, Colombia, Mexico, Peru.
Source: IMF *World Economic Outlook* (various issues).

lytical framework I propose provides relevant coordinates to events and permits comparison between countries.

2 Asian growth and setbacks

In most crisis countries the balance on current account was a source of worry, that is, the flow dimension was a concern. Many countries – Malaysia, Korea and Thailand – suffered large deficits, and in some countries, Thailand and Korea but not Indonesia, the government deficit was a major concern. At a time of crisis, a sudden huge reversal of capital flows (Radelet and Sachs, 1998) occurs. This can be interpreted as a shift of portfolio preference from assets denominated in local currency to assets denominated in US$. Thus, in considering the economic mechanism of a currency crisis, we must consider both the flow and the stock aspect. As the driving force of financial crises, it is probable that the dislocation of stock demand plays a direct and more immediate role than the erosion of flows. For example, Indonesia's current account deficit was less serious than either Malaysia's or Thailand's, but its currency depreciation was greatest. whereas the Philippines with a large current account deficit escaped severe crisis.[1] What made Indonesia's crisis nearly catastrophic was the sudden shift in asset preferences ignited by a loss of confidence in political and economic stability.

3 The portfolio approach to exchange-rate depreciation

There has been wide discussion of the relationship between stock equilibrium and flow equilibrium. The flow relationship describes economic activity during a given period of variables such as savings, GDP and the balance of payments.[2] These flow variables affect the speed of asset accumulation in a national economy and its international credit and debt position, and the flow-dimension variables determine the speed of change in the stock variables. The imbalances in government current-account deficits are imbalances in the flow dimension. On the other hand, the asset balance is the equilibrium in stocks, that is, outstanding assets, denominated in different currencies. Thus the IMF recommendation to balance the government budget or the current account balance was an attempt to remedy the flow side of the problem, while the recommendation to adjust the asset market by raising interest rates was an attempt to remedy the stock side of the problem.

Whatever the causes, the common phenomenon is a sudden dislocation of asset preference, and Radelet and Sachs (1998) refer to the sudden, huge reversal of capital flows. As a phenomenon, the stock rather than the flow aspect is the most important. Regardless of whether or not disequilibria existed in the flow market, the sudden dislocation of asset demands was the *sine qua non* of the Asian currency crisis, and the flow imbalances were primarily important because of the linkages to stock problems.

This conceptual framework is basically the portfolio (asset) approach to the determination of exchange rates discussed in Kouri (1970). Branson and Henderson (1984), for example, study the dynamics of the exchange rate resulting from a stabilizing flow equation and a destabilizing stock equation. Alternative versions exist for the formulation of the portfolio approach to exchange-rate determination. The model varies depending on alternative assumptions, for example whether agents have rational expectations, whether residents have an own-currency bias in asset choice, or whether agents in one country hold another country's assets in a cross-country way. My model using Indonesian rupiah is similar to Kouri (1979).

Assume that Indonesians hold only one asset denominated in rupiah, but that residents in the rest of the world hold assets in both rupiah and US$. This is a simplifying assumption, but the qualitative nature of the results will hold even if Indonesians held US$-denominated assets, provided each nation has a national-currency bias. The national-currency preference implies that, other things being equal, Indonesians would hold a higher proportion of their portfolio in rupiah.

Let us denote the exchange rate in rupiah in terms of US$ as e, in such a way that $e = 1/8,000$, meaning that one rupiah is worth US$1/8,000 (note that this is the reverse of the usual expression of the exchange rate as US$ in terms of rupiah – 8,000 rupiah = US$1). Let the rest of the world's total assets be Z rupiah. Then Indonesia's balance of payments will be a function of the exchange rate e and the level of indebtedness Z. In terms of the increase in Z, that is, the negative of the balance of payments of Indonesia, one can obtain:

$$dZ/dt = f(Z,e) \tag{1}$$

where $f_z < 0$ and $f_e > 0$

The portfolio-balance equation expresses the relationship that the rest of the world holds a higher proportion of the Indonesian asset in their portfolio when the expected rate of appreciation of the value of the Indonesian currency is higher than other currencies. That is, denoting the expectation by operator E,

$$(eZ)/(W + eZ) = g(\pi), \text{ where } \pi = E[(de/dt)/e], \text{ and } g'(\pi) > 0 \tag{2}$$

If we impose the assumption of rational expectations such that $E[(de/dt)/e] = \pi = de/dt)/e$, we obtain from equation (2) the following:

$$de/dt = h(Z, e) \tag{3}$$

where $h_z > 0$, $h_e > 0$

Strictly speaking, the portfolio balance is meaningful for the nominal exchange rate e, and the current account balance is meaningful for the real exchange rate, because the current account is considered to respond to the real exchange rate. This aspect is not considered further.

Figure 1.1 shows the portfolio approach to the exchange rate. The phase diagram of simultaneous equations (1) and (3) is drawn as *CC* and *PP*. *CC* shows the combination of e and Z that keeps the Indonesian current account in balance, or maintains the value of Indonesian assets held by the rest of the world constant. *PP* indicates

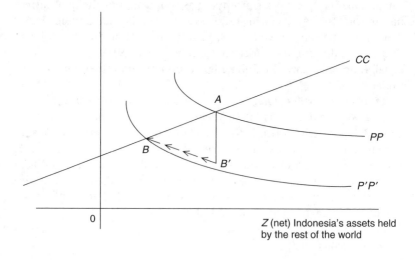

Figure 1.1 The portfolio approach to the exchange rate

the combination of *e* and *Z* that keeps the portfolio balance of the rest of the world. This is an intrinsically *unstable* relationship, so that *e* increases above *PP* and decreases below. The combination of these two balances creates a phase diagram around the intersection of *CC* and *PP* at point *A* – the well-known saddle-point diagram. Under changes in exogenous factors, exchange rate *e* jumps to the saddle-stable path and the balance of payments adjusts gradually to a new equilibrium.

Before the crisis, the Indonesian economy appeared so bright that Indonesians borrowed from abroad to invest and lenders concurred with this view. The rest of the world was willing to hold much of the Indonesian debt; the country risk was considered small. Thus portfolio balance *PP* was located to the right. Equilibrium was at a point such as *A*, where Indonesian debt was large and the value of the rupiah high. Suddenly, the asset demand for assets in rupiah declined precipitously; the new equilibrium shifted to a point such as *B*. Since *Z* moves only slowly, only *e* jumped, the path of variables took the trajectory from *A* through *B'* to *B*. This situation occurred in many countries including Thailand and South Korea.

The model predicts, first, the sudden overshooting depreciation of the Asian currency resulting from the dislocation of demand for the currency, and, second, the gradual current account recovery of the

Asian country. The predictive element of this model applies surprisingly well to the Asian experience, as well, perhaps, as to that of Latin American countries. Figure 1.2 shows the change in exchange rates after the dislocation of currency demand, and the ensuing slow adjustment of current accounts. In most countries (except Mexico) in Figure 1.2 one can detect jumps in exchange rates, and the reversal of the current account from deficit to surplus.

Technically, this model of stock–flow interactions could be analysed more rigorously. Merton (1969) and Samuelson (1969) showed that under the specification of constant relative risk-aversion utility, the consumption decision in the flow dimension and the wealth-holding decision in the stock dimension can be analysed separately. Using this formulation, Branson and Henderson (1985, equation 3.19, p. 787) derived the optimal wealth composition of foreign currency in the international portfolio. The portfolio depends on the deviation from the interest parity, the variance of the exchange rate, and the covariance between the future exchange rate and the future price level. This last term reflects the fact that the exchange rate works as the insurance against inflation.

We can interpret this as follows. When market participants suddenly realize that they have been overoptimistic about a country's future income, then the flow relation, equation (1), that is *CC* in Figure 1.1, shifts to the left because participants no longer regard borrowing as reasonable; the stock relation, equation (3), that is *PP* in Figure 1.1, shifts drastically downward. The analysis also describes the dramatic fall in the exchange rate.

This model analyses a floating exchange-rate regime where the exchange rate is freely determined, a regime often recommended by the IMF to ailing nations. While it might implicitly have endorsed fixed exchange rates before the onset of the crisis, in Asia after the crisis it recommended a flexible exchange-rate regime with fiscal and monetary austerity to induce a shift in the national economy, *CC* and *PP* above. The economy should return to a new, less-extravagant, equilibrium position. In any economy, residents would experience hardship from this sudden change in the exchange rate and the adjustment process.

It is well-known that the impossible trilogy – a fixed exchange rate, free capital mobility and an autonomous monetary policy – cannot be sustained. The flexible exchange-rate regime abandons the fixed exchange rate. However, this is not the only possible regime. Alternatives are: the 'capital-control regime' and the 'currency-board

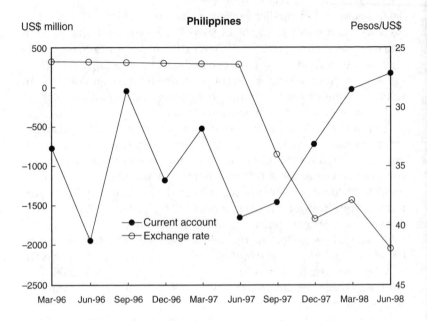

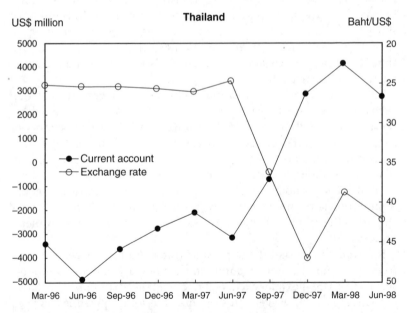

Figure 1.2 Exchange rate movements after dislocation
Source: Author's calculations

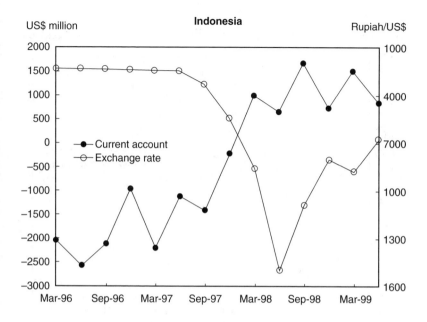

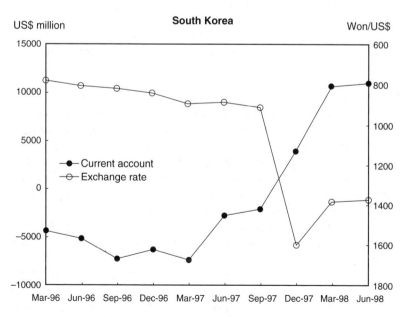

Figure 1.2   Exchange rate movements after dislocation (*continued*)

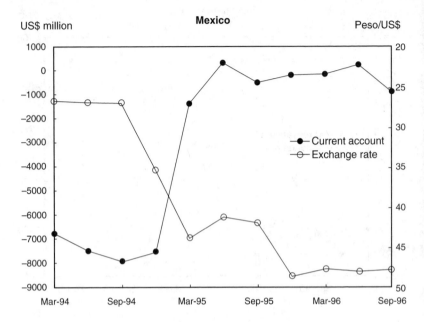

Figure 1.2   Exchange rate movements after dislocation (*continued*)

regime'. The capital-control regime changes the slope of the portfolio relationship and the speed of adjustment. A proportionate Tobin tax rate τ on all capital transactions will substitute $g((1 - \tau)\pi)$ for $g(\pi)$. It is easy to see that the arrows in the phase diagram become steeper. In this portfolio-asset model, a capital transaction tax will *increase* rather than decrease the volatility of exchange rates.[3] On the other hand, with controlled capital outflows, as imposed in Malaysia, the portfolio relation *PP* will shift to the right, and the equilibrium exchange rate for local currency will initially appreciate. Whether this increase is offset by a reluctance of potential investors to invest in the country because of the imposition of controls remains to be seen. Naturally, controls tend to reduce the value of the home currency.

With a fixed exchange rate under the currency-board system, the exchange rate becomes the policy variable controlled by the monetary authority. This changes the nature of the above system. The exchange rate is no longer an endogenous, forward-looking variable; exchange rates are no longer jumping variables; and the money supply is no longer a policy variable. The flow equation *CC* and the stock relation *PP* are forced to intersect at the intersection of a predetermined value of the exchange rate. This means that domestic price levels and the domestic interest rate will vary. A speculative attack occurs where confidence in the fixed parity is less than perfect, and reserves are rapidly drawn on to push up the domestic interest rate. In Hong Kong and Argentina, technical devices were introduced to broaden the money base. In summary, the currency-board system imposes a burden of high interest rates.

4 Experience of flexible exchange rates

Asian countries

Asian countries showed that currency crises could occur even where economies controlled inflation and pursued sound fiscal and monetary policies. The following Asian countries adopted a more or less floating exchange-rate policy in line with IMF recommendations. For a general view, see Krugman (1994) and Roubini (2000).

Thailand

The crisis broke in July 1997, and on 27 July of that year Thailand requested assistance from the IMF. Thailand is considered to have triggered the Asian crisis. Basically, the fiscal balance was in order; price levels were under control, but the current account was in deficit. Thus the flow dimension suffered a symptom in the balance of payments to which the first-generation approach to the causes of the currency crisis might apply (see Table 1.2). The baht was pegged to a currency basket in which the US$ was overrepresented; and the yen depreciated by about 50 per cent against the US$, which blunted the competitiveness of the Thai trade sector. The baht declined 36 per cent. In. May 1998, the IMF agreed a rescue package, including standby loan facilities worth approximately US$4.0 billion, effective for 34 months. That was equivalent to 505 per cent of Thailand's IMF quota or around 2 per cent of GDP.

Indonesia

Indonesia was also a high-saving country, but with higher inflation. Fundamentally, in 1997 the economy appeared quite sound; fiscal balance was in surplus and current account deficits within a permissible range. This suggests that it was speculative attacks on the asset market that triggered the currency crisis, and an element of contagion worked through the *PP* balance. On 4 August 1997, one month after Thailand's crisis, Indonesia floated the rupiah, and in early October Indonesia started negotiations with the IMF.

Table 1.2   Thailand economic indicators

	1994	1995	1996	1997	1998
Real GDP growth (%)	8.6	8.8	5.5	−0.4	−8.0
CPI inflation (%)	5.1	5.8	5.9	5.6	8.1
Money supply growth (%)	12.9	17.0	12.6	16.5	9.6
Savings (% of GDP)	34.9	34.3	33.1	32.9	35.9
Fiscal balance (% of GDP)	2.0	2.6	1.6	−0.4	−2.5
Current account balance /GDP (%)	−5.6	−7.9	−7.9	−2.0	−11.5
Official reserves (US$ billion)	29.3	36.0	37.7	26.2	28.8
External debt (% of GDP)	45.8	49.7	49.3	62.6	n.a.
Share of short-term external debt (%)	44.5	49.4	41.4	37.3	n.a.

Source: Author's computation

Political instability fuelled speculative pressure, and the rupiah spiralled downwards as shown in Figure 1.2. The exchange rate fell 600 per cent from 2,500 rupiah = US$1 to 15,000 rupiah = US$1, although by 1999 it was back to around 7,000 rupiah = US$1. The recovery process was slow and painful. The Indonesian case shows that even reasonably sound economies are vulnerable to speculators. The shift in asset balances was aggravated by the loss of public confidence in the rupiah because of political turmoil. At the end of 1996, the external debt stood at US$129 billion, nearly 60 per cent of GDP. Unlike other Asian countries, nearly half – 46 per cent – of the national debt was owned by the public sector,[4] 75 per cent in long-term maturities.

The 1998 IMF rescue package of a standby loan worth some US$10 billion, effective for three years, was equivalent to 494 per cent of Indonesia's IMF quota, or 4.4 per cent of GDP. The IMF did not approve the adoption of the currency-board system. In my view, the rupiah was grossly overvalued and, given the limitations of the currency board system when attacked by speculators, the IMF was fully justified. Table 1.3 presents some economic indicators for Indonesia.

South Korea

South Korea was an active growth engine in East Asia; people saved a high proportion of income and investment was vigorous. Price levels were stable and the government budget of South Korea was more or less balanced. The current account of the balance of payments, shown in Table 1.4, had a deficit below 5 per cent in 1996 – an acceptable level. Again the economy appeared sound. The contagious speculative attacks caused short-term speculators, mainly Japanese, to move funds

Table 1.3 Indonesian economic indicators

	1994	1995	1996	1997	1998
Real GDP growth (%)	7.2	8.0	7.4	5.5	−13.7
CPI inflation (%)	8.5	9.4	7.9	6.6	58.2
Money supply growth (%)	20.0	27.4	27.2	52.7	62.3
Savings (% of GDP)	29.2	29.0	28.8	29.9	19.1
Fiscal balance (% of GDP)	0.5	0.8	0.2	0.0	−4.7
Current account balance (% of GDP)	−1.7	−3.3	−3.3	−1.4	1.1
Official reserves (US$ billion)	12.1	13.7	18.3	16.6	22.7
External debt (% of GDP)	61.0	61.5	56.7	65.3	n.a.
Share of short-term external debt (%)	18.0	20.9	25.0	26.4	n.a.

Source: Author's computation

Table 1.4 South Korea economic indicators

	1994	1995	1996	1997	1998
Real GDP growth (%)	8.6	8.9	7.1	5.5	−5.5
CPI inflation (%)	6.3	4.5	4.9	4.5	7.8
Money supply growth (%)	18.7	15.6	15.8	14.1	27.9
Saving (% of GDP)	34.6	35.1	33.3	32.9	42.3
Fiscal balance (% of GDP)	0.3	0.6	0.5	−1.4	−5.0
Current account balance (% of GDP change)	−1.2	−2.0	−4.9	−2.0	13.2
Official reserves (US$)	25.6	32.7	34.0	21.1	52.0
External debt (% of GDP)	24.9	25.4	29.4	32.8	n.a.
Share of short-term external debt (%)	n.a.	n.a.	49.9	37.5	n.a.

Source: Author's computation

as well as other speculators, and South Korea became the victim of an asset-market-initiated currency crisis. The rigid industrial and financial structure added to the burden. The crisis started in early November 1997, and Korea requested IMF help on 19 November. The won exchange rate fell about 37 per cent. The IMF's high-interest-rate policy caused hardship, and the IMF tried to shift the *PP* schedule in Figure 1.1 upwards. The cyclical trough was deep but, fortunately, recovery was swift.

South Korea's total external debt at the end of 1996 was US$158 billion, some 33 per cent of GDP, with 98.5 per cent held by the private sector and 63 per cent in short-term maturities. The nationalist policy of restricting foreign direct investment may have exacerbated the unfavourable effects. In May 1998, The IMF extended a rescue package including standby facilities of approximately US$21 billion, effective for three years. This was equivalent to 1,939 per cent of South Korea's IMF quota and about 4.3 per cent of GDP. Economic indicators are shown in Table 1.4.

Latin American countries

Mexico

Mexico was in many ways the forerunner of the Asian-type crisis. In 1994, the current account deficit was 7.7 per cent of GDP. Capital market liberalization preceded trade liberalization, and this deficit was more or less funded by capital inflows, but in 1994 this became difficult. The flow fundamentals, as in Thailand, were in trouble, but unlike Thailand national savings were not high and the government deficit remained high. Short-term debt denominated in US$ was the major trigger of the Mexican crisis. A combination of human error, myopia and cognitive dissonance contributed to the debacle.

The value of the peso fell drastically from mid-1993; international reserves were depleted, and in December 1994 the peso exchange rate was floated. In 1996, it was devalued by 50 per cent. Foreign investors withdrew from government holdings, mainly *Tesobonos*, dislocating the stockmarket. Between December 1994 and September 1995, US foreign investments of US$21 billion fell by two-thirds (Griffith-Jones, 1996). Nevertheless, in 1996 the current account was almost in equilibrium, underlining the robustness of the portfolio approach, but the adjustment entailed a sharp decline in GDP of over 6 per cent.

Brazil

At the end of 1994 Brazil devalued the real drastically. This was partly in response to the Mexican crisis and partly to remedy its own disequilibrium. The current account had been in surplus until the third quarter of 1994, but then the pattern no longer seemed to conform to the paradigm of the portfolio approach. Brazil was another case of government rather than market failure, and the government struggled to control inflation. Between 1994 and September 1998, inflation was brought down from 2,700 per cent a year to under 3 per cent. This remarkable achievement was helped by strict fiscal discipline and structural reform. An IMF package of US$41 billion was released in November 1998, about 2.3 per cent of GDP. In addition to the IMF standby arrangement, the World Bank, the Inter-American Development Bank and other governments participated.

Table 1.5 Malaysia economic indicators

	1994	1995	1996	1997	1998
Real GDP growth (%)	9.3	9.4	8.6	7.7	−6.2
CPI Inflation (%)	3.7	3.4	3.5	4.0	5.3
Money supply growth (%)	14.7	24.0	20.9	16.5	4.7
Saving (% of GDP)	35.0	35.2	33.7	33.1	42.3
Fiscal balance (% of GDP)	2.5	0.9	0.7	1.8	−3.4
Current account balance (% of GDP)	−7.8	−10.0	−4.9	−4.8	8.1
Official reserves (US$ billion)	25.4	23.8	27.0	21.7	25.6
External debt (% of GDP)	40.4	39.3	40.1	50.5	n.a.
Share of short-term external debt (%)	21.1	21.2	27.8	31.6	n.a.

Source: Author's computation

5 Capital control measures

Capital control measures in Malaysia and Chile differed considerably.

Malaysia

Malaysia experienced similar difficulties to Thailand, Indonesia and South Korea, but Premier Mahathir Mohamad, however, did not appeal to the IMF. Highly critical of the behaviour of international speculators and reluctant to conform to IMF conditionality, he instead opted for a policy of capital control. In September 1998, the government prohibited the repatriation of foreign capital with a maturity of less than one year. In February 1999, this embargo was relaxed, but a tax imposed on capital repatriation (see Kaplan and Te, 1998).

This measure shifted *PP* in Figure 1.1 upwards in the short run by making it difficult for foreigners to offload assets denominated in ringgits. In the long run this could reduce foreign investment in Malaysia, and if Malaysia wishes to rely on Western, Chinese or Japanese capital this scheme cannot continue indefinitely but will need to be gradually phased out. The rapidity of recovery has been impressive, and as a short-term device this measure merits further study. Malaysian economic indicators are shown in Table 1.5.

Chile

In 1991, the Chilean government required 20 per cent of foreign borrowing to be deposited interest free for a period of one year. This was effectively a tax on capital inflows, with a heavier burden on short-term funds. From 1989 capital inflows caused the Chilean peso to appreciate and generated a current account deficit which fuelled inflation (Dornbusch and Edwards, 1994). Right or wrong, as a former central banker told me, it was believed that a current account surplus was necessary for Chile's economic development. The interest-free level was increased in 1992 to 30 per cent, and the legal coverage increased. The effect of this measure was to push down the *PP* curve in Figure 1.1, and prevent any sudden dislocation of demand for Chilean pesos. Initially it created considerable prosperity and economic growth, but eventually discouraged inward flows to such an extent that the measure was suspended.

Chile pursued a cautious policy of an *ex ante* character compared to Malaysia, by preventing already-invested capital from being repatriated Laban and Larrain (1994). By holding down the *PP* curve, the balance-of-payments deficit and international indebtedness were kept under control. Malaysia tried to prevent the *PP* curve from shifting downwards, but uncertainty meant that the curve would inevitably shift downwards. The Chilean policy meant that the tax burden was known to investors, while the Malaysian policy encouraged surprise attacks. Agosin and Ffrench-Davis (1998) suggest that in the long run the effects evened out, but that short-run dynamics were more disturbed by Malaysia's actions.

6 Currency-board systems

Hong Kong and Argentina are considered typical examples of the currency-board system.

Hong Kong

Hong Kong has a long tradition of using the currency-board system, first pegging to sterling, then with a floating exchange rate later pegging the HK\$ to the US\$, at HK\$7.8 = US\$1. In principle, under the currency-board system, HK\$s are issued only in exchange for US\$s; thus Hong Kong relinquishes autonomy of monetary policy.

The classical specie-flow mechanism was supposed to work here. Under the gold standard, the mechanism worked slowly as the flow relationship. Overextended domestic activity generated a balance-of-trade deficit which led to an outflow of gold, which reduced the monetary base and level of traded goods, but led to speculation, which triggered a financial crisis. Speculators usually bet against the whole system of the currency board, and, if not the system, at least the existing parity, and speculative moves can rapidly drain reserves leading to rapid increases in the domestic interest rate. In autumn 1997, the

Table 1.6   Hong Kong economic indicators

	1994	1995	1996	1997	1998
Real GDP growth (%)	5.4	3.9	4.9	5.3	−5.1
CPI Inflation (%)	8.1	8.7	5.2	6.5	2.8
Money supply growth (%)	11.7	10.6	12.5	8.4	11.8
Saving (% of GDP)	33.1	30.4	30.6	31.8	30.5
Fiscal balance (% of GDP)	1.3	−0.3	2.2	6.5	−2.5
Current account balance (% of GDP)	1.6	−3.9	−1.3	−1.5	−0.4
Official reserves (US$ billion)	49.8	55.4	63.8	92.8	89.6
External debt (% of GDP)	15.6	n.a.	n.a.	n.a.	n.a.
Share of short-term external debt (%)	n.a.	n.a.	n.a.	n.a.	n.a.

Source: Author's computation

stockmarket index fell 23 per cent between 20 and 23 October, and the overnight call rate between banks in Hong Kong rose more than 300 per cent Lo and Chow (1998). Speculators would still have found it profitable to borrow because a 10 per cent devaluation within one week created an investment opportunity of more than 500 per cent. China decided to protect the HK$.

In August 1998 there were renewed speculative attacks, and stockmarket, real estate and hotel values fell by over 50 per cent. The Hong Kong government engaged in price-keeping operations in the stockmarket, essentially using its foreign reserves – the principle of a free market. It introduced measures to broaden the monetary base, so that speculative attacks affected only part of the money base. The discount window was introduced to lend HK$s in exchange for exchange fund bills and notes. These were backed by the US$. In effect, by using their ample foreign reserves the monetary base was broadened while deposits continued to be backed by reserves. The credibility of the currency-board system was strengthened, greater flexibility in monetary policy was encouraged, and the check to interest rate movements moderately successfully curbed (Yam, 1998; Kwan, Lui and Cheng, 1999). Economic indicators for Hong Kong are given in Table 1.6.

Argentina

A brief mention must be made of Argentina. The 1994 Mexican crisis created speculative waves against the Argentinian peso, depleting reserves by about 40 per cent between December 1994 and March 1995. Interest rates soared.

In December 1996, in order to avoid a liquidity crisis, the central bank negotiated standby agreements with foreign banks; Argentine government bonds denominated in US$ were used as collateral. At the end of 1997, the standby limit was increased to US$7.4 billion, some 10 per cent of total domestic deposits, and nearly 3 per cent of 1995 GDP. The difference in the level of foreign reserves accounted for the difference between a sort of domestic funding and the external funding in Argentina.

7   Conclusions: are there any stylized patterns in Asia and Latin America?

Across the Pacific, we observed similar patterns that exemplified the universality of economic mechanisms. At the same time, subtle differences reflected differences in economic systems – differences in philosophy, in the objectives and instruments of economic policy, and crucially differences in the initial state of each economy. Our observations are summarized below with some possible policy implications:

1   In Latin America, countries subject to currency crises had macroeconomic difficulties, particularly high inflation. Thus the first-generation model of currency crises focusing on economic fundamentals will explain the causes of the crisis. On the other hand, Asian countries mostly enjoyed stable prices and a reasonable fiscal and monetary policy. Here, fundamental theory needs to be supplemented by a more sophisticated strategic or expectations-oriented explanation of the causes of the financial crisis.

2   Asian countries were high-saving, high-investment countries. The major mistake by these countries and their lenders was overconfidence in the future. This led to an overappreciation of the local currency and fuelled overborrowing. When their rosy optimism was shaken, the currency collapsed.

3   IMF theory is suited to a fundamentals-triggered crisis. If a change in the prospect of asset markets triggers the crisis, flow measures such as balancing fiscal budgets are not sufficient or even necessary. The asset-market-oriented measure of raising interest rates might work in principle, but should be accompanied by a policy directed at changing the future outlook itself.

4   Except for Indonesia, the external debt in Asia was mostly owed by the private sector. Overborrowing occurred by the mismatch of private lenders' and private borrowers' expectations. Lenders also

made mistakes about the capacity of borrowers to repay by themselves or with the help of their government, or indirectly through financial organizations. On the other hand, the external debt in Latin America was mostly owed by governments. Private lenders overestimated the capacity of governments to repay either through taxation or by being bailed out by another nation or international financial institution.

5 The Wall Street = Treasury = IMF conspiracy theory maintains that the IMF is guided by the intentions of the US Treasury, Wall Street and Western governments. Hamada (1998) showed that the analytical results using the common-agency theory predicted a similar pattern by studying the incentives structure facing agents involved in the rescue plan. A related opinion held that the IMF helped Latin American countries more than Asian countries because of Latin America's proximity to Wall Street. Comparing the magnitude of IMF and other international agency support relative to the size of national economies in Asia and Latin America, we failed to establish sufficient quantitative support for this view.

I had intended to try to stylize the characteristics of the Asian and Latin American types of crisis, but this proved difficult. Instead, I propose a few concluding thoughts. Asian institutions are the product of historic experience, but Confucionism, Buddhism and Islam by encouraging saving, which promoted growth, may have deepened the financial crisis. Turning to the costs of adjustment, my main finding is that there is no obvious way to adjust. The IMF method brings widely fluctuating exchange rates and high domestic interest rates, although it does not impair the intertemporal resource-allocating function of the capital market. Capital controls disrupt this function, but restore monetary autonomy. The currency-board system relinquishes monetary autonomy, but is subject to volatile interest-rate fluctuations.

I once asked Kazushi Ohkawa, an eminent historian who might be called the Kuznets of Japan,[5] 'Does economic theory as developed in Western economies apply to other parts of the planet?' He replied simply, 'Yes it does. But you must study carefully the institutional environment when you analyse individual countries, because economic conditions differ from country to country.' My conclusion, maybe, should be: while the economic mechanism at work in a currency crisis may be universal, initial conditions are so different that any remedy will function differently.

Notes

1 It is interesting to see why the Philippines were less affected. Consumer-oriented attitudes may have prevented a large investment–savings gap, and, further the country's financial sectors were already malfunctioning so that the contagion effect was absent.
2 Those flow variables affect the speed of asset accumulation in a national economy and its international credit and debt position. The flow-dimension variables determine the changes in the stock variables.
3 That may be the reason that Indonesia has some similarity to Latin American countries, they all tightly control or manage capital.
4 In this sense, Indonesia resembles Latin American cases.
5 He enjoyed the game of Go, and always remembered me in the economists' Go tournament; when I met him at academic conferences he often forgot who I was.

References

Agosin, M. R. and R. Ffrench Davis (1998) 'Managing Capital Inflows in Chile' (mimeo).

Branson, W. H. and D. W. Henderson (1985) 'The Specification and Influence of Asset Markets', in W. J. Jones and P. B. Kenen (eds), *Handbook of International Economics*, Vol. II, ch. 15 (Amsterdam, NL: North-Holland).

Dornbusch, R. and S. Edwards (1994) 'Exchange Rate Policy and Trade Strategy', in B. P. R. Bosworth, Dornbusch and R. Laban (eds), *The Chilean Economy: Policy Lessons and Challenges* (Washington DC: Brookings Institution).

Griffith-Jones, S. (1996) 'The Mexican Peso Crisis', UN ECLAC paker.

Hamada, K. (1998) 'Incentive Mechanisms Surrounding International Financial Institutions', *Asian Development Review*, vol. 16, no. 7 pp. 126–50.

Hayek, F. A. von (1949) *Individualism and Economic Order* (London: Routledge & Kegan Paul).

International Monetary Fund (1995, 1999) *World Economic Outlook* (Washington, DC: IMF).

Kaplan, I. and A. K. Te (1998) 'Malaysia', in K. Wong (ed.), *The Asian Crisis: What has Happened and why*, the Economic Research Group on Southeast and East Asia (ERGSEA).

Kouri, P. J. K. (1976) 'The Exchange Rate and the Balance of Payments in the Short Run and in the Long Run', *Scandinavian Journal of Economics*, vol. 78, pp. 280–304.

Krugman, P. (1994) 'The Myth of Asian Miracle', *Foreign Affairs*, vol. 73, pp. 62–78.

Kwan, Y. K., F. T. Lui and L. K. Cheng (1999) 'Credibility of Hong Kong's Currency Board: The Role of Institutional Arrangement', paper presented at the 10th Annual East Asian Seminar in Hawaii.

Laban, R. and F. B. Larrain (1994) 'The Chilean Experience with Capital Mobility', in B. P. Bosworth, R. Dornbusch and R. Laban (eds), *The Chilean Economy: Policy Lessons and Challenges* (Washington, DC: Brookings Institution).

Lo, M. C. and J. Chow (1998) 'Hong Kong', in K. Wong (ed.), *The Asian Crisis: What has Happened and Why*, the Economic Research Group on Southeast and East Asia (ERGSEA).

Merton, R. C. (1969) 'Lifetime Portfolio Selection under Uncertainty: The Continuous Time Case', *Review of Economics and Statistics*, vol. 31, pp. 247–56.

Radelet, S and J. D. Sachs (1998) 'The Onset of the East Asian Financial Crisis', Harvard Institute for International Development.

Roubini, N. (2000) Nouriel Roubini's Asian Crisis Website www.stern.nyu.edu/-nroubini/asia

Samuelson, P. A. (1969) 'Lifetime Portfolio Selection by Dynamic Stochastic Programming', *Review of Economics and Statistics*, vol. 31, pp. 239–46.

Yam, J. (1998) 'Review of Currency Board Arrangements in Hong Kong', Hong Kong Monetary Authority Sub-Committee on Asian Financial and Capital Markets.

2

Latin America and the External Crisis of the Second Half of the 1990s

*Vittorio Corbo**

1 Introduction

Latin America suffered a series of external shocks in the second half of the 1990s. The first shock, which followed the initiation of the 1997 Asian crisis, took the form of a sharp deterioration in the terms of trade, due to a sharp fall in the price of primary commodities in international markets. Following the Russian crisis, the region received a second external shock in the form of higher costs and reduced access to foreign financing. The external crisis surfaced in Brazil in early 1999, following a severe attack on its currency which forced the country to abandon the defence of its peg exchange-rate system and adopt a floating exchange rate. The response to the crisis was twofold. First, macroeconomic policies were altered to avoid excessive current account deficits that could not be financed, and, second, protective measures were introduced to mitigate the effects of a capital flow reversal. When the crisis came, Latin American countries were better prepared than at the time of the debt crisis of the early 1980s, as a result of the deep reforms implemented in recent years. The policy response to these shocks was more appropriate.

The rest of this chapter is divided into four sections. Section 2 reviews the prevailing conditions in Latin America when the crisis hit.

* An earlier version of this chapter was written while the author was visiting the Center for Research on Economic Development and Policy Reform at Stanford University. I am grateful to Eduardo Engel, Leonardo Hernández, Nicholas Hope, Anne O. Krueger, Assaf Razin and seminar participants at Stanford University and at the University of California at Berkeley for useful comments, and to Óscar Facusse and José Antonio Tessada for research assistance.

Section 3 analyses the special case of Brazil, the country most affected by the crisis. Section 4 studies the main policy responses employed to adjust to the crisis and make countries less vulnerable to external shocks, and considers new issues which resulted from the crisis such as the choice of exchange-rate system and ways to implement monetary policy. Finally, section 5 presents some conclusions.

2 Latin America on the eve of the Asian crisis

At the time of the Asian financial crisis, Latin American economies were in better shape than at the outset of the debt crisis in the early 1980s. By the end of 1997, an important group of Latin American countries – Argentina, Chile, El Salvador, Mexico and Peru – had transformed their economies; another group of countries – Bolivia, Brazil, Colombia, Costa Rica and Nicaragua – had made important changes, but still had a way to go; Ecuador, Venezuela, Guatemala and Honduras lagged far behind. The change in economic philosophy was radical. After pursuing economic policies based on a deep distrust of markets, heavy government intervention and isolation from foreign trade, as described by Edwards (1995) and Corbo (2000a), Latin American countries introduced policies that emphasized macroeconomic stability, competitive market structures, integration into the world economy (outward orientation) and a new role for government. These changes followed a new development model, discussed by Williamson (1989) and Corbo and Fischer (1995),[1] according to which the government was responsible for establishing the institutions necessary for the proper functioning of a market economy, together with the provision of public goods and improved access of the poorest in the population to social services.

These changes were initiated in Chile in the mid-1970s, and subsequently extended to most countries in the region. This policy revolution resulted in a frontal attack on public-sector deficits, and drastically changed the traditional import-substitution cum government-intervention model which had prevailed in most of the region from the great depression up to the debt crisis of the early 1980s.[2]

As a direct consequence of these policy changes, macroeconomic stability improved during the 1990s: the annual average inflation rate, that had been over 100 per cent in the 1980s, fell to less than 10 per cent by the end of the 1990s, and several large economies experienced inflation below 5 per cent. A sharp fiscal adjustment was behind the reduction of inflation (Tables 2.1 and 2.2). Chile, before its short-lived

Table 2.1   Annual average inflation rate (%)

Country	1980–85	1986–90	1991–97	1996	1997	1998	1999
Argentina	335.6	1192.7	30.8	0.2	0.8	0.9	−1.2
Bolivia	2249.9	68.0	11.8	12.4	4.7	7.7	2.2
Brazil	141.9	1056.9	823.6	15.5	6.0	3.2	4.9
Chile	23.8	19.4	11.9	7.4	6.2	5.1	3.3
Colombia	23.1	25.0	23.9	20.8	18.5	18.7	10.9
Mexico	56.4	75.7	20.8	34.4	20.6	15.9	16.6
Peru	97.4	2341.4	83.8	11.6	8.6	7.3	3.5
Latin America and the Caribbean*	107.1	321.9	110.11	22.3	13.1	10.2	9.3

* GDP weighted average.
Source: Burki and Perry (1997) and *World Economic Outlook* Database, IMF, September 2000.

Table 2.2   Non-financial public sector balance (percentage of GDP)

Country	1980–85	1986–90	1991–97	1996	1997	1998	1999
Argentina	−14.5	−6.4	−1.8	−3.2	−2.1	−2.1	−4.1
Bolivia	−10.3	−6.3	−3.7	−1.9	−3.3	−4.0	−3.9
Brazil	−4.3	−3.9	−1.8	−5.9	−6.1	−8.0	−9.5
Chile	−1.2	1.9	2.0	2.1	1.0	−1.2	−2.5
Colombia	−5.7	−1.1	−1.5	−2.0	−3.1	−3.4	−6.0
Mexico	−11.3	−10.6	−0.2	−0.1	−0.6	−1.2	−1.1
Peru	−8.0	−7.7	−1.9	−1.0	−0.1	−0.6	n.a.[1]
Latin America and the Caribbean*	−8.6	−7.0	−2.8	−1.1	−1.3	−2.5	−3.1

n.a.:   not available; [1]the 1999 Peru central government balance was −3.0 per cent of GDP; * GDP weighted average.
Source: Banco Central de Bolivia (1997), Banco Central de la Reserva del Perú (1998), Burki and Perry (1997) and IMF, *World Economic Outlook*, various issues.

recession of 1999, had enjoyed a fiscal surplus for over 10 years, and fiscal deficits were low to moderate in Mexico, Argentina and Peru. However, they remained high in Brazil, Ecuador, Colombia and Venezuela, as did inflation in Venezuela, Colombia, Ecuador and Mexico.

In all countries, independent of the policy used to reduce inflation (exchange-rate-based, money-based or inflation-targeting), the reduction of inflation was accompanied by an increase in the GDP growth rate, as shown in Table 2.3. Thus, the observed 'sacrifice ratio' was positive rather than negative. This result is not so surprising if one consid-

Table 2.3   Real annual GDP growth rate (%)

Country	1980–85	1986–90	1991–97	1996	1997	1998	1999
Argentina	−1.1	0.4	6.2	4.2	8.4	3.9	−3.1
Bolivia	−1.4	2.3	4.0	4.1	4.3	4.7	2.5
Brazil	2.5	2.0	3.0	2.8	3.0	−0.1	0.5
Chile	2.3	6.5	7.4	7.2	7.1	3.4	−1.0
Colombia	2.6	4.6	4.0	2.0	3.2	0.4	−5.1
Mexico	3.1	1.5	2.9	5.2	7.0	4.8	3.7
Peru	0.6	−0.8	5.4	2.6	7.5	0.3	3.5
Latin America and the Caribbean*	1.8	3.4	3.7	3.6	5.4	2.2	0.3

* GDP, weighted average.
Source: Burki and Perry (1997) and *World Economic Outlook* Database, IMF, September 2000.

ers the high growth costs of the debt crisis and the extreme inflation experienced in the region during the 1980s.

Following the Mexican crisis of 1994, a set of initiatives was developed to avoid similar situations. That crisis had provided an early warning of the importance of strong financial systems, of avoiding the build-up of short-term debt and large current account deficits. In response to these concerns, countries improved their macroeconomic management policies and strengthened institutions related to the regulation and supervision of the financial system. At the same time, Latin America countries altered their exchange-rate policies, moving away from fixed but adjustable pegs, towards more flexible arrangements. The exception to this was Argentina which continued with its currency board.

Although Argentina was still vulnerable because of its monetary and exchange-rate system, its financial system had been substantially strengthened. This was necessary given that in the early 1990s, as a result of hyperinflation and with banking revenues highly dependent on the deposit base, Argentina's banking system was fragmented and included a number of weak banks. At the time of the 'tequila crisis', many banks either went into liquidation or were consolidated into larger banks.

After the Mexican crisis, regulation and supervision were upgraded and capital requirements for banks in Argentina raised above international standards. An offshoot of this effort was an important restructuring and consolidation of the banking system. Foreign ownership increased substantially, and by the end of the 1990s over 60 per cent of bank deposits were in foreign-owned banks or foreign bank sub-sidiaries. To protect the financial system from a sudden reversal of capital flows, a liquidity requirement of 20 per cent of the deposit base – held in highly liquid international assets – was introduced. Argentina signed a line of credit with a group of commercial banks for close to 10 per cent of the deposit base, to be drawn against selected banking assets which would serve as collateral. The margin-call requirements for this line of credit were further strengthened with the approval of a contingency facility financed by the World Bank and the IDB. In addition, extra protection against a sudden deterioration in the external environment, which could restrict access to international financial markets, was obtained through two large Special Adjustment Loans, totalling US\$ 4.5 billion, from the World Bank and the IDB.

Chile and Peru took precautionary measures to avoid large current account deficits, with Chile, Colombia, Mexico and Peru maintaining a managed float exchange-rate system. Efforts were made by these countries to improve the information, regulation and supervision of the financial system. In particular, loan classification systems and currency matching of assets and liabilities were improved; lending to related parties was curtailed and bank capital requirements raised.

Mercosur was the one development which might have spread contagion as trade linkages in Latin America increased, so that shocks in a large country – Argentina or Brazil – within the common market might have been more contagious than before. Thus, although the danger of contagion was greater than during the 1980s, as shown below, this was only a problem for Argentina, as trade with Brazil and Argentina remained relatively low for other countries.

3 The special case of Brazil

The economy most affected by the deterioration in the external environment was also the largest and most vulnerable – Brazil. Brazil's vulnerability was the result of many years of large fiscal deficits, which resulted in a large domestic debt, with short maturity periods. Between 1994 and 1997, an exchange-rate-based stabilization strategy, which combined a loose fiscal policy and a restrictive monetary policy, resulted in high real interest rates and a sharp real appreciation of the domestic currency, the *real*. High *real* interest rates might also have reflected doubts about the continuity of the exchange-rate-based stabilization programme in place until early January 1999.

Brazil experienced an attack on its currency in October of 1997 as the Asian crisis gained strength. In the third quarter of 1997, Taiwan devaluated its dollar and there were speculative attacks on the Hong Kong dollar and Korean *won*. The Brazilian government responded by raising interest rates and announced a programme to reduce the fiscal deficit. As a result, the narrow exchange-rate-band system survived the attack. However, as the presidential election approached, the promised fiscal adjustment did not take place resulting in increased vulnerability. Pressure on the Brazilian currency intensified with the onset of the Russian crisis. As Brazil was unable to implement a full adjustment programme in the middle of a presidential election, high real interest rates and a loss of foreign reserves defended the attack on the currency. This situation could not continue for long without creating insuperable real costs or exhausting international reserves, so shortly after the elections the authorities introduced a fiscal package. On the strength of this fiscal programme, Brazil was able to mobilize US$41 billion as part of an IMF programme.

This adjustment programme, supported by the IMF, was supposed to restore confidence and to contribute to a substantial reduction in real interest rates. The latter, through its effects on the interest component of the budget, was intended to make the fiscal situation more sustainable. But slow implementation of the adjustment programme and conflict between the federal government and some state governors made the fiscal programme less credible. As a result, pressure on the currency intensified. Brazil's case is close to the characterization used in Krugman's (first)-generation model of a currency crisis. That is, the fiscal fundamentals were incompatible with a semi-fixed exchange rate, which was the main anchor of the exchange-rate-based stabilization programme. This caused economic agents to anticipate a depreciation. Then, probably, elements of a second-generation currency-crisis model set in as agents started to anticipate the government's abandonment of the high interest rates that were necessary to defend its exchange-rate system. As pressure on the currency increased, the government abandoned its exchange rate before exhausting reserves.

Matters were made worse by a poorly implemented devaluation, with inadequate progress on approving the fiscal programme, which was the central component of the IMF-backed programme, and the lack of any clear monetary policy. Not surprisingly, the initial devaluation intensified the speculative attack against the currency. After another substantial loss of foreign reserves, the Central Bank decided to abandon the recently modified exchange-rate band in favour of a floating rate. As no programme followed on the fiscal and monetary front, the currency went into free fall which resulted in a nominal depreciation of over 60 per cent in just two weeks. Thus, the Brazilian crisis was little different from the Russian crisis in 1998, which is well-documented by Kharas, Pinto and Ulatov (2001).

To the surprise of many, the exchange-rate crisis helped to mobilize enough political support to win approval for a substantial fiscal adjustment that yielded a primary surplus of over 3.0 per cent of GDP in 1999, which was planned to increase in 2000 and 2001. In parallel, a new well-qualified team was brought in to run the Central Bank, and the foreign commercial banks renewed their short-term credit lines. This set of actions allowed Brazil to stabilize its financial markets, halt the loss of reserves and start to reduce short-term interest rates. It is important to recognize that before the currency crisis Brazil had started restoring macroeconomic stability and initiating important structural reforms. In particular, trade barriers were reduced, first unilaterally and later as part of Mercosur negotiations. The steel, petrochemical, electricity generation and distribution, banking and telecommunication sectors started to be privatized. Of course, much remained to be done to complete the restructuring and privatization of the public sector. In particular, the state pension system, which had been abused and is still a major source of fiscal imbalance, needed major reform in order to reduce benefits or increase contributions. Brazilian pensions are extremely generous, and the government wisely concentrated on pension reform and, despite heavy political opposition, the government won a major battle by taxing higher-rate pensions.

The sharp reduction in real interest rates that took place in Brazil following the adjustment programme made the internal debt dynamics less explosive and reduced the risk of domestic debt restructuring, setting in motion a virtuous circle.

4   The effects of the crisis and the response

The external crisis had three main effects in the region:

- a severe negative shock to commodity prices;
- an income (interest-rate) and terms-of -trade shock; and
- a credit-rationing shock.

In time sequence, commodity prices and terms-of-trade effect hit first, while the other two effects struck with force after the Russian crisis.

Table 2.4 International price movements (%)

	1981–90	1991–97	1997	1998
Non-fuel products	−2.3	1.3	−0.4	−17.8
Petroleum	−4.7	−2.5	−6.1	−28.5
G5 – manufactures: export prices	3.3	1.1	−5.1	−3.8

Source: *Global Economic Prospects*, World Bank (1999).

Table 2.5 Stripped spreads

Country	1997	1998				1999		
	31/3	31/7	28/8	28/9	30/12	12/2	12/3	7/5
Argentina	502	531	1,419	882	697	742	707	578
Brazil	471	626	1,451	1,185	1,246	1,288	1,247	850
Mexico	509	553	1,131	1,044	748	692	630	535
Poland	173	191	400	303	266	233	244	225
EMBI*	507	644	1,494	1,177	1,135	1,170	1,136	870

* Emerging markets bonds index.
Source: J.P. Morgan, *Global Data Watch*.

Indeed, after an initial jump in October 1997, when the Asian crisis started to pressure Hong Kong, the spreads on Latin American government bonds stayed almost constant until mid-August 1998.

Table 2.4 presents the evolution of commodity prices showing the severe deterioration in terms of trade, especially for oil-exporting countries. Table 2.5 shows the stripped spread of the sovereign debt of the largest countries in Latin America. As can be observed from this table, the spreads were almost the same in late March 1997 and late July 1998, one year after the initiation of the Asian crisis. It was only after the Russian crisis that the spreads experienced a large jump that was almost fully reversed by the end of the year.

The first two effects resulted in a reduction of national disposable income. The third effect, although it had an equivalent income loss, worked through the capital account of the balance of payments, setting in motion a reduction in the current account deficit and putting pressure on the foreign-exchange market.

The total terms-of-trade effects – commodity and income – reduced national disposable income, which is a function of the size of the initial trade volumes and of the magnitude of the drop in terms of trade. By late 1997, the trade deficit as a share of GDP was over 4 per cent of GDP in Chile, Peru and Colombia. The terms-of-trade loss was highest in Chile, followed by Peru and Mexico. The income reduction, in turn, generated a reduction in domestic absorption, consumption plus investment, as consumers and producers adjusted to their reduced income level. Typically, the reduction in absorption was smaller than the reduction in income and, as a result, the current account tended to deteriorate.[3] However, reduced access to external financing, or a deliberate decision to adjust to avoid having to face this option (to reduce vulnerability to capital reversals), led to the need to introduce measures to reduce domestic absorption. This was the route chosen by most Latin American countries. Consequently, fiscal and monetary policies were employed to obtain a larger reduction in the current account deficit than that induced by the private response to the terms-of-trade effect.

In the short run, macroeconomic policy was adjusted to control the current account deficit, that is the difference between domestic expenditure and national income; falling national income called for policy measures to reduce expenditure rather than boosting output, which takes effect more slowly. Thus, adjustment programmes were dominated by stabilization components, often with the support of the IMF and other international financial institutions.

The well-known Meade–Salter–Swan–Dornbusch model of the dependent economy illustrates that, in reducing a current account deficit, expenditure-reducing policies must be accompanied by expenditure and output-switching policies to keep internal balance (or unemployment) under control (Dornbusch, 1980, ch. 6). A real exchange-rate depreciation, which is the main switching component of an adjustment programme, is also required by the loss in terms of trade. Expenditure-reduction policies took the form of more restrictive monetary policies and a tightening of fiscal policy throughout Latin America. This was accomplished by a combination of expenditure reduction and tax increases. In Mexico, a series of fiscal adjustment plans were introduced to maintain a sustainable fiscal situation in spite of the drastic reduction in oil prices. Peru, and to a lesser extent Argentina, also pursued more restrictive fiscal policies. In contrast, in Chile most of the stabilization was done through monetary policy as fiscal policy became expansionary.

Next, for a given demand adjustment, the degree of switching accomplished was mainly determined by the existing exchange-rate system. By mid-1998, exchange-rate systems in Latin America were extremely diverse. They varied from the rigid Argentinean currency board, to Mexico's and Peru's flexible systems. Between these extremes, Chile and Colombia operated wide exchange-rate bands, as did Brazil on paper, although in practice it used the exchange rate as the monetary anchor for an exchange-rate-based stabilization programme – the *real* plan. In Argentina the government tried to facilitate switching through wage flexibility, but, given the political difficulties involved in approving labour reforms, it resorted to facilitating switching through a reduction in labour taxes. As non-tradable goods and services are usually more labour-intensive than tradables, this policy had an implicit switching effect.

Real exchange-rate depreciation is determined by the change in fundamentals – in the short run, that is, the demand correction and the drop in terms of trade – flexibility of relative prices and extent of the initial misalignment. The countries that achieved larger corrections in the real exchange rate were those with the greatest misalignment (Chile, Colombia and Peru), those that had suffered the largest terms-of-trade losses (Colombia, Mexico, Peru and Chile), and those with a more flexible exchange-rate system (all of the above). In the special cases of Brazil and Ecuador, the real depreciation came through an exchange-rate crisis, while Chile and Colombia abandoned exchange-rate bands in favour of a flexible system. In contrast, Venezuela resisted any nominal devaluation of its currency by intervening in the exchange-rate market.

The use of monetary policy also varied throughout the region. In Argentina's currency-board system, interest rates are not a matter of policy and are mostly determined by the operational rules of the currency board: when money flows out, the monetary base contracts and the interest rate rises. In Brazil, Chile, Colombia and Mexico, all countries with flexible exchange-rate arrangements, monetary policy follows an inflation-target framework. In this framework, the target rate of inflation is the monetary anchor and monetary (and fiscal) policies are geared towards achieving this target. Thus, the announced target is the ultimate policy objective, and forecast inflation, sometimes not made public, is the intermediate objective, using interest rates as the main policy instrument. When the conditional forecast inflation, made with the existing policies and the expected path of the exogenous variables, is above the target inflation, the level of the intervention interest rate is raised accordingly.

All countries except Argentina used monetary policy as an integral component of expenditure-reduction programmes. In Bolivia and Peru, monetary policy followed the monetary-target approach closely. In

Chile, restrictive monetary policy was introduced early on to reduce the current account deficit, and through this make the economy less vulnerable to a sudden reversal of capital flows. After some initial hesitation, the exchange-rate policy was made more flexible and the central bank reduced its intervention in the exchange market. Brazil, Peru and Colombia also introduced more restrictive monetary policies. However, policy responses were not restricted to expenditure and exchange-rate adjustment only; structural measures were also introduced (or attempted) to make the economies more resilient to a much less favourable external environment.

In Argentina, a fiscal convertibility law was approved. This law would increase fiscal responsibility and provide for a liquidity fund to cope with unexpected capital reversals in order to restore the solvency of the public sector. The law set a series of objectives. First, the size of the government deficit was to be gradually reduced, to achieve balance by 2002. Second, the rate of growth of government expenditure was to be below the rate of GDP growth. Third, a large share of the proceeds from new privatizations was to be invested overseas in a contingency fund to be used, eventually, for fiscal stabilization purposes. Brazil also approved a sort of fiscal responsibility law that increased the accountability of public officials and the states. In Peru the fiscal responsibility law restricted the fiscal deficit and government spending during an election year.

In Chile – at the request of producers' associations – integration into the world economy was strengthened by a law introduced in 1998 to gradually reduce import tariffs. The law stipulates a gradual reduction in the uniform tariff by one percentage point per year down to 6 per cent in 2003. Through this initiative, the country renewed its commitment to an export-led development strategy.

The Brazilian devaluation induced another shock in Latin America. However, the precautionary measures protected the region from any major contagion effects. Surprisingly, in terms of the cost of foreign borrowing and capital reversal, the Brazilian crisis had a much smaller effect in the region than the Russian crisis. This was partly due to the fact that the devaluation was, most likely, anticipated and to the precautionary adjustment measures already in place. However, given the size of Brazil' economy – bigger than Mexico's and more than twice the size of Argentina's – whatever happens in Brazil has indirect effects throughout the region. Thus, inevitably, the exchange-rate crisis in Brazil resulted in a general slowdown. Argentina suffered the largest impact; because of its loss of competitiveness vis-à-vis Brazil, its sizeable trade with Brazil, and the higher cost of foreign borrowing. Trade with Brazil was only important for full members of Mercosur, particularly Argentina (in 1998, 28 per cent of Argentina's exports were destined for Brazil, compared to 6 per cent of Chile's, 1 per cent of Colombia's and Mexico's, and 4 per cent of Peru's and Venezuela's). Even in Argentina, the overall economic impact was less than the export figures suggest, because Argentina remains a very closed economy; total exports were (and are) less than 9 per cent of GDP, and exports to Brazil were only 2.4 per cent of GDP.

Thanks to its serious fiscal adjustment Brazil was able to stabilize its economy and avoid a major crisis. Furthermore, with the stabilization of the Brazilian financial markets the spreads in foreign debt started to come down again. Indeed, as shown in Table 2.5, after an initial jump (not shown) the stripped spreads on Latin American sovereign bonds returned to the pre-Brazilian crisis levels.

The crisis, however, raised important questions about the appropriate institutions and the appropriate macroeconomic policies that would make individual economies more resilient to external shocks, and facilitate adjustment in the event of a shock. On the macro side two other issues emerged: the choice of exchange-rate regime and the choice of monetary regime to reduce inflation to the levels observed in industrial countries.

A large body of literature has appeared recently on the choice of exchange-rate regime for emerging markets. The emerging consensus is that for countries with access to international capital markets, the main options are either to establish a credibly fixed exchange-rate system (dollarization or the weaker version of a currency board), or to have a floating exchange-rate system with instruments to cover exchange-rate risks (Obtsfeld and Rogoff, 1995; Summers, 2000; Mussa *et al.*, 2000, and Edwards and Savastano, 2000; Calvo, 2000; Edwards, 2000; Corbo, 2001; Fischer, 2001).[5]

In practice, in countries with poor records of monetary stability resulting in widespread currency substitution, the domestic currency is rarely used either as a medium of exchange or as an accounting unit, and, therefore, there is not much room for monetary policy. Furthermore, in these cases, an exchange-rate adjustment could have substantial economic costs due to balance-sheet effects (Calvo and Reinhart, 2000). For such countries, the benefits of adopting a rigid exchange-rate system could outweigh its costs. In contrast, in countries with a reputation for financial prudence the benefits of exchange-rate flexibility and retaining the option to use monetary policy for stabilization purposes could be an important asset.

For countries that choose to use a floating exchange-rate regime there is the issue of which monetary policy regime to use to anchor inflation.[6] Here there are two options: a money target, or an inflation target. In the latter option, the anchor for inflation is the inflation forecast.

The use of a monetary anchor runs into trouble when the demand for money is highly unstable. This is a problem where there is considerable financial innovation or when there is a sudden change in the rate of inflation. Due to these problems, some countries adopted an inflation-targeting anchor. In inflation targeting, the target rate of inflation serves the purpose of a monetary anchor, and monetary and fiscal policies are geared towards achieving the inflation target at the lowest cost. The appeal of this system is that its effectiveness does not rely on a stable relationship between a monetary aggregate and inflation, and, at the same time, it avoids problems associated with the fixing of the exchange rate reviewed above (Bernanke *et al.*, 1999; Corbo and Schmidt-Hebbel, 2001).

5 Conclusions

The international financial crisis of the second half of the 1990s occurred when most Latin American countries were in the process of a major overhaul of their economic models. These new models emphasize achieving and maintaining macroeconomic stability, creating a more open trade regime with fewer distortions, the development of a safer and healthier financial system, the development of competitive market structures, and the restructuring of the public sector. A drastic reduction in public-sector deficits led to substantial reduction of inflation together with an increase in the rate of output growth. On the eve of the Asian crisis, Latin America was beginning to reap the benefits of a decade of reforms.

The recent international crisis put some stress on economic policies in the region. In particular, the crisis resulted in a sharp drop in terms of trade, a substantial increase in borrowing spreads and a sudden reduction in capital in flows. The latter put pressure on current accounts and exchange-rate regimes, forcing the introduction of restrictive fiscal and monetary policies. The economy most affected by the deterioration in the external environment – Brazil – was also the most vulnerable. Brazil's vulnerability was the result of many years of large fiscal deficits that resulted in a large domestic debt with short maturity periods. During 1994–97, an exchange-rate-based stabilization strategy, combined with a loose fiscal policy and a restrictive monetary policy, resulted in a high real interest rate and a sharp real appreciation of the real. However, after the exchange-rate crisis in early 1999, Brazil introduced an adjustment programme to stabilize its financial market. The Brazilian crisis also had important negative effects on Argentina where the combination of a currency board and a rigid labour market made the adjustment difficult.

However, unlike previous crises, this time the policy reaction of most Latin American countries has avoided action to seal the economy off and to introduce expansionary fiscal and monetary policies in an attempt to stabilize output. The typical response was to introduce restrictive macroeconomic policies to restrain current account deficits and facilitate the real depreciation required by a drop in terms of trade. Some countries went further by reinforcing the movement towards becoming an open-market economy. Thus, Chile approved a gradual tariff reduction, providing a clear signal that the opening-up process would continue, while Mexico, Peru, Colombia and Chile have all introduced restrictive fiscal and monetary policies to curb the increase in the current account deficit.

As to exchange-rate regimes, the typical pattern has been a move towards more flexible systems. As more countries moved to the use of more flexible exchange-rate regimes, there emerges the issue of the how to conduct monetary policy. Here, an increasing number of countries have decided to use the inflation-target framework. Fiscal discipline and central bank independence provide the institutional underpinnings for the inflation-target strategy.

Notes

1 For a critical view of this consensus see Baker, Epstein and Pollin (1998).
2 For a review of economic policies in Latin America in an historical perspective, see Diaz-Alejandro (1982, 1983) and Corbo (1988).
3 For an analysis of the effects of terms-of-trade shocks, see Gavin (1990).
4 The interest rate that is the instrument of monetary policy can be the real rate, as in the much indexed Chilean economy until 2001, or the nominal rate as in most other countries, including Chile since 2001.
5 For minority views in favour of exchange-rate bands, see Williamson (1996) and Frankel (1999).
6 On monetary anchors, see Calvo and Vegh (1999), and Bernanke and Mishkin (1997). On the choice of monetary anchors in Latin America, see Corbo, Elberg and Tessada (1999), Corbo (2000b) and Mishkin (1999). On the Latin American experience with inflation targeting, see Corbo and Schmidt-Hebbel (2001).

References

Baker, D., G. Epstein and R. Pollin (1998) *Globalization and Progressive Economic Policy: What Are the Real Constraints and Options?* (New York: Cambridge University Press).

Banco Central de Bolivia (1997) 'Memoria'.

Banco Central de Reserva del Perú (1998) 'Nota Semanal' (weekly reports), various issues.

Bernanke, B. S. and F. S. Mishkin (1997) 'Inflation Targeting: A New Framework for Monetary Policy', *Journal of Economic Perspectives*, vol. 11. no. 2, pp. 97–116.

Bernanke, B. S., T. Laubach, F. S. Mishkin and A. Posen (1999) *Inflation Targeting* (Princeton, New Jersey: Princeton University Press).

Burki, S. and G. Perry (1997) *The Long March. A Reform Agenda for Latin America and the Caribbean in the Next Decade* (Washington, DC: The World Bank).

Calvo, G. (2000) 'Reflections on Dollarization', in A. Alesina and R. Barro (eds), *Currency Unions* (Stanford, CA: Hoover Institution Press).

Calvo, G., and C. Reinhart (2000) 'Fear of Floating', NBER working paper no. 7993 (November).

Calvo, G. and C. Vegh (1999) 'Inflation Stabilization and BOP Crisis in Developing Countries', NBER working paper no. 6925 (February).

Corbo, V. (1988) 'Problems, Development Theory and Strategies of Latin America', in G. Ranis and T. P. Schultz (eds), *The State of Development Economics: Progress and Perspectives* (London: Basil Blackwell).

Corbo, V. (2000a) 'Economic Policy Reforms in Latin America', in A. O. Krueger (ed.), *Economic Policy Reform: The Second Stage* (Chicago: University of Chicago Press).

Corbo, V. (2000b) 'Monetary Policy in Latin America in the 1990s', in N. Loayza and K. Schmidt-Hebbel (eds), *Monetary Policy Rules and Transmission Mechanisms* (Chile: Central Bank of Chile), mimeo.

Corbo, V. (2001) 'Is it Time for a Common Currency for the Americas?', *Journal of Policy Modelling*, vol. 23(3), pp. 241–8.

Corbo, V. and S. Fischer (1995) 'Structural Adjustment, Stabilization and Policy Reform: Domestic and International Finance', in J. Behrman and T. N. Srinivasan (eds), *Handbook of Development Economics, Vol. III* (New York: Elsevier).

Corbo, V., A. Elberg and J. Tessada (1999) 'Monetary Policy in Latin America: Underpinnings and Procedures', *Cuadernos de Economía* (December).

Corbo, V. and K. Schmidt-Hebbel (2001) 'Inflation Targeting in Latin America', paper presented at the Latin American Conference on Fiscal and Financial Reforms, Stanford University, CA. (January).

Díaz-Alejandro, C. (1982) 'Latin-America in Depression, 1929–1939', in M. Gersovitz, C. Díaz-Alejandro, G. Ranis and M. Rosenzweig (eds), *The Theory and Experience of Economic Development* (London: George Allen & Unwin).

Díaz-Alejandro, C. (1983) 'Stories of the 1930s for the 1980s', in P. Aspe *et al.* (eds), *Financial Policies and the World Capital Market: The Problem of Latin American Countries* (Chicago: University of Chicago Press).

Dornbusch, R. (1980) *Open Economy Macroeconomics* (New York: Basic Books).

Edwards, S. (1995) *Crisis and Reform in Latin America. From Despair to Hope* (Oxford: Oxford University Press).

Edwards, S. (2000) 'Exchange Rate Regimes, Capital Flows and Crisis Prevention', paper presented at the NBER Conference on Crisis Prevention (December).

Edwards, S. and M. Savastano (2000) 'Exchange Rates in Emerging Economies: What Do We Know? What Do We Need To Know?, in A. O. Krueger (ed.), *Economic Policy Reform: The Second Stage* (Chicago: University of Chicago Press).

Fischer, S. (2001) 'Exchange Rate Regimes: Is a Bipolar View Correct?' (mimeo) January.

Frankel, J. (1999) 'No Single Currency Regime is Right for all Countries or at all Times', NBER working paper no. 7338 (September).

Gavin, M. (1990) 'Structural Adjustment to a Terms of Trade Disturbance: The Role of Relative Prices', *Journal of International Economics*, vol. 28, nos 3/4, pp. 217–43.

International Monetary Fund, *World Economic Outlook* (various issues) (Washington, DC: IMF).

Kharas, H., B. Pinto and S. Ulatov (2001) 'An Analysis of Russia's 1998 Meltdown: Fundamentals and Market Signals', World Bank (mimeo) February.

Mishkin, F. S. (1999) 'International Experiences with Different Monetary Policy Regimes', NBER working paper no. 7044 (March).

Mussa, M., P. Masson, A. Swoboda, E. Jadresic, P. Mauro and A. Berg (2000) 'Exchange Rate Regimes in an Increasingly Integrated World Economy', IMF occasional paper no. 193.

Obtsfeldt, M. and K. Rogoff (1995) 'The Mirage of Fixed Exchange Rates', *Journal of Economic Perspectives*, vol. 9 (Fall), pp. 73–96.

Summers, L. (2000) 'International Financial Crises, Causes, Prevention and Cures', *American Economic Review*, vol. 90, no. 2, pp. 1–16.

Williamson, J. (1989) *Latin American Adjustment* (Oxford: Oxford University Press).

Williamson, J. (1996) *The Crawling Band as an Exchange Rate Regime: Lessons from Chile, Colombia and Israel* (Washington, DC: Institute for International Economics).

World Bank (1999) *Global Economic Prospects* (Washington, DC: The World Bank).

3
Banking Crises in Latin America in the 1990s: Lessons from Argentina, Paraguay and Venezuela

Alicia García-Herrero *

1 Introduction

This chapter analyses the banking crises in three Latin American countries – Argentina, Paraguay and Venezuela – in the mid-1990s, presenting an overview of the crisis in each country, with some lessons and consequences.

2 The Argentine banking crisis

Situation prior to the crisis

Argentina's banking crisis cannot be divorced from the currency crisis that the country experienced after the devaluation of the Mexican peso in December 1994, which adversely affected confidence in the Argentine economic and financial sectors. Since the early 1990s Argentina had been running current account deficits, and the drying up of external financing due to the Mexican crisis made it difficult to finance the public sector and meet external obligations. While the soundness of the banking system had generally improved in the 1990s following stricter bank supervision and regulation, problems with provincial banks remained. The deteriorating fiscal situation of the provinces and the poor management of most provincial banks resulted in a mounting volume of non-performing loans (NPLs) in these banks.

* This chapter is a shortened version of an IMF 1997 paper. My thanks go to J. T. Baliño, L. Catão, D. Dueñas, A. Ize, A. Leone, H. Mejia, E. Milne, C. Muñiz and R. Rosales for helpful comments, and L. Moore for research assistance.

Crisis developments

The crisis was triggered by the collapse of one small bond trader, with only 0.2 per cent of total Argentine deposits. The trader was closed down on 18 January 1995, and credit lines to other banks were cut. This triggered financial panic and capital flight as foreign investors and bank depositors feared that banks and government would renege on their obligations. The crisis spread rapidly throughout wholesale banks, which held large bond stocks and were dependent on large corporate deposits. Extensive withdrawals of deposits together with cuts in interbank lending forced some banks into liquidation. Flight from weak provincial cooperative and small retail banks created a major banking crisis. The interbank interest rate peaked at 70 per cent, while peso and US$ loan rates rose to 40 and 19 per cent respectively. Deposit rates rose sharply from 9 to 20 per cent for peso-denominated deposits and from 6 to 10 per cent for US$-denominated deposits. The situation was aggravated by capital flight. The central bank's international reserves slumped and the demand for peso-denominated deposits fell. The more stable funds were re-deposited in foreign-owned banks, or converted into foreign currency deposits. However, at the peak of the crisis, fears of devaluation spread and the credit lines of foreign banks with their headquarters were cut. US$ deposits started to fall resulting in massive capital flight.

The authorities' response

The government responded to fears of devaluation by reasserting its exchange-rate policy. The Convertibility Law severely restricted the central bank's role as lender of last resort (LLR), so in January 1995 the Central Bank of Republica Argentina (CBRA) persuaded the top five domestic banks to establish a safety net – initially of US$250 million but later raised to US$790 million – to buy the assets of illiquid wholesale banks. In exchange these banks were allowed to lower their reserves at the CBRA, and these freed funds were transferred to the Banco de la Nación (BN) to advance collateralized money to illiquid banks, in effect replacing the CBRA's LLR role. On 26 January 1995, the CBRA allowed '*numerales*', that is, the trading of excess legal reserve positions between financial institutions. As fears of devaluation grew, the government amended the CBRA Charter to allow it to lengthen the maturities of its swap and rediscount facilities. These measures are summarized in Table 3.1.

Deposit runs intensified due to the public's mistrust of the government's macroeconomic programme, and interest rates on peso and

Table 3.1   Measures to ensure banks' liquidity

Date	Measures
Jan. 1995	A$250 million safety net required from top 5 banks in exchange for reduced reserve requirements
Jan. 1995	A$790 million safety net from transfer of 2 per cent of pre-crisis deposit base from top 25 banks to BNC
Jan. 1995	Trading of excess legal reserve positions between banks allowed
Feb. 1995	Swaps and rediscounts allowed longer maturities and amounts exceeding the net worth of the borrowing bank
Mar. 1995	Banks with insufficient credit balance at Central Bank allowed to cover themselves with documents drawn on them to the amount necessary for a positive balance in that account

Source: National authorities

US$ deposits doubled. When several banks and bond traders stopped honouring deposits, concern increased over the solvency of the entire banking system. Memories of the 1989 banking crisis, when deposits were frozen and converted into bonds, added to the public's fears. By mid-March the CBRA had lost about US$5 billion of its international reserves which put the level of reserves below the monetary base, effectively breaking the Convertibility Law. The CBRA had to adopt further measures to reduce deposit runs on banks. On 13 March, the CBRA authorized banks to use up to 50 per cent of cash in vaults to purchase the assets of troubled banks. On 17 March, banks with insufficient credit at the CBRA were authorized to cover their 24-hour clearing balances, by presenting documents to the CBRA. This ensured positive balances and avoided the CBRA financing overdrafts that might jeopardize the Convertibility Law. Some banks were forced, therefore, to restructure their deposits, the *'pisada'*, by renewing term deposits and limiting withdrawals of current and deposit accounts. Meanwhile, the CBRA continued to provide rediscounts and swaps; in March 1995 these reached A$1.7 billion or 0.6 per cent of GDP.

The next, more comprehensive, step was a new IMF-supported programme, funded by a US$3.7 billion package from international financial institutions. In addition, two trust funds were set up to facilitate the restructuring of private banks and the privatization of provincial banks. Deposits at private banks were to be covered by a limited private deposit insurance scheme for local and foreign currency

Table 3.2 Measures to encourage banking confidence

Date	Measures
Apr. 1995	US$1.95 billion trust fund for privatization of provincial banks
Apr. 1995	US$2.50 billion trust fund for restructuring private banks
Apr. 1995	Limited private deposit insurance introduced
Apr. 1995	Financial Institution Act amended to increase CBRA's involvement in bank restructuring
Jan. 1997	US$6 billion medium-term line of credit for banks needing liquidity

Source: National authorities

deposits of less than 90 days up to a limit of A$20,000, which covered about 80 per cent of accounts.

These steps slowed down deposit runs, although a further loss of A$2.3 billion – nearly 1 per cent of 1995 GDP – occurred in the run up to the general election of 15 May 1995. After the election, measures were taken to free up more liquidity. The Financial Institution Act was amended to increase the CBRA's involvement in bank restructuring, increasing its powers to penalize individuals breaking banking regulations. Reserve requirements were replaced by liquidity requirements, which allowed banks to invest reserves previously held at the CBRA without remuneration in low-risk assets, thereby increasing bank profitability. After the May 1995 election, the deposit base recovered to its pre-crisis level at the end of 1995. This allowed for some cancellation of the CBRA's rediscounts and swaps and some recovery in the banks' cash assets. Finally, in early 1997, a US$6 billion medium-term line of credit with a group of foreign banks was established in order to secure liquidity for domestic banks in case of future need. These measures are summarized in Table 3.2 above.

The impact of the crisis

The CBRA succeeded in controlling inflation, largely through the reduction in public-sector credit. As regards interest rates, the measures taken by the authorities to inject liquidity and restore confidence somewhat reduced interbank rates although they stabilized on a high plateau. This, coupled with the sharp fall in private credit, temporarily pushed the economy into recession. NPLs doubled to reach 10 per cent of total credit by October 1995. Bank credit to the private sector fell 5 per cent in 1995, compared to growth rates of

19 per cent in the previous four years, as the high risks and liquidity regulations made lending to the public sector more attractive. Further, the concentration of bank activity in fewer banks (only 160 financial institutions out of 205 remained at the end of 1995) reduced the level of private credit offered. Real GDP declined by 4.5 per cent in 1995. Unemployment jumped from 12.5 per cent in October 1994 to a high of 18.6 per cent in May 1995. The government, however, maintained its economic programme, and a gradual recovery began in1996. The alternative strategy would have been to devalue, which would have fuelled inflation and been very costly due to the large share of debt denominated in foreign currency and the dollarization of the banking system.

3 Paraguay

Situation prior to the crisis

During most of the 1980s, the Paraguay financial system was adversely affected by an unstable macroeconomic environment and repressive financial policies. In addition, lax entry requirements during the 1980s, coupled with a poor legal framework and supervision system encouraged numerous relatively weak institutions to enter the market. In 1989, a new political regime introduced new economic policies. Reforms included the unification of the exchange rate and the floating of the guaraní (G), liberalization of interest rates, the introduction of market-based monetary instruments, and the partial removal of selective credit controls. From October 1990, the Central Bank of Paraguay (CBP) carried out open-market operations using its own short-debt instrument and reduced rediscount operations at subsidized rates, causing monetary expansion during the 1980s. In 1992, reforms included the authorization of foreign-currency loans by local banks, although only for export or import-substituting activities, followed during 1992–4 by the harmonization and gradual reduction of reserve requirements.

Improved economic conditions and financial liberalization reversed the declining trend in financial deepening, as shown by the ratio of broad money (M2) to GDP, which increased from 17 per cent in 1988 to 30 per cent in 1993. However, the major source of this growth in deposits was the transfer of public enterprise deposits and the Social Security Institute to private financial institutions. Although the informal private sector continued to be important, perhaps the more relevant financial channel, the volume of credit handled by banks increased from 10 per cent of GDP in 1988 to over 20 per cent in 1994, as a result of sizeable private capital inflows and central-bank rediscounts to agriculture and commerce sectors. At the same time, the degree of dollarization, in terms of US$ deposits to total deposits, rose from 3 per cent in 1988 to 32 per cent in 1993, as a consequence of positive real interest rates on US$-denominated time deposits. In 1994, however, dollarization decreased as new reserve requirements favoured guaraní deposits. Finally, financial liberalization led to a sharp increase in the real interest rates on guaraní-denominated certificates of deposit from negative to positive.

Despite the favourable environment, the level of capitalization in the banking system remained low. Interest-rate spreads widened sharply, reflecting the implicit tax arising from the higher reserve requirements and the need to cover losses from NPLs, which doubled in the seven months prior to the crisis. The Superintendence of Banks, although aware that about one-third of the system was virtually insolvent, was not empowered to apply appropriate sanctions. Meanwhile the CBP continued granting credit to problem banks since shareholders refused to provide additional capital. In December 1992, a system of loan classification was introduced but was resisted by the banking system. Indeed, several institutions obtained a 5-year grace period to comply with the loan risk classification. There was increased evidence of high credit concentration and insider lending practice, and in March 1995, two months before the onset of the crisis, 10 out of 34 banks were undercapitalized. Table 3.3 illustrates this.

Crisis developments

The crisis broke in May 1995 when a discrepancy of US$4 million was discovered in the CBP reserve holdings. Public confidence was shaken. Additionally, Banco General and Bancopar, the third and fourth largest commercial banks which had been identified as capital-deficient and had been pursuing an aggressive lending policy, announced that they could not meet their clearing obligations. The CBP intervened. This was the first of numerous interventions by the CBP. On investigation, widespread mismanagement and fraudulent practice were revealed in both banks: many of the recorded assets did not exist; over half the loans had been granted to related parties, and only a fraction of the banks' liabilities were registered. Unrecorded deposits found in a second book-keeping system, were either 'grey' in that adequate documentation only existed off-balance-sheet, or 'black' where no off-balance-sheet documentation existed. These tactics were intended either to evade the high reserve requirements or taxation on earnings.

Table 3.3   Selected balance sheet items, December 1994 and October 1996 (% of total)

Balance-sheet items	Private domestic banks	Foreign banks	Government banks	Total banks	Finance companies	Total financial sector (guaraní billion)
Assets						
Dec. 1994	41	36	16	93	7	5,263
Oct. 1996	32	42	17	92	10	
Deposits						
Dec. 1994	38	43	12	93	7	3,493
Oct. 1996	34	44	13	93	9	
Net worth						
Dec. 1994	37	33	14	84	16	856
Oct. 1996	49	29	10	85	12	

Source: National authorities

From May 1995 there was a massive withdrawal of deposits from private domestic banks, particularly from intervened banks. To avoid a run on the entire system and a failure to meet payments, the BCP provided distressed banks with massive liquidity. About half of this was used to offset deposit withdrawals, while the remainder was used to meet short-term external obligations and loans outstanding with other financial institutions. Even so, as a result of the large liquidity injection, flight to more secure foreign and government banks, and improved recording, total deposits only declined by about 2 per cent. The closure of five financial companies increased the loss of confidence, as investment bills issued by them had been widely used as a means for retail payment. Concern grew over the validity of post-dated cheques, frequently used in the retail sector. Delays in payments to depositors by the intervened banks led to withdrawals from any bank perceived as weak.

The authorities' response

The government assumed ownership of the four banks closed in mid-1995. These continued to operate under new management, but share-holders lost their stake. To reestablish public confidence and halt deposit withdrawals, CBP announced that it would honour the recorded deposits of intervened banks, a measure that later had to be extended to all banks and to unrecorded deposits. As the situation did not improve, in June 1995 the CBP introduced the so-called 'Bank Safety Net', to recycle liquidity from banks with increasing deposits to banks experiencing losses, with the CBP acting as broker. However, banks with excess reserves were reluctant to lend to distressed banks, so the CBP was forced to provide liquidity through rediscounts to distressed institutions. In practice rediscounts were given more freely than planned and by end-1995 CBP credit to intervened and distressed banks reached G700 billion, or 4 per cent of GDP. Despite these measures the banks' situation failed to improve. This led, in June 1996, to the introduction of a rehabilitation plan for distressed banks, and in November 1996 to a CBP programme to repurchase bad loans. Table 3.4 shows these confidence-boosting measures.

The impact of the crisis

Despite the massive liquidity injection, and a sharp increase in currency in circulation in mid-1995, caused by the run on deposits, there was an effective contraction of money in 1996. This was the result of the sharp fall in international reserves and the increase in bank reserves, reinforced by the measures taken by the authorities to sterilize excess liquidity, such as the reduction in net public-sector credit and the aggressive use of open-market operations to sterilize

Table 3.4 Measures to increase confidence in the banking system

Date	Measures
July 1995	Intervention in 4 banks, 6 finance companies and a savings & loans association (kept open to honour all registered deposits)
July 1995	BCP implicitly guarantees all deposits in financial system
Mid-1995	Congress law to honour unrecorded deposits vetoed by President
Mid-1995	Creation of 'bank safety net' – a special LLR facility to provide liquidity
June 1996	New banking law makes deposit insurance compulsory for banks. US$2,500 guaranteed per account
Nov. 1996	CBP purchase of loans to distressed banks
Dec. 1996	Adoption of Congressional law granting restitution of unrecorded deposits to US$1,500 per account

Source: National authorities

Table 3.5   Use of monetary instruments to manage liquidity

Instruments to inject liquidity	Instruments to absorb liquidity
CBP overdraft	Central bank paper
Bank safety net	High reserve requirements
CBP longer-term credit linked to banks' rehabilitation programmes	Sale of foreign reserves
CBP purchases banks' loans	Reduction of CBP credit to the public sector

Source: National authorities

the liquidity injection. Table 3.5 above shows the monetary instruments applied.

This non-accommodative monetary policy was supported by a cautious fiscal stance, which helped to dampen inflation to 10.5 per cent in 1995 compared to the 12 per cent official projection. However, restrictive economic policies, coupled with a shortage of private credit following the closure of banks, and the breakdown of the retail payments system resulted in low rates of growth in monetary aggregates and slowed economic activity. Bank lending stagnated and real interest rates remained high, as the banks were reluctant to lend.

Bank interest rate spreads widened reflecting growing uncertainty. Real interest rates rose at first, then fell back largely as a result of injections of liquidity. The impact of the crisis on the banking system was uneven leading to greater concentration and segmentation, as shown in the second row of Table 3.3. Private domestic banks reduced their share of deposits in the financial system, while foreign banks increased theirs but were reluctant to lend to small local borrowers. This was one of the reasons for the slow recovery in private credit.

4 Venezuela

Situation before the crisis

The Venezuelan economy performed poorly throughout the 1980s. Between 1980 and 1988, annual GDP growth averaged only 1 per cent, while average inflation increased from 6 to 24 per cent a year. Monetary policy was aimed at maintaining low, stable interest rates and subsidizing priority sectors. Real interest rates became increasingly negative, which encouraged strong capital outflows. Domestic deposits were transferred to offshore banks which contributed to a sharp fall in intermediation. In 1989 a major stabilization programme was introduced, supported by the IMF. Measures included the unification and floating of the exchange rate, a shift to market-based instruments for monetary control, and the removal of interest rate controls. Interest rates increased sharply and the measure of broad money (M2) recovered in 1990–91. Two attempted coups in 1991 and continued political instability contributed to a renewed decline in real M2 and capital flight. A currency crisis broke out in October 1992. At the beginning of 1993, a weak oil market, persistently lax fiscal policy and increasing political tension affected public confidence increasing pressure on the bolivar.

Before 1989, the Venezuelan banking system comprised numerous specialist banks owned by private domestic financial groups. These groups were virtually outside the control of the Superintendency of Banks. Banking suffered from low capitalization, and several banks failed as a result of excessive loan concentration, insider lending and weak management. As the government always bailed these banks out, depositors never bore the costs of failure. This practice encouraged excessive risk-taking by banks. Until the end of 1993 the financial sector remained largely unchanged, owing to delays in implementing any comprehensive financial reform programme designed to abolish barriers to the entry of foreign banks and to strengthen regulation and supervision. In this context, private banks, as shown in Table 3.6, still retained 90 per cent of assets; while government-owned banks accounted for less than 10 per cent and foreign-owned banks less than 1 per cent. Lax supervision, a high cost structure, inefficiency and poor reporting of data continued. Problem loans or losses were diverted to related affiliates, particularly offshore branches, so as to evade the regulations on loan concentration and reserve requirements.

In 1993, in response to a dramatic loss of international reserves, interest rates rose sharply. This increased the ratio of NPLs to

Table 3.6 Structure of the banking system (December 1993)

Type of bank	No. of banks	Per cent of total deposits
Private banks	36	90.2
National public banks	2	3.1
Foreign banks	4	0.7
Public regional banks	9	6.0
Total	51	100.0

Source: National authorities

10 per cent from about 4 per cent in 1991. Because of the reduction in credit, banks accumulated large excess reserves and used most of these funds to buy central bank or government bonds. Meanwhile, political and economic instability led to a fall in bank deposits. Banks, especially distressed banks with liquidity problems, increased their interest rates on saving deposits yet again to attract additional funds. Banks also took measures to attract savings to their offshore branches. This reduced the demand for domestic deposits and the liquidity of domestic banks. At end-1993, the CBV was forced to step up LLR facilities for those distressed banks, who were net borrowers in the interbank market (specially banks from the same financial group). Rumours of problems affecting whole financial groups spread contagion to sound banks.

Crisis developments

The banking crisis was triggered by the collapse in early 1994 of one of the oldest and largest banks in Venezuela, the Banco Latino, which caused widepread deposit withdrawals from the whole financial group. There was an attempt to meet these withdrawals by a sale of assets and borrowing from the CBV, but eventually the whole group whose assets totalled over 10 per cent of all commercial bank deposits had to be closed down.

The runs spread to other banks considered financially weak. The Deposit Guarantee Fund (FOGADE) reacted by offering massive financial assistance, financed through the LLR facilities of the CBV. Reserve requirements were reduced from 15 per cent to 12 per cent to channel funds to illiquid banks. In March 1994, increasing deposit withdrawals, capital flight and a sharp fall in CBV foreign reserves forced the government to legislate to protect depositors and nationalize the Banco Latino, which reopened within three months. FOGADE injected additional funds, valued at 3.6 per cent of the 1994 GDP, into the Banco Latino, whose losses were higher than envisaged following high-risk off-balance-sheet activities. Market expectations worsened, as did the public perception of the solvency of several banks. By the end of March, seven banks and one financial company had been virtually excluded from the interbank market. Runs also affected the trading desks and offshore operations of these banks. FOGADE continued to assist them without imposing any restructuring plan. In early June, the CBV stopped lending to FOGADE, causing a further loss of confidence, and intervened in the eight distressed financial institutions which had over 20 per cent of total deposits.

Table 3.7   Banking measures

Date	Measures
Feb. 1994	FOGADE's resources depleted following credit given to ailing banks after closure of Banco Latino
March 1994	Special law to protect depositors enforced, raising possibility of rehabilitating insolvent institutions
April 1994	Nationalization of Banco Latino
June 1994	Financial Emergency Board set up
July 1994	Fixed exchange rate, exchange rate controls and price controls introduced
Aug. 1994–Jan. 1995	Nationalization of several banks, and closure of four banks, and deposits transferred to newly nationalized banks
July 1995	Financial Emergency Law passed

Source: National authorities

To restore public confidence, in June the government established the Financial Emergency Board, a high-ranking executive body including Ministers of Finance, the Governor of the CBV and three senior officials. However, there was still no clear, consistent coping strategy. Money demand fell sharply, and capital flight dramatically reduced reserves. In July, the government fixed the exchange rate against the US$ and imposed strict controls on current and capital accounts. Price controls were imposed, and certain constitutional rights were suspended to enable the state to take over banks.

From August 1994 until February 1995 the situation worsened; three additional banks had to be nationalized, four closed and their deposits migrated to the nationalized banks without any corresponding assets. This raised the financial costs of the receiving banks. The government and FOGADE issued bonds which were transferred to the nationalized banks, effectively passing the costs on to taxpayers. Some former shareholders took legal action against the government. In July 1995, Congress finally passed the Financial Emergency Law, giving wider powers to the Financial Emergency Board, including control of the Superintendency and FOGADE. Still confidence did not return. Table 3.7 above summarizes the measures taken to deal with the crisis.

Macroeconomic impact

Prior to the crisis, Venezuela's tight monetary policy contributed to controlling inflation. Real interest rates were high and liquidity scarce. When runs on the Banco Latino started, the CBV provided massive

Table 3.8   Monetary instruments used to manage liquidity

Instruments to inject liquidity	Instruments to withdraw liquidity
CBV rediscount facilities	Sales of CB bonds
CBV loans to FOGADE for long-term loans to distressed banks	Sale of government bonds
Reserve requirements reduced	Sale of foreign reserves
Mechanism to free reserve requirements temporarily to sound banks to on-lend to distressed banks in inter-bank market	

Source: National authorities

liquidity, and reserve requirements were reduced to free additional liquidity. Interest rates declined to negative levels in real terms notwithstanding the efforts made by the CBV to absorb it through sales of central bank paper. However, there was concern over the large quasi-fiscal losses which prevented the CBV from stepping-up bond placements as needed. This period of excess liquidity allowed some banks to survive despite virtual insolvency, but increased inflation to about 100 per cent in 1996, compared to about 6 per cent in 1993. Table 3.8 above summarizes the CBV's use of monetary instruments.

The fiscal position of the public sector was weakened by the closure of and nationalization of failing banks, at a cost equal to about 17 per cent of GDP. Domestic public debt during the crisis rose from 7 per cent in 1993 to 16 per cent in 1995, and the financial position of the CBV was weakened by this increase in domestic debt. Despite negative real interest rates, GDP fell by 2.4 per cent in 1994 – oil being the growth sector. The recession was made worse by government intervention in non-financial enterprises connected to the failed banks, which increased bankruptcies. The imposition of exchange-rate controls created additional distortions, which further restricted growth.

The banks' asset structure was dramatically changed by the crisis. While the share of loans to total assets fell, public-sector credit increased sharply in the form of government and central-bank paper. Credit to the private sector shrank significantly owing to the decline in demand for loans and to the banks' increasingly conservative lending policy. The solvency of the banking sector was adversely affected by the economic recession. However, through a combination of fortuitous events in 1996, such as a sharp increase in the world price of oil, banks

Table 3.9   Bank structure before, during and after crisis (% of total commercial banks' deposits)

	December 1993	December 1994	September 1996
Private banks	90.2	58.4	58.9
Public national banks	3.1	4.4	5.6
Foreign banks	0.7	1.7	2.0
Regional public banks	6.0	7.6	9.4
Nationalized banks	n.a.	n.a.	23.1
Intervened banks	n.a.	19.5	0.5^2
Closed banks	n.a.	8.4^1	0.5^2

Notes: [1]Deposits of all banks closed between December 1994 and January 1995; [2] deposits on balance sheets of banks intervened or closed. n.a.: not available
Source: National authorities

improved their solvency and liquidity position. Devaluation of the bolivar also benefited several weak banks as they were allowed to accumulate long US$ positions. With nationalization the number of state-owned banks and their share of deposits increased sharply. The flight to quality tripled the share of deposits in foreign-owned and government-owned banks, which were perceived as safe. These developments are summarized in Table 3.9 above.

5 Lessons from these crises

Given the small number of countries reviewed, the lessons drawn here cannot be extrapolated to all countries. Nevertheless, these points may prove useful as a benchmark for future crises, as long as a country's individual characteristics are not overlooked:

1 *Banking crises caused by macroeconomic and bank-specific factors had the largest negative macroeconomic impact*
   The crisis was most severe in Venezuela where it was caused by a combination of macroeconomic imbalances, incomplete financial liberalization and a lack of adequate banking supervision. The banking system was saddled with problems, such as high levels of insider lending and loan concentration as well as outright fraud. Several banks had embarked on aggressive expansion resulting in accumulated losses. The unstable political environment and high real interest rates contributed to the eruption of the crisis.
   The contagion effect was most severe in Argentina where it originated as an external shock spread from Mexico; the banking crisis

coincided with a currency crisis, but had a lesser macroeconomic impact, particularly as regards inflation. In Paraguay, the banking crisis arose from bank-specific problems, stemming from financial liberalization with inadequate bank regulation and supervision and governance problems. Both the Venezuelan and Paraguay cases point to the need for an appropriate incentive structure and strong supervision and regulation, including exit policies.

2 *Without tough exit policies banks tend to take higher risks; history matters*

The extent of deposit runs will partly depend on past history. Fully honouring deposits, either through bail-outs or a generous deposit guarantee, boosts public confidence in the banking system, which should limit financial flight. Memory of Argentina's previous banking and balance-of-payments crises partly explains the depth of the 1995 crisis and the rapidity of deposit withdrawals. In Paraguay, few banks had experienced any official intervention, and banks needing liquidity competed for financial resources regardless of risk. Considering the Venezuelan banking crisis in terms of the number of institutions and deposits affected, the macroeconomic impact might have been expected to be more severe. But a past history of bail-outs and limited inflation mitigated the severity of deposit runs. Nevertheless, as neither banks nor shareholders carried the cost of bank failure, the environment was conducive to high risk-taking.

3 *In a country with a fixed-exchange rate and currency-board control, a balance-of-payments crisis easily becomes a banking crisis and exchange–rate controls are not a panacea*

In Argentina, the crisis was the direct result of massive capital outflows that followed the Mexican peso devaluation. Argentina's high degree of dollarization together with substantial public and private foreign currency-denominated debt would have increased the negative impact on the crisis had the country devalued. In Venezuela, at the peak of the crisis the government introduced exchange controls and a fixed exchange rate; this failed to stop financial flight or contain inflation, but weakened external financing prospects.

4 *Dollarization may help to stabilize the deposit base during a banking crisis*

Argentina, the most dollarized of the three countries reviewed, at first, succeeded in limiting capital flight. These US$ deposits acted as a buffer until confidence drained, leading to a run on US$

deposits. The same, although to a lesser extent, happened in Paraguay. In Venezuela, where US$ deposits were not allowed there was substantial capital flight, helped by the offshore market closely connected to the domestic system. This fostered instability, deepened the crisis and increased the adverse macroeconomic impact.

5 *Foreign and government banks helped to stabilize the deposit base*
   In Argentina and Paraguay the large number of foreign and government-owned banks encouraged flight into quality rather than capital flight. In Venezuela, where there were few foreign-owned or government banks, capital flight was greater. The existence of an unsupervised offshore banking system in both Paraguay and Venezuela accelerated capital flight. Consolidated financial bank statements, including offshore and off-balance-sheet operations, might have helped the supervisory authorities avert a crisis.

6 *Contagion effects among banks may stem from excessive specialization*
   In Argentina, bond traders and wholesale banks suffered from contagion effects when one small bond trader failed in December 1994. The abrupt loss of value in bonds following the Mexican crisis encouraged contagion. This highlights the risk of non-diversified portfolios financed by volatile deposits. In Paraguay, the contagion effects probably arose from problems in the payments system. Depositors with intervened banks endured months of delay before they could withdraw funds. This delay increased the perception of other banks as distressed, exacerbating withdrawals.

7 *Delays by the authorities in responding to a banking crisis may reduce public confidence, create a failure in the payments system, aggravating negative macroeconomic consequences*
   Argentina responded the most quickly and comprehensively to signs of major weaknesses in the banking sector. Deposit withdrawals were contained by enlarging the role of the central bank as lender of last resort and establishing trust funds to restructure the banking system. Venezuela's response was slower and lacking in strategy. In Paraguay, delays to distressed and intervened banks disrupted the payments system, which affected economic growth. The lack of a comprehensive rehabilitation programme added to the public's lack of confidence in the domestic banking system.

8 *Well-functioning lender-of-last-resort facilities reduce the negative macroeconomic impact of a banking crisis*
   The case of Argentina shows the importance of being able to adopt lender-of-last-resort policies when the banking system is hit by a shock. In Paraguay and Venezuela aid was not directed at the

soundest institutions and the provision of liquidity to insolvent banks increased costs associated with the crisis. In Paraguay and Venezuela, the provision of liquidity to insolvent banks increased risks and insider withdrawal of deposits, made worse by a lack of regulation and supervision. The costs associated with the failure of institutions were higher because banks were not closed when problems emerged. The deposit insurance scheme had insufficient funds to meet its obligations, which intensified deposit runs. In Paraguay, the massive financial assistance given to intervened and distressed banks was given without conditionality or collateral. The establishment of the Bank Security Net, as lender of last resort, helped restore confidence, but at a high cost because of lax credit mechanisms.

9 *Sound macroeconomic and anti-inflation policies are essential to resolve a banking crisis*
   In Paraguay favourable macroeconomic conditions and a cautious fiscal policy helped to offset the impact of extended credit by the central bank to distressed banks, and reduced pressure on the foreign-exchange market and interest rates. In Argentina, however, the situation was complicated by underdeveloped capital markets, and the inflexibility of the currency board. In Venezuela, inadequate macroeconomic policies before the crisis contributed to an unsustainable asset boom in the early 1990s, macroeconomic instability with episodes of capital flight and an erosion of real money demand. During the crisis, monetary and fiscal policy was too expansionary and, therefore, inconsistent with stability. Negative real interest rates increased pressure on the bolivar adding to the costs of the crisis.

10 *How liquidity levels are managed will be crucial to controlling the crisis*
   In Argentina, the high legal reserve requirements before the crisis enabled the system to cope with massive withdrawals. The establishment by Argentina of a line of credit with foreign banks was viewed positively during the crisis.

   High reserve requirements can be distortionary, as in Paraguay. The high reserve requirements led rapidly to the development of an informal financial sector, including off-balance sheet operations and offshore banking. In Venezuela, reserve requirements were reduced during the crisis, which contributed to excess liquidity. Sales of central-bank paper were not enough to absorb the excess liquidity, and so the central bank lost monetary control and inflation surged.

11 *Recovery of private credit may depend on structural change*
The experience of Argentina and Paraguay shows that high bank concentration and many foreign-owned banks may delay the recovery of private credit. This is more marked where the crisis is accompanied by flight to foreign-owned banks. An economic recession will further reduce the level of private credit, as happened in Venezuela.

12 *Quasi-fiscal losses should be borne by the government*
Typically, central banks find it difficult to transfer the quasi-fiscal losses incurred during a banking crisis to the government. While these losses remain on the central bank's balance sheet, they reduce the central bank's ability to control inflation. In Paraguay, the assistance to distressed institutions was nearly twice the level of deposits withdrawn; often this was in non-collateralized overdrafts or the collateral was non-performing loans. In Venezuela, the central bank lent large sums to the Deposit Guarantee Fund, which provided distressed banks with liquidity without any conditionality and little or no collateral. However, as the crisis worsened the Deposit Guarantee Fund itself became insolvent, and the central-bank was unable to provide central-bank paper for monetary control which itself fuelled inflation.

4
On the Causes of the Latin American and Asian Currency Crises of the 1990s

*Marcel Fratzscher**

1 Introduction

Asia's 1997 severe financial crisis surprised many policy-makers, economists and investors; as did the Latin American crisis in December 1994. These crises shocked not only by their severity, with large currency devaluations, widespread financial-sector failures and sharp output contractions, but also by their contagious character – spreading among regional economies. One controversial issue remains as to the factors responsible for this spread of currency crises. Could the weakness of economic fundamentals in affected countries explain their transmission, or was it the acts of speculators, and of panic and herding behaviour by investors fearful of financial loss fleeing regional markets? This chapter attempts to shed light on this question by comparing the spread of the Thai crisis in 1997 and the Mexican crisis in 1994–95.

Many observers of both crises blamed presumably unsustainable policies and poor economic performance for the transmission. To evaluate this assertion critically, we present and test a model linking the transmission of currency crises with contagion based on economic fundamentals, and with contagion resulting from factors independent of fundamentals. The role of various economic fundamentals is analysed:

- Misalignments of the real exchange rate and current account deficits as measures of the viability of a country's exchange-rate regime.

* I would like to thank Markus Diehl for comments as well the office of the Harvard Institute of International Development (HIID) in Jakarta, Indonesia, for accommodating me while researching this topic in November 1997 and April 1998. An earlier version of this chapter was published in *Weltwirtschaftliches Archiv*, vol. 134, no. 4.

- Bank lending to the private sector as a proxy for the health of the banking and financial system.
- The size and composition of capital inflows and foreign debt to indicate a country's vulnerability to capital flow reversals.

The integration of financial markets and the degree of export competitiveness among emerging markets was included to determine whether countries suffered a financial crisis because they were financially closely integrated with, or were competitors of, the country where the crisis originated.

The empirical tests of the model refute the hypothesis that unsustainable policies and weak economic fundamentals alone explain the transmission of these crises. Our findings show that financial and trade integration among affected countries were important in accounting for the spread of both crises, suggesting that transmission is partly explained by factors unrelated to the soundness of economic fundamentals. Moreover, the vulnerability to capital-flow reversals and weak financial sectors in Asia, and the unsustainability of exchange-rate policies and unsound financial systems in Latin America, contributed to the transmission of the crises.

The chapter is organized as follows. Section 2 surveys some of the theoretical and empirical literature on currency crises and contagion, and section 3 analyses and compares the Latin American and Asian crises. A basic model of currency crises and their underlying causes is presented and tested in section 4; a modified model is outlined to test whether contagion affected primarily countries with weak fundamentals. Sections 5 and 6 discuss policy implications and conclusions.

2 Currency crises and contagion: an overview of the literature

Models and literature on currency crises

Currency crises have traditionally been analysed from one of two theoretical perspectives. The first-generation approach, originating from Krugman's (1979) seminal work, implied that the unsustainability of economic policies was the ultimate cause of financial crises. Unwise fiscal and monetary policies, excessive credit expansion, an overvalued exchange rate, and a worsening current account confirmed macroeconomic imbalances and signalled to investors and speculators that exchange-rate policies were incompatible with economic fundamentals, ultimately leading to a speculative attack on the currency.

Second-generation models extended the first-generation approach, as discussed by Garber and Svensson (1994) and Agenor, Bhandari and Flood (1992), emphasizing governments' sometimes multiple and contradictory policy goals. If ensuring currency stability conflicts with other policy objectives, such as maintaining steady output growth, full employment and low inflation, a government may relax its exchange-rate regime. For instance, a government may devalue in response to a speculative attack in order to protect the banking sector from higher interest rates. A government's decision to alter its exchange-rate policy does not necessarily require domestic policy failures. Changes in economic conditions in neighbouring countries or large trading partners may alter expectations, which will affect domestic output, wages and employment levels. The government may decide to let the currency devalue to lessen adverse consequences, leading to self-fulfilling expectations yielding multiple equilibria.[1]

A third more recent type of literature focuses on the interaction between banking crises and balance-of-payments crises, or 'twin crises'. This literature emphasizes the role of the banking sector and the reversal of capital flows before crises. Kaminsky and Reinhart (1996) showed that many balance-of-payments crises were preceded by a rapid expansion in banking activity, and often a domestic banking crisis. Their findings reveal that financial liberalization and deregulation are closely linked to banking crises, which suggests that inappropriate deregulation and insufficient supervision of the financial sector may be contributary factors.

On the empirical side, a rich literature on financial crisis episodes has emerged since the late 1980s,[2] and there is a broad consensus that most crisis countries had previously faced some fundamental macroeconomic imbalance. However, attempts to identify a predictive set of variables so far lack success, or as Dornbusch (1998) puts it: 'Of six crises predicted by experts, five never happen'. Kaminsky, Lizondo and Reinhart (1997) suggest a methodology that tracks the behaviour of economic variables prior to crises and identifies them as 'signals' of a future crisis occurring if they deviate significantly from usual levels. If accurate, such models could become invaluable tools for policymakers.

Contagion

Various studies have attempted to analyse the spread among economies of financial crises.[3] Contagion effects can broadly be categorized into four groups: 'fundamentals contagion', 'real integration contagion', 'herding contagion' and 'institutional contagion', the former two being based on real factors in an economy and the latter two relating to financial phenomena.

'Fundamentals contagion' implies that the transmission of a crisis occurs if affected countries have similar economic fundamentals or face common external shocks. If a financial crisis occurs in one country, investors and speculators become sensitive to similar risks in other countries, and reduce their exposure in those countries with 'weak' fundamentals thus spreading the crisis among economies.

'Real integration contagion' refers to the phenomenon that investors and speculators reduce their exposure in countries closely integrated with the crisis economy. The reason is that a crisis in one country may have important real effects for related economies. If a currency collapses in a closely related country, a government may actually want to devalue its currency to regain competitiveness.

'Herding contagion' refers to the behaviour of investors who simply follow other investors blindly. Herding behaviour is not necessarily 'irrational', but this behaviour is not justified by economic fundamentals. Acquiring information to make a more informed decision may be costly, making it rational for smaller investors to follow large investors with superior information.[4] Herding behaviour also explains how a few large investors and speculators move markets, and how a few pessimistic expectations become a vicious cycle of self-fulfilling expectations. In particular, herding behaviour can be crucial for the success of speculative attacks, if enough investors are persuaded to sell the domestic currency and run down international reserves, forcing a government to devalue.

Frankel and Schmukler (1996) argue that the incentive structure for fund managers and traders may encourage them to act in a way contrary to the broader macroeconomic perspective. The performance of fund managers is often measured relative to that of other fund managers, which may make them more risk-averse and induce them to optimize short-run returns. To follow common investment strategies can therefore be optimal from an individual manager's point of view, but sub-optimal from a longer-term perspective.

A fourth type of contagion may be called 'institutional contagion' where a financial crisis in one country, usually accompanied by a decline in stockmarket returns, may induce investors to reduce asset holdings in other countries. Fund managers may lower asset holdings in other countries either to balance portfolios and to optimize the overall risk/return ratio, or to raise cash to meet redemptions as investors withdraw funds. 'Institutional contagion' helps explain how financial crises spread among countries without weak real economic fundamentals.

In the empirical literature, many studies link the onset of currency crises with 'fundamentals contagion', but with no general consensus as to the key factors. Fewer studies have attempted to identify sources for other types of contagion. Calvo and Reinhart (1996) argued that stock-market returns during the Latin America 1994–95 crisis were partly explained by economic fundamentals and partly due to high financial integration with Mexico. Frankel and Schmukler (1996) looked at the prices and net asset values of country funds for Latin America and found that the spread of the Mexican funds was substantially based on herding and institutional contagion. Eichengreen, Rose and Wyplosz (1996) showed that trade integration and linkages largely explained the spread of currency crises among industrialized countries.

3   Comparing the Latin American crisis and the Asian crisis: some stylized facts

Various internal and external imbalances made both Mexico in 1994 and Thailand in 1997 natural targets for speculators. Both countries had received large capital inflows and foreign investment; export growth deteriorated sharply and the current account deficit rose significantly the year before the crisis. High foreign debt and worsening current account deficits meant a rapid rise in short-term, US$-denominated debt. Both countries experienced a significant real appreciation of their exchange rates, strengthening the perception that fixed exchange-rate regimes were becoming unsustainable in the medium term. A combination of speculative attacks, investor panic and an obviously overvalued exchange rate made devaluation inevitable.The controversial question is which transmission channels spread the Mexican and Thai crises to other emerging markets.

Analysts of the Latin American crisis were quick to identify external imbalances, and in particular overvalued exchange rates, to explain why the crisis spread among regional economies. Table 4.1 provides a comparison of key economic indicators. Argentina and Brazil had run current account deficits and experienced real currency appreciations prior to the crisis; nevertheless, why other Latin American countries with similar imbalances escaped the crisis is puzzling. Chile and Colombia, for instance, experienced real currency appreciations but were barely affected. A fixed exchange-rate regime as in Brazil and

Table 4.1 Comparison of economic indicators prior to crises

	Prior to Latin American crisis 1994						Prior to Asian crisis 1997					
	RER 1990–94	% change 1992–94	CE 1990–94	CA % 1994	RES % Nov 1994	DEBT % Dec 1994	RER 1990–97	% change 1995–97	CE 1990–96	CA % 1996	RES % June 1997	DEBT % June 1997
Latin America												
Argentina	9.0	−6.1	8.4	−3.6	6.8	6.7	19.2	10.5	8.7	−1.3	8.4	8.0
Brazil	26.1	40.3	10.4	−0.2	9.6	4.5	20.5	5.7	9.6	−3.3	11.0	5.9
Chile	13.9	−1.1	5.8	−3.1	11.5	12.8	33.2	8.0	12.4	−5.4	10.6	10.6
Colombia	19.1	11.3	2.7	−4.5	6.9	7.4	36.0	17.5	3.9	−5.5	9.2	7.7
Mexico	11.1	−1.1	21.9	−7.0	1.5	7.9	0.1	20.0	−1.8	−0.6	3.5	8.4
Peru	−3.1	8.9	8.9	−5.3	9.9	4.5	3.7	8.4	15.8	−5.9	14.1	8.8
Venezuela	5.4	17.7	−7.1	4.3	9.8	6.2	34.1	−2.4	−7.7	12.6	14.5	5.5
Asia												
India	−22.7	−7.0	−0.6	−0.6	8.4	2.4	−18.3	9.0	−1.2	−1.5	6.5	2.3
Indonesia	−1.1	−1.7	1.5	−1.6	4.5	12.0	7.2	9.5	6.1	−3.3	5.0	15.4
Korea	−17.0	−5.1	4.7	−1.0	2.5	10.5	−13.4	−0.5	9.7	−4.8	2.3	14.3
Malaysia	7.1	−2.9	4.3	−6.2	5.4	9.3	17.5	9.8	15.9	−4.9	3.8	18.5
Pakistan	4.2	5.4	−0.9	−3.5	3.6	3.8	9.9	5.3	−0.8	−6.5	0.9	4.7
Philippines	5.8	3.9	10.8	−4.6	3.1	4.9	19.5	21.6	30.1	−4.7	3.3	9.9
Sri Lanka	5.7	−4.3	5.8	−6.5	5.1	4.5	15.0	−1.6	7.1	−4.7	3.5	2.9
Thailand	−1.6	−1.8	27.9	−5.6	5.8	21.6	10.2	13.1	34.3	−8.1	6.3	24.9
Africa/Middle East												
Jordan	1.0	0.2	2.5	−6.6	6.7	n.a.	1.4	3.0	3.2	−3.1	5.6	n.a.
Nigeria	50.8	126.7	0.3	−5.1	1.0	n.a.	45.9	67.2	0.3	4.4	15.7	n.a.
South Africa	−4.4	−5.9	−2.5	−0.3	0.6	4.3	−3.3	3.8	−4.5	−1.6	0.8	10.4
Turkey	−29.3	−23.8	−2.3	1.9	3.2	n.a.	−24.2	−1.4	0.8	−0.8	4.3	n.a.
Zimbabwe	−25.5	−11.6	3.2	−6.2	2.4	n.a.	−19.2	−1.6	3.2	n.a.	3.2	n.a.

Notes: RER = real effective exchange rate (positive number means appreciation); CE = credit to private sector/GDP; RES = reserves/imports; DEBT = short-term foreign debt/GDP; na = not available

Sources: IMF; JP Morgan; BIS

Argentina clearly makes a speculative currency attack more likely; however, most Latin American countries had similar regimes, and the Philippines, the country hardest hit in Asia, had one of the more flexible currency regimes.

In the case of the Asian crisis in 1997–98, many analysts blamed overvalued currencies and inflexible exchange-rate regimes for part of the problems. This critique, however, seems misplaced. Although there was some real appreciation of exchange rates in many Southeast Asian countries, many Latin American exchange rates were even more overvalued. The only measures where Asian countries performed worse was credit expansion to the private sector, the size of short-term foreign debt and short-term capital inflows. This suggests that dependence on foreign capital may have made many Asian economies vulnerable.

These Southeast Asian countries were the showcase of emerging markets: except for the Philippines, they had been growing at rates of over 6 per cent a year for the past decade, had extraordinary savings and investment rates, low inflation rates, and a reputation for sound economic policy management. Given this perspective, moderate current account deficits had not been considered unsustainable. Therefore, the severity of the crisis in Southeast Asia came as a surprise, and attempts to blame 'weak' economic fundamentals alone for the crisis are unconvincing.

4 An empirical analysis of currency crises and contagion

The stylized facts of the two crises raise doubts about the hypothesis that differences in macroeconomic factors can explain why the crises spread to other emerging markets from Mexico in 1994 and Thailand in 1997. Was contagion random? We consider this question from an analytical point of view.

A basic model of contagion

First, one needs to define the term 'currency crisis'. If investors perceive weaknesses in an economy or consider government policies unsustainable, they come to expect a devaluation. Capital inflows dry up and investors convert domestic assets into foreign-currency-denominated assets. The demand for foreign exchange increases, putting pressure on the domestic currency to depreciate. A government has two options for dealing with capital flow reversals and pressure to devalue: either it can devalue and incur capital losses on investors holding domestic currency, or it can fend off the attack on currency by servicing the demand for foreign exchange and running down reserves, and/or raising interest rates to discourage capital flight and to increase the demand for the domestic currency.

Given these options, a crisis index was calculated using the weighted average of the percentage devaluation of the domestic currency above trend, the percentage loss in reserves and the percentage change in short-term real interest rates over the five-month period during which the crisis occurred:[5] for Latin America, December 1994 to April 1995; and for Asia, July to December 1997. Unlike many empirical models of currency crises, the basic model did not choose a random cut-off point above which a devaluation is defined as a currency crisis.[6] The two main advantages of the measure used here are that the severity of a currency crisis can be determined by using a continuous variable, and all three defining elements (devaluation, fall in reserves, and rise in interest rate) are included.[7]

To test for the dominant type of contagion transmitting the crisis from Mexico and Thailand, the model expresses the currency crisis measure (CC) as a function of various economic fundamentals (FUN_i), as well as a function of financial market integration (INT) and trade competitiveness (COMP) with the country where a currency crisis first occurred (with Mexico in 1994 and with Thailand in 1997). The two time periods included ($t = 1$) for Latin American and ($t = 2$) for Asia. The basic model is:

$$CC_t = \alpha + \beta_t FUN_{i,t} + \chi RES_t + \delta INT_t + \gamma COMP_t + \varepsilon_t \qquad (1)$$

The economic fundamentals variable (FUN_i) is used to indicate 'fundamentals contagion', whereas financial market integration (INT) is employed to proxy 'herding contagion' and 'institutional contagion', and competitiveness (COMP) measures 'real integration contagion'. Before testing this model empirically, we consider the intuition of including these variables in the model.

'Fundamentals contagion'

A number of macroeconomic factors may help to explain why a country experiences a balance-of-payments crisis. I distinguish between three groups of fundamentals: misalignments of the real exchange rate and current account deficits as measures of a country's ability to sustain its exchange-rate regime; bank lending to the private sector as an indicator of the health of the banking and financial system; the size and composition of capital inflows, and foreign debt to measure a country's vulnerability to capital flow reversals.

Concerning the first group, an overvalued real exchange rate (*RER*) and a large current account deficit (*CA*) make a currency crisis more likely and more severe. *RER* is measured as the appreciation of the real exchange rate relative to a country's main trading partners over a number of years pre-crisis. The obvious difficulty in generating a meaningful measure is to determine what constitutes an overvaluation. Three different measures were tested: the change in the real exchange rate between 1990 and the onset of the crisis, a two-year span, and one year prior to the crisis. The choice of the *RER* measure, however, did not make a significant difference as all three *RER* measures yielded similar results. The idea of including the current account (*CA*) is that the larger this deficit, the higher the demand for foreign currency and the risk that borrowers will be unable to repay their debts. Once investors reduce their financing of a country's external deficit, the country may be forced to devalue, thus reducing the ability of domestic borrowers to repay foreign loans even further.

The credit expansion (*CE*) variable is used to measure the weakness of a country's banking system. Ideally, one would like to measure the vulnerability of banking systems as the share of bad loans relative to total credit, but these data were not available across countries. Instead, following the example of Sachs, Tornell and Velasco (1996), the increase in bank lending to the private sector as a share of GDP was used. The idea is that if bank lending expands rapidly, the ability of banks to monitor lending activities is limited, and credit to higher-risk areas such as the property sector and consumer loans increases. This increases the share of bad loans in banks' portfolios making the sector more vulnerable to a financial crisis.[8]

Third, we tested whether increased vulnerability to capital flow reversals increased the likelihood of a transmission of the currency crises. Countries that rely heavily on short-term capital inflows (*CAP*)[9] are more vulnerable to capital flow reversals and need to make larger adjustments if a balance-of-payments crisis occurs. Similarly, if a country has high short-term foreign-currency-denominated debt (*DEBT*),[10] the size of the capital flow reversal will be more substantial, leading to larger devaluations. A large government deficit as a share of GDP (*GOV*) may increase the likelihood of a financial crisis. An excessive fiscal deficit often contributes to a current account deficit and a real appreciation of the domestic currency, making a balance-of-payments crisis more likely.

Finally, the level of a country's reserves (*RES*) may be important in discouraging speculative attacks, and in determining the severity of a financial crisis. Speculative attacks are less likely if a central bank has sufficient international reserves to back its currency, and even if there is a run on reserves it may be able sustain the exchange-rate regime without raising interest rates to prohibitive levels. The reserve measures tested in the model were the ratio of reserves to imports and the ratio of reserves to M2 in the month prior to the crisis (November 1994 for Latin America and June 1997 for Asia).

'Herding contagion' and 'institutional contagion'

To determine whether the transmission of balance-of-payments crises was based on factors other than fundamentals, this model used the correlation of weekly stockmarket returns (*INT*) in the the country of origin (Mexico in 1994 and Thailand in 1997) and other emerging markets as a proxy for 'herding contagion' and 'institutional contagion'. High correlations of stockmarket returns result if investors consider that a group of countries have similar risks and prospects. If one country is hit by a financial crisis, investors may leave the financial markets of connected countries either to adjust their investment holdings and to raise cash ('institutional contagion'), or because they fear the spread to connected countries and follow the example of other investors ('herding contagion'). This measure of contagion implies that the greater the financial integration with the crisis country, the greater the contagion.

A shortcoming of this measure is that stockmarket returns may primarily be the result of common fundamentals and not due to financial integration. To correct for this potential bias, stockmarket returns (*RET*) for each country were regressed on a number of economic fundamentals for the tranquil period between January 1992 and six months prior to the respective crises in Mexico (*t* = 1) and Thailand (*t* = 2):

$$RET_{i,t} = \pi_0 + \pi_1\,CA_{i,t} + \pi_2 CAP_{i,t}\ \pi_3 E_{i,t} + \pi_4 r_{i,t} + \pi_5 P_{i,t} + \varepsilon_{i,t} \qquad (2)$$

with the independent variables being the current account (*CA*), portfolio capital inflows (*CAP*), the nominal exchange rate (*E*), the change in a country's interest rate (*r*) and the rate of inflation (*P*) for each country *i* at time *t*.

The correlations of the residuals indicate the degree of financial-market integration after controlling for fundamentals. If high correlations of returns were mainly due to similarities of economic fundamentals, then the correlations of these residuals should be significantly lower than the correlations of returns. The evidence refutes this hypothesis. In fact, correlations of the residuals were in some cases higher than the correlations of the returns, especially for Asian countries. Table 4.2 presents these results. The residual correlations reveal that financial markets of most Southeast and East Asian economies are highly integrated with Thailand. This finding holds to a lesser extent for Mexico and Latin American markets prior to the Mexican crisis.

'Real integration contagion'

Currency crises may be transmitted not only between economies that are integrated financially, but also between those that have similar economic structures and are closely integrated via trade flows. I refer to this phenomenon as 'real integration contagion'. The argument is that a currency crisis is more likely to spread to a country that is trading or competing strongly with the crisis country. A devaluation in one country is likely to worsen the trade balance of close trading partners, putting pressure on these countries to adjust their policies and possibly to devalue. However, this effect is not usually strong among developing countries as bilateral trade is relatively small and most exports are directed at industrialized countries. The more important effect for developing countries results from competition between economies for export market shares in industrialized countries. If one country devalues, closely integrated countries may devalue to regain competitiveness or may be unable to withstand speculative pressure on their currencies.

To test whether countries were affected by the Mexican or Thai crisis as a result of their close trade integration with these two countries, an index of trade competitiveness was constructed for each of the countries in the sample using the following formula:

$$COMP_j = \sum_c \sum_d \left(\frac{X_{id}^c}{X_d^c} \times \frac{X_{jd}^c}{X_j} \right)^{d \neq i,j} + \sum_c \left(\frac{X_{ij}^c}{X_{\cdot j}^c} \times \frac{X_{ji}^c}{X_{j\cdot}} \right) \qquad (3)$$

or for simplicity: $COMP_j = (A * B) + E$. Term $(A * B)$ measures the degree of competition between country j and country i (i being either Mexico or Thailand) in all third markets d. Term B calculates how large the export share of one commodity c to one region d is of total exports for country j, weighted by term A, which is the market share Mexico or Thailand have in this commodity market in region d. As an example, if both Indonesia and Thailand sell a large share of their total exports as footwear in the USA, then the index yields a relatively high number indicating that Thailand is a strong competitor in an important Indonesian market. This calculation was done for all commodity exports X^c to all regions d and then summed for each country. World Trade Database data were aggregated to three-digit SITC categories of manufacturing exports for 1993/4 to six regions (Africa/Middle East, Latin America, USA/Canada, Europe, Asia/Australia, and 'other'). Term E measures the bilateral manufacturing trade of country j with either Mexico or Thailand. The nominator calculates total exports to and imports from country i for country j. The denominator sums total exports and imports for country j. If country j's trade with country i is a large share of total trade, the index yields a large number and vice versa. One problem in calculating the total index $COMP_j$ was how to weight bilateral trade and third-market trade relative to each other. Indices with different weights were tested in the empirical analysis – equal weights or giving either bilateral trade or third-market trade double weights – with robust results. Table 4.2 lists the standardized competitiveness indices (average = 100) for each country vis-à-vis Mexico and vis-à-vis Thailand, confirming that regional economies are mostly close competitors, with similar export structures and export destinations.

Empirical results of the basic model

To measure contagion effects, the analysis covered emerging markets with a relatively open capital account that allowed foreign investors to invest relatively freely as defined by the International Finance Corporation's *Emerging Stock Market Factbook*. Table 4.3 presents the results of the empirical analysis of the basic model for 20 open emerging markets in the two crisis episodes that began in Mexico in 1994–95 and in Thailand in 1997. Transition economies are excluded partly due to data comparability and availability. The table shows the results of the standard OLS regressions for the Latin American crisis, the Asian crisis, and both crises combined.[11] The combined regression (1) finds little evidence that the transmission of the two crises was based on differences in economic fundamentals. Only the current account (*CA*) variable is significant. On the contrary, lower reserves (*RES*), and both higher financial integration (*INT*) and trade competitiveness (*COMP*) with the country where the crisis originated made a balance-of-payments crisis more likely and more severe.

The key finding of the model is that the spread of the Mexican crisis in 1994–95 and the Thai crisis in 1997 were fundamentally different. An overvalued real exchange rate (*RER*), a worsening of the current account (*CA*) and insufficient reserves (*RES*) were important factors in

Table 4.2 Comparison of financial integration (*INT*) and trade integration (*COMP*)

	Integration with Mexico 1994		Integration with Thailand 1997	
	Financial integration (INT)	Trade integration (COMP)	Financial integration (INT)	Trade integration (COMP)
Latin America				
Argentina	0.48	169.2	0.24	47.1
Brazil	0.66	293.2	0.08	97.4
Chile	0.43	138.9	0.26	17.6
Colombia	−0.01	220.3	−0.06	67.5
Mexico	–	–	0.60	51.7
Peru*	0.38	302.9	0.38	31.2
Venezuela	−0.48	235.8	0.03	10.4
Asia				
India	0.05	33.1	0.04	126.1
Indonesia	0.09	44.4	0.49	157.6
Korea	0.11	103.8	0.36	187.2
Malaysia	0.10	74.2	0.64	287.6
Pakistan	−0.34	35.2	−0.31	104.1
Philippines	0.37	70.0	0.63	180.6
Sri Lanka*	0.45	46.9	−0.03	192.6
Thailand	0.36	69.7	–	–
Africa/Middle East				
Jordan	−0.16	1.7	−0.18	44.9
Nigeria*	n.a.	n.a.	−0.94	n.a.
South Africa*	−0.67	33.9	−0.61	28.4
Turkey	−0.18	12.9	0.02	65.8
Zimbabwe*	n.a.	n.a.	0.06	n.a.

Notes: Correlations of stockmarket return residuals (*INT*) are based on quarterly regressions prior to each crisis. *INT* for countries with * are based on a somewhat reduced time span due to data availability. *COMP* uses equal weights for bilateral weights and third-country trade and is standardized to average 100; n.a. = not available

inducing the spread of the Mexican crisis to other emerging markets in 1994–95, but only the reserve variable was significant for the spread of the Thai crisis in 1997. Moreover, trade competitiveness with Mexico was a highly significant factor behind the Latin American crisis, compared to financial integration for the Asian crisis.

Conclusions about the role of fundamentals in inducing the transmission of the two crises cannot be drawn from this evidence alone. Possibly economic fundamentals are important in explaining the occurrence and the severity of a crisis in some countries but not others.

Table 4.3 Regression results for the basic model

(Dependent variable: CC) Independent variables	Latin American and Asian crises (1)	Latin American crisis (2)	Asian crisis (3)
RER	0.135	*0.304	−0.133
	(0.246)	(0.177)	(0.609)
CE	0.464	0.477	0.200
	(0.302)	(0.297)	(0.521)
CA	* −1.215	* −1.106	−1.877
	(0.622)	(0.549)	(1.537)
CAP	0.777	0.539	0.293
	(0.528)	(0.351)	(1.073)
GOV	0.452	0.096	−0.346
	(0.909)	(0.291)	(0.935)
DEBT	0.416	−0.791	*2.022
	(0.582)	(0.482)	(1.030)
RES	* −1.208	* −1.255	* −1.793
	(0.644)	(0.515)	(0.941)
INT	* 0.123	0.046	* 0.279
	(0.079)	(0.056)	(0.147)
COMP	* 0.041	* 0.049	0.085
	(0.025)	(0.024)	(0.080)
R-squared	0.360	0.703	0.529

Note: * indicates the rejection of the null hypothesis at the 10 per cent level

One would expect a country with sound economic fundamentals, for instance a low current account deficit, a competitive real exchange rate and low credit expansion, to be less affected by a currency crisis even if these three variables worsened somewhat prior to a crisis. Below we analyse whether countries were affected differently by the crises depending on the strength of their fundamentals.

The modified model

Were countries hit harder by a crisis if they had 'weak' economic fundamentals? As argued in section 3, an overvalued exchange rate and a credit boom were widely blamed for the transmission of both the Mexican and Thai crises to other emerging markets. To test the validity of this assertion, our analysis defined a country as having 'weak' fundamentals if it experienced a substantial credit expansion (*CE*) and a real exchange-rate appreciation (*RER*) prior to the crisis.[12] The intuition is that a crisis was more likely to occur in a country with 'weak' fundamentals.

Similarly, a crisis would be more severe and require larger adjustments if foreign reserves (RES) were low, while a country with high reserves might be able to withstand a temporary loss in investor confidence by reducing reserves. The hypothesis is that a financial crisis is more devastating for a country with weak fundamentals and low reserves, and less severe for a country with low reserves but sound economic fundamentals.

We not only tested how significant the real exchange rate and the credit expansion variables were, but also how each of the other variables affected the likelihood of the crisis spreading and its severity, depending on the strength of a country's previous fundamentals and reserves. These hypotheses can be expressed as follows:

$$
\begin{aligned}
CC_t = \ &\beta_0 + \beta_1 RER_t + \beta_2(RER_t * D_{RES_t}) + \beta_3(RER_t * D_{RES_t} * D_{FUN_t}) \\
&+ \beta_4 CE_t + \beta_5(CE_t * D_{RES_t}) + \beta_6(CE_t * D_{RES_t} * D_{FUN_t}) \\
&+ \beta_7 var_t + \beta_8 (var_t * D_{RES_t}) + \beta_9 (var_t * D_{RES_t} * D_{FUN_t}) + \varepsilon_t \quad (4)
\end{aligned}
$$

with *var* representing all variables other than RER and CE in the basic model above. D_{RES} is the dummy variable for low reserves with $D_{RES} = 1$ if a country has low reserves and $D_{RES} = 0$ if it has strong reserves. D_{FUN} is the dummy variable for weak fundamentals with $D_{FUN} = 1$ if a country has weak fundamentals and $D_{FUN} = 0$ if the fundamentals are strong.

The hypothesis that financial crises only spread to countries that have both weak fundamentals and low reserves implies that only $\beta_1+\beta_2+\beta_3$ and $\beta_4+\beta_5+\beta_6$, $\beta_7+\beta_8+\beta_9$ should be statistically significant in the regression analysis. All other coefficients that either indicate weak reserves but strong fundamentals, namely $\beta_1+\beta_2$, $\beta_4+\beta_5$ and $\beta_7+\beta_8$, or imply strong fundamentals and high reserves, β_1, β_4 and β_7, should be statistically insignificant for this hypothesis to be verified.

Empirical results of the modified model

The empirical analysis produced little evidence that countries with weak fundamentals and low reserves were more likely to experience a more severe financial crisis. Table 4.4 shows that countries with weak fundamentals and low reserves were affected more strongly by a crisis only if they had had rapid credit expansion (CE) prior to the crisis. This is the case for both Latin America and Asia.

However, there was no proof that a real appreciation (RER) had a worse impact on countries with weak fundamentals and low reserves. Indeed, in Latin America, the analysis showed that countries more

Table 4.4   Regression results for the modified model (*RER*) and credit expansion (*CE*)

Dependent variable: CC Independent variables		Latin American and Asian crises (1)	Latin American crisis (2)	Asian crisis (3)
RER	β_1	0.194 (0.332)	* 0.438 (0.134)	−0.330 (0.658)
RER *D_{RES}	β_2	−0.185 (0.489)	−0.467 (0.267)	0.575 (1.021)
RER *D_{RES}* D_{FUN}	β_3	−0.410 (0.942)	0.048 (0.551)	−6.702 (4.897)
CE	β_4	0.084 (0.425)	0.008 (0.357)	−0.143 (0.724)
CE* D_{RES}	β_5	0.153 (0.562)	0.004 (0.393)	2.896 (1.697)
CE* D_{RES}* D_{FUN}	β_6	* 0.867 (0.528)	* 1.247 (0.411)	−0.890 (1.653)
R-squared		0.499	0.675	0.483
Joint coefficients & hypothesis tests:				
$\beta_1+\beta_2$		0.009	−0.029	0.245
$\beta_1+\beta_2=0$ (p value)		0.982	0.895	0.840
$\beta_1+\beta_2+\beta_3$		−0.409	0.019	−6.457
$\beta_1+\beta_2+\beta_3=0$ (p value)		0.640	0.968	0.194
$\beta_4+\beta_5$		0.237	0.012	2.753
$\beta_4+\beta_5=0$ (p value)		0.558	0.949	0.160
$\beta_4+\beta_5+\beta_6$		* 1.114	* 1.259	* 1.863
$\beta_4+\beta_5+\beta_6=0$ (p value)		0.009	0.009	0.067

Note: * indicates the rejection of the null hypothesis at the 10 per cent level

affected by a real appreciation of their currency generally had relatively strong fundamentals prior to the crisis. In the case of the Asian crisis, the real exchange rate was not statistically significant for either countries with strong or weak fundamentals.

Table 4.5 shows the results of extending the model to include the other variables. Overall, there is no evidence that countries with 'weak' fundamentals and low reserves were more likely to be affected by the crises. The current account (*CA*) variable shows significance only for countries with low reserves in the combined regression and for countries with strong fundamentals during the Latin American crisis.

The important finding of the regression analysis is that it was the vulnerability to capital flow reversals that lay behind the spread of the

Table 4.5 Extended regression results for the modified model: current account (CA), short-term capital inflows (CAP), government deficit (GOV), short-term foreign debt (DEBT), financial integration (INT) and trade integration (COMP)

Dependent variable: CC

Independent variables		Latin American crisis and Asian crisis						Latin American crisis					
		CA	CAP	GOV	DEBT	INT	COMP	CA	CAP	GOV	DEBT	INT	COMP
var	β_7	−0.114	0.304	−0.411	−0.210	−0.167	−0.006	*−0.529	−3.689	−0.624	−0.666	−0.253	0.087
		(0.869)	(0.461)	(0.775)	(0.978)	(0.187)	(0.035)	(0.453)	(2.475)	(0.566)	(0.697)	(0.816)	(0.117)
var*D_{RES}	β_8	−2.036	2.252	0.319	*1.816	*0.361	*0.079	1.208	1.111	0.507	0.549	*1.849	0.062
		(1.417)	(1.529)	(0.558)	(0.845)	(0.212)	(0.046)	(1.353)	(2.909)	(0.376)	(0.545)	(0.841)	(0.113)
var*D_{RES}*D_{RUN}	β_9	2.593	6.796	1.019	−0.969	−0.149	−0.036	−1.417	−12.58	−0.102	0.470	−1.173	−0.023
		(1.790)	(5.749)	(1.028)	(0.957)	(0.255)	(0.065)	(1.433)	(11.28)	(0.764)	(1.280)	(0.392)	(0.058)
R-squared		0.388	0.408	0.407	0.447	0.413	0.439	0.835	0.643	0.807	0.842	0.948	0.881
Joint coefficients & hypothesis tests:													
$\beta_7+\beta_8$		*−2.150	*2.556	−1.962	*1.606	*0.294	*0.073	0.679	−2.578	−0.117	−0.117	*0.596	*0.148
$\beta_7+\beta_8=0$ (p value)		0.066	0.078	0.428	0.042	0.040	0.079	0.613	0.196	0.719	0.879	0.001	0.023
$\beta_7+\beta_8+\beta_9$		0.443	9.351	0.799	0.637	0.145	0.037	−0.738	−15.15	−0.219	0.353	0.423	*0.125
$\beta_7+\beta_8+\beta_9=0$ (p value)		0.759	0.125	0.810	0.475	0.861	0.490	0.289	0.270	0.803	0.813	0.127	0.033

Note: *indicates the rejection of the null hypothesis at the 10 per cent level

Thai crisis to other emerging markets. Countries that experienced a large surge in short-term capital inflows (*CAP*) prior to the Thai crisis were hit more severely if they also had low reserves. Similarly, short-term debt (*DEBT*) was a significant factor behind the spread of the Thai crisis. Both of these results indicate that the large short-term obligations and short-term capital flows encouraged speculative attacks in the affected countries, and contributed to the severe decline in exchange-rate values duing the Asian crisis.

The other main finding is the high significance of the financial integration variable (*INT*) and the competitiveness index (*COMP*). This suggests that other types of contagion were present in both the Latin American and Asian crises. Although the competitiveness index is relevant for the Asian crisis, the dominant channel of contagion was financial integration for both crisis episodes. Again, financial integration primarily affected countries with strong fundamentals and low reserves, and not those that already had significant external imbalances prior to the crises.

To summarize, three key results stand out. First, the spread of both the Mexican and Thai crises was not caused by the affected countries having 'weak' economic fundamentals. While an overvalued real exchange rate and current account deficits played some role in explaining the Latin American crisis, in Asia countries were crisis prone if they were vulnerable to capital flow reversals, that is, if they had experienced large short-term capital inflows and had significant short-term foreign debts prior to the crisis.

Second, and equally important, is that the transmission of both crises was based on other types of contagion than 'fundamentals contagion'. In particular, a high degree of financial integration with Mexico or Thailand meant that countries were hit harder by the crisis.

The third major result is highlighted by the difference between the contagion effects of the Latin American and the Asian crises. The real exchange rate did not matter for the spread of the Asian crisis; the size of the effects of other economic fundamentals, such as the credit boom and the composition of capital inflows, proved significantly larger in the case of the Asian crisis. The importance of financial integration for contagion was much higher in the Asian case. This leads to the overall conclusion that 'non-fundamentals contagion' was even more dominant for Asia.

5 Policy implications

As an immediate response to the crisis, Thailand, Indonesia and South Korea were forced to ask for IMF support, just as Mexico had in December 1994. The IMF is often criticized by policy-makers and academics alike for the restrictiveness of its prescribed orthodox policies of tight monetary and fiscal policies together with other economic reform measures. Although there is a broad consensus that this policy stance worked reasonably well for Latin America in 1995, by helping to restore confidence and attract foreign capital back into the region, IMF conditionality for the bail-out of Asia's economies is more controversial. Critics argue that the case of Asia is fundamentally different, and that the problem here lies mainly with the private sector and not with unsustainable government policies. Tight fiscal and monetary policies, it is argued, lead to the insolvency of banks and other private firms undermining confidence rather than restoring it.[13] Advocates of IMF-style policies, on the other hand, claim that only fundamental economic reforms and tight fiscal and monetary policies can ultimately stabilize an economy and restore confidence. It is still too early to pass judgement on this debate as the Asian crisis is not over, and only time will tell which of these two schools of thought was closer to the truth.

The findings of our empirical analysis have some important longer-term policy implications. The results suggest that the reason countries were affected in particular by the Asian crisis was a high vulnerability to capital flow reversals and weak financial sectors. The key policy failure in this respect, and in particular for the Asian crisis, seems to be an inability or reluctance of governments to adopt a sound regulatory and supervisory framework for the financial sector following deregulation and liberalization in the early 1990s. Large capital inflows and an insufficient regulatory framework helped to nurture an asset-price bubble which contributed to the weakening of the financial sector with a rising share of non-performing loans and a worsening of a maturity mismatch where longer-term investment was financed through short-term loans. These factors further tied governments' hands in dealing with speculative attacks and financial crises as monetary and fiscal tightening can have disastrous effects for the financial sector and the real economy.

While the desirability of a sound financial regulatory system seems unanimous, it has been in particular the financial meltdown in Asia that led numerous policy-makers and economists to question the virtues of unrestricted capital flows.[14] It is, however, questionable how far measures of capital-account liberalization can be reversed and what the economic consequences would be. After all, foreign capital had been an inevitable source for fuelling the regions' economic growth in both Asia and Latin America. Moreover, an equally important issue is how to reform affected economies internally. Further, Southeast Asian economies which had enjoyed years of economic growth are still often characterized by weak internal competition, with monopolies, strong family ties and close links between business and government leaders. Without reform to make the economies more competitive and efficient, it is unlikely that Asian economies can resume the impressive growth rates they enjoyed in the early 1990s.

While the previous two points indicate an optimistic policy lesson, namely that governments and private-sector agents can indeed learn from the financial crises, there is also a pessimistic policy lesson. That is, that currency crises can spread to other countries even if these have otherwise sustainable economic fundamentals. This chapter has shown that close financial integration and trade integration increase the likelihood of a crisis being transmitted to related economies. The only thing a government can do about this is to foster cooperation with governments of closely related countries to encourage economic stability and hope that neighbouring countries take wise policy decisions.

6 Summary and conclusions

This chapter presents evidence in support of the hypothesis that the Mexican crisis of 1994–95 and the 1997 Thai crisis were 'contagious' in affecting other emerging economies. The main findings are that, first, it was not a currency misalignment and excessive current account deficits, but rather the vulnerability to capital flow reversals that explained the transmission of the Asian crisis. Second, unhealthy financial and banking sectors are shown to have contributed significantly to the severity of the financial crises in affected countries for both the Latin American crisis and the Asian crisis.

Third, we found strong support for the hypothesis that the transmission of the two crises was based on contagion that had nothing to do with the strength of the economic fundamentals in affected countries. High financial integration and close trade integration were central in explaining the spread of the crises among mostly regional economies.

The policy lessons are instructive but pessimistic. It is essential to reduce vulnerability to capital flow reversals; this requires avoiding an excessive dependence on short-term capital for funding domestic investment and consumption, and the creation of a sound regulatory framework for financial institutions. The challenge is to attract longer-term investment and foreign direct investment while discouraging the inflow of short-term and 'hot' money subject to investor sentiment. The pessimistic lesson that emerges from this study is that it may nevertheless be beyond a government's control to prevent currency crises from affecting its economy. Economic problems in neighbouring economies or other closely connected markets may be contagious even for countries that follow otherwise sustainable economic policies.

Notes

1 Garber and Svensson (1994) and Agenor, Bhandari and Flood (1992) provide an overview of these models.

2 Obstfeld (1994 and 1996) analyses how expectations affect wages, employment and interest rates, inducing a government to change policy and devalue.

3 Dornbusch, Goldfajn and Valdes (1995) and Edwards and Santaella (1993) compare different countries' experience during currency crises. Other studies, such as Eichengreen, Rose and Wyplosz (1995), Frankel and Rose (1996) and Edin and Vredin (1993), estimate how different factors, mostly macroeconomic variables, affect the probabality of a currency crisis occurring.

4 See Frankel and Schmukler (1996), Calvo and Reinhart (1996), Gerlach and Smets (1994) and Bordo, Mizrach and Schwartz (1995).

5 Calvo (1995) provides a model of herding contagion that is partly based on these arguments.

6 The weights used for the three variables are the relative precisions, measured as the inverse of the variance, of a country's series over the past seven years. The trend of the exchange rate is measured as the average rate of nominal depreciation or appreciation prior to the crisis.

7 The case of Argentina reveals the weakness of such a measure of currency crises: Argentina was able to avoid a devaluation of its currency following the Mexican crisis in 1994–95 but at the cost of raising interest rates and losing substantial amounts of reserves, leading to a serious economic downturn in 1995. A crisis measure that is exclusively defined as a substantial currency devaluation would not have identified Argentina as a crisis case.

8 The methodology developed in this model and in the modified model below partly builds upon that used by Eichengreen, Rose and Wyplosz (1996), Sachs, Tornell and Velasco (1996) and Kaminsky and Reinhart (1996).

9 See Rojas-Suarez and Weisbrod (1995) who present evidence for this argument.

10 Short-term capital inflows are defined as 'portfolio investment', plus 'other short-term inflows' plus 'errors and omissions,' using the IMF's *International Financial Statistics* as data source.

11 Four measures of this variable were tested in the empirical analysis: Short-term foreign debt with maturity of less than one year as a share of total foreign debt, and short-term debt as a share of GDP prior to the respective crises. It was also tested whether a worsening in these two ratios was an indication for a crisis to be more likely to occur. The measures that showed most significance were the levels of short-term debt rather than the changes.

12 Note that because we are interested in contagion effects, Mexico and Thailand are excluded from the regression for that episode where the crisis originated in their country.

13 Sachs, Tornell and Velasco (1996) use a similar measure. However, they define a country with 'weak' fundamentals as a country that is both not in the quartile of countries with the strongest real depreciation, nor in the quartile of countries with the lowest credit expansion/GDP ratio. Such a definition of 'weak' fundamentals seems too wide because it defines countries such as Jordan, Indonesia and Malaysia, for instance, as having 'weak fundamentals' in 1994 although, according to the data Sachs, Tornell and Velasco (1996) use, all three countries experienced a significant real depreciation and almost no credit expansion until 1994.

14 This line of thought is summarized by an article by Jeffrey Sachs, entitled 'The Wrong Medicine for Asia' (*New York Times*, 3 November 1997), where he argues: 'The region does not need wanton budget cutting, credit tightening and emergency bank closures. It needs stable or even slightly expansionary monetary and fiscal policies to counterbalance the decline in foreign loans.'

15 See, for instance, Bhagwati (1998).

References

Agenor, P.-R., J. S. Bhandari and R. P. Flood (1992) 'Speculative Attacks and Models of Balance of Payments Crisis', International Monetary Fund, Staff Papers no. 39, pp. 357–94.

Bhagwati, J. N. (1998) 'The Capital Myth', *Foreign Affairs*, vol. 77(3), pp. 7–12.

Bordo, M. D., B. Mizrach and A. J. Schwartz (1995) 'Real Versus Pseudo-International Systemic Risk: Some Lessons from History', NBER working paper no. 5371.

Calvo, G. A. (1995) 'Varieties of Capital Market Crises. Center for International Economics,' working paper no. 15, University of Maryland.

Calvo, S. and C. Reinhart. (1996) 'Capital Flows to Latin America: Is There Evidence of Contagion Effects?' Policy research working paper no.1619, World Bank (June).

Dornbusch, R. (1998) *Asian Crisis Themes*, Massachusetts Institute of Technology (mimeo).

Dornbusch, R., I. Goldfajn and R. O. Valdes (1995) *Currency Crises and Collapses*, Brookings Papers on EconomicActivity, no. 2, pp. 219–95.

Edin, P.-A. and A. Vredin. (1993) 'Devaluation Risk in Target Zones: Evidence from the Nordic Countries, *The Economic Journal*, vol. 103, pp. 161–75.

Edwards, S. and J. Santaella (1993) 'Devaluation Controversies in the Developing Countries: Lessons from the Bretton Wood Era', in M. D. Bordo and B. Eichengreen (eds), *A Retrospective on the Bretton Woods System: Lessons for International Monetary Reform* NBER project report. pp. 405–55.

Eichengreen, B., A. Rose and C. Wyplosz (1995) 'Exchange Rate Mayhem: The Antecedents and Aftermath of Speculative Attacks', *Economic Policy*, vol. 21, pp. 249–312.

Eichengreen, B., A. Rose and C. Wyplosz (1996) 'Contagious Currency Crises', EUI working paper EUF no. 96/2.

Frankel, J. A. and A K. Rose (1996) 'Currency Crashes in Emerging Markets: An Empirical Treatment', *Journal of International Economics*, vol. 41, pp. 351–66.

Frankel, J. and S. Schmukler (1996) 'Crisis, Contagion, and Country Funds: Effects on East Asia and Latin America', Pacific Basin working paper series no. PB96-04, Federal Reserve Bank of San Francisco.

Garber, P. M. and L. E. O. Svensson (1994) 'The Operation and Collapse of Fixed Exchange Rate Regimes', NBER working paper no. 4971.

Gerlach, S. and F. Smets (1994) 'Contagious Speculative Attacks', CEPR discussion paper no. 1055.

Goldfajn, I. and R. O. Valdes (1997) 'Capital Flows and the Twin Crises: The Role of Liquidity', International Monetary Fund working paper no. 87.

Kaminsky, G. and C. Reinhart (1996) 'The Twin Crisis: The Causes of Banking and Balance-of-Payments Problems', International Finance, discussion paper no. 544, Board of Governors of the Federal Reserve.

Kaminsky, G., S. Lizondo and C. M. Reinhart (1997) 'Leading Indicators of Currency Crises', International Monetary Fund, working paper no. 79.

Krugman, P. (1979) 'A Model of Balance of Payments Crises', *Journal of Money, Credit, and Banking*, vol. 11, pp. 311–25.

Obstfeld, M. (1994) 'The Logic of Currency Crises', NBER working paper no. 4640.

Obstfeld, M. (1996) 'Models of Currency Crises with Self-fulfilling Features', *European Economic Review*, vol. 40, pp. 1037–47.

Rojas-Suarez, L. and S. R. Weisbrod (1995) 'Financial Fragilities in Latin America: The 1980s and 1990s', Occasional Paper no. 132, International Monetary Fund.

Sachs, J. (1997) 'The Wrong Medicine for Asia', *The New York Times*, 3 November.

Sachs, J., A.Tornell and A.Velasco (1996) 'Financial Crises in Emerging Markets: The Lessons from 1995', *Brookings Papers on Economic Activity*, no. 1, pp. 147–215.

5
Contagion in Emerging Markets: When Wall Street is a Carrier

*Guillermo A. Calvo**

1 Introduction

Prior to the Tequila crisis of 1994–95 in Mexico, balance-of-payments crises in emerging-market economies were quickly attributed to macroeconomic mismanagement – the first and foremost suspect always being an 'unsustainable' fiscal deficit. The Mexican crisis questioned this conventional view because the country was emerging from a long period of stability during which important structural reform had been undertaken and, on the whole, fiscal deficit had been brought under control. However, conventional wisdom started to shift towards focusing not just on fiscal deficit, but also on the current account deficit – undoubtedly a more encompassing measure of a country's deficit. Mexico showed some weakness in this respect, as its current account deficit was about 8 per cent in 1994 and was programmed to rise to 9 per cent in 1995. This was considered 'unsustainable' for Mexico, given its poor growth record.[1]

The new crisis paradigm had hardly begun when Asia fell into disarray. The unsustainability flag could not easily be raised in this instance, especially for countries like Korea and Indonesia. For the first time, conventional wisdom turned its attention to what is likely to be central to all recent crises, namely, financial-sector weaknesses.

Looking at the financial sector, one begins to find threads common to all emerging markets. A salient aspect was the existence of short-

A draft version of this chapter was presented to the AEA 1999 New York Meetings, and the Winter Camp in International Finance, organized by the Center for International Economics (University of Maryland) and the Faculty of Economics (Universidad de los Andes, Bogotá, Colombia) in Cartagena, Colombia, 7–11 January 1999. I would like to acknowledge with thanks useful comments by Enrique Mendoza, Maury Obstfeld, and other seminar participants.

term debt, mostly denominated in foreign exchange (and, thus, could not be liquidated through devaluation) and, in several instances, a weak and poorly supervised domestic financial system. However, before the pieces of the puzzle could be put together, in August 1998 Russia announced a surprise partial repudiation of its public debt. Russia's trade with most emerging markets is insignificant (particularly with those located in Latin America), and its GDP represents a scant 1 per cent of world output. However, the shock wave spread throughout emerging markets, and even hit financial centres. What happened?

The dominant theory is that – as a result of market incompleteness and financial vulnerability – many economies, especially emerging-market economies, exhibit multiple equilibria. No one has yet provided a good theory about equilibrium selection, but multiple-equilibria models encouraged statements to the effect that: 'upon seeing Russia default, investors thought that other emerging-market countries would follow suit, tried to pull out and drove those economies into a crisis equilibrium'. Moreover, in a formal model exhibiting multiple equilibria the crisis can be rationalized; models that can be adapted to provide that kind of explanation include Obstfeld (1994), Calvo (1998b), Cole and Kehoe (1996).

I propose a different tack, and explore the underpinnings of a model in which a key factor behind the spread of the Russian shock lies at the heart of the capital market. I do not shift the focus away from the financial sector, but explore the possibility that Wall Street helped spread the virus. The basic ideas have been summarized in an informal way in Calvo (1998c and d). This chapter provides a more formal discussion of the central insights.

The key notion underlying the models is that knowing about emerging-market economies involves large fixed costs relative to the size of investment projects. Learning about an individual country is costly: one needs information on its economy and politics, and this requires a team of experts to monitor those variables. Economies change rapidly, especially emerging-market economies with incipient political systems. Thus, monitoring has to be frequent and in depth. However, there is little cost difference between learning about macro variables in the USA and, say, a small country like Paraguay. In fact, a large country may exhibit more stability in its macro variables, making frequent monitoring less necessary. Therefore, fixed learning costs may be especially relevant for small emerging-market economies.

Fixed costs generate economies of scale and, hence, the financial industry is likely to organize itself around *clusters of specialists*. It seems plausible, therefore, to assume that there exists a set of informed and a set of uninformed investors. The former probably leverage their portfolios (those who know better about a given project have incentives to borrow to finance it) and, thus, are potentially liable to margin calls.[2] In fact, it seems, important specialists invested in Russian debt and were subject to margin calls as its value plunged after repudiation. Section 2 starts from this observation and presents two models to explain the behaviour of the uninformed. In both models, the problem faced by the uninformed is that they can only observe price and, occasionally, some details of the investment strategy followed by specialists. However, if they see the latter selling emerging-market securities, or, more simply, staying out of auctions of new bonds, for example, they could not know exactly whether it reflected negative information about those securities or whether the specialists were subject to margin calls. Thus, they face a 'signal-extraction' problem. The first model shows an example where if the volatility of emerging-markets returns is high relative to, say, margin calls, then it will be rational to attach high probability that the signal received by the uninformed reflects conditions in emerging markets. The second model obtains essentially the same result in terms of a more elementary setup. These models help to rationalize a situation in which the capital market – the uninformed part of it – assumed the events surrounding the Russian shock indicated fundamental problems with emerging markets in general, and tried to remove their funds from all of them.[3] Unlike Grossman and Stiglitz (1980), I assume that the uninformed can observe informed investors' trades, albeit imprecisely.

Section 3 explores 'multiplier' effects that magnify the initial shock. It develops ideas in Calvo (1998d) where a sudden stop in capital inflows (provoked by the Russian shock, for example) can wreak havoc on financial systems, unless financial contracts are indexed to the sudden-stop state of nature (which is unlikely when the shock comes via Russia and margin calls in Wall Street). It is argued that this channel may give rise to multiple equilibria, but the relatively novel insight is that, even under equilibrium uniqueness, the sudden-stop channel may produce multiplier effects that help to magnify the initial shock. Section 4 concludes, and discusses possible extensions.

2 Signal extraction: two simple models

Two simple models are presented in which rational but imperfectly informed individuals may take a signal emitted by informed investors as a good indicator of prospects in emerging markets. The signal is imperfect and sometimes reflects conditions available to informed investors – such as the margin calls that reportedly took place after Russia repudiated some of its debt – but provides no information on emerging markets. Thus, these models show that emerging markets could be innocent victims of shocks that lie completely outside their realm and control.

Model 1

Informed investors take an observable (for the uninformed investors) action y (for example, buying emerging-markets bonds). This action is motivated by a combination of the following two variables: s and m. Variable s is an accurate signal of returns on emerging-market securities: the larger is s, the larger is the return. This is the variable that uninformed investors would like to know (not y). In turn, variable m reflects factors that are relevant only for the informed (for example, margin calls, profitability of investment projects available to informed investors only, see Wang, 1994). For simplicity, we assume that:

$$y = s - m \tag{1}$$

Uninformed individuals are able to observe y, and are assumed to know the unconditional distribution of s and m. Informed individuals know the exact value of the two variables.

Let $\bar{s} \sim n(\bar{s}, \sigma^2)$ and $m \sim n(0, \tau^2)$ where function n denotes normal distribution and, as usual, the first argument denotes the mean and the second the variance of the associated random variable. These are the *unconditional* distributions of s and m. Upon observing y, however, the uninformed can compute the *conditional* distribution of s and m (conditional on y, of course). In particular, it can be shown that if m and s are stochastically independent, the conditional distribution for s is:

$$n(\theta y + 1 - \theta)\, \bar{s},\ \theta \tau^2) \text{ where } \theta = \frac{\sigma^2}{\sigma^2 + \tau^2}$$

The intuitive plausibility of the result can be appreciated in limiting cases.[4] Thus, for example, if τ is very close to zero, the idiosyncratic variable m would be nearly a constant and, hence, it is plausible to attribute most of the change in y to changes in s. That is precisely what the formula implies since in that case $\tau^2 \approx 0$ and $\theta \approx 1$. Notice that while the conditional mean of *s* is a function of the observed variable *y*, its conditional variance is not.

The case $\theta \approx 1$ is interesting because it shows the possibility that uninformed investors will react strongly even though the change in *y* is provoked, say, by margin calls. Our formal results imply that one can get $\theta \approx 1$ *even though* τ^2 is 'large'. For, what is actually required is that τ^2 be small *relative* to σ^2. A characteristic of emerging-markets is the relatively high volatility of variables such as terms of trade (see Hausmann and Rojas-Suarez, 1996), which will be reflected in large σ^2. On the other hand, margin calls and serious liquidity problems in Wall Street are more likely to be the exception than the rule. Consequently, the case for large σ^2/τ^2 is not hard to make. In this context, the Russian shock can be interpreted as the outcome of a large positive shock to *m*, for example, large margin calls, which resulted in a sizeable cut in observed *y*.

Model 2

In contrast to the previous model, we assume that *s* and *m* can take two values indicated by $x^L < x^H$, x = s, m. Observable variable *y* also takes two values $y^L < y^H$ as follows:

$$y = y^H \text{ if } s = s^H \text{ and } m = m^L \qquad (2)$$
$$y = y^L, \text{ otherwise}$$

This captures the situation in which the informed send a negative signal (that is, $y = y^L$) if they get negative information about the profitability of emerging-market securities (that is, $s = s^L$), or if they are subject to, say, margin calls (that is, $m = m^H$). Otherwise, they send a positive signal (that is, $y = y^H$). Again, we assume that variables *m* and *s* are stochastically independent; hence the set of possible events:

$$\Omega = \{(s^L, m^L), (s^L, m^H), (s^H, m^L), (s^H, m^H)\} \text{ and}$$
$$P(s^L / y^L) = \frac{P(s^L)}{1 - P(s^H)P(m^L)} \qquad (3)$$

where *P* is the probability measure on Ω. As a result, as $P(m^L) \to 1$, we have $P(s^L/y^L) \to 1$. Therefore, again, uninformed investors are going to attach a large probability to the 'bad' outcome (that is, $s = s^L$) after observing $y = y^L$ if the 'bad' idiosyncratic shock (that is, m^H) has low probability.

3 Sudden stop: multiplier effect

Extensions to a dynamic setting could rationalize positive and negative shocks to emerging markets coming from Wall Street but, unless one introduces serial correlation, there will be a quick reversion to the mean. Serial correlation could be introduced through random variables s and/or m, but this is not a satisfactory modelling strategy. Much better would be to obtain serial correlation from fundamental economic considerations. Moreover, if the analysis rested there, large shocks to emerging markets would be predicated on the existence of equivalently large Wall Street shocks. This is possible, but more interesting would be to identify mechanisms that *magnify* Wall Street shocks. The present section will identify 'multiplier' effects, and channels that might contribute to serial correlation in dynamic settings.

I have argued in Calvo (1998c) that a sudden stop (that is, a sizeable and largely unanticipated stop) in capital inflows could result in a collapse of the marginal productivity of capital in emerging-market economies. One can formalize this situation by postulating that the unconditional mean of s, $\bar{s}$, is a decreasing function of the (relative) size of the sudden stop. Let production in emerging-market economies be proportional to their capital stock, k, and the factor of proportionality be given by s. Consider Model 1 above. Suppose that the return on projects outside emerging-market economies is normally-distributed. Thus, in the context of a one-period portfolio-choice model, one could write the demand for k as a function of the conditional expectation of s only (recall that the variance of the conditional distribution for s is constant with respect to y and $\bar{s}$). The higher y or $\bar{s}$, the larger will be the demand for emerging-market securities. More specifically:

$$k = K(\theta y + (1 - \theta)\bar{s}), \, K' > 0 \tag{4}$$

for some differentiable function K.

The sudden-stop effect can be captured by postulating that the unconditional expectation of s is a positive function of the difference between k and, say, its expected value from the previous period's perspective. Taking the latter as given, one can simply write:

$$\bar{s} = \Phi(k), \, \Phi'(k) > 0 \tag{5}$$

for some differentiable function Φ. Function Φ is likely to be concave as a drop in k is likely to have a larger impact than an equivalent rise.

By equations (4) and (5):

$$k = K (\theta y + (1 - \theta) \Phi (k)) \tag{6}$$

The expression on the right-hand side of equation (6) is an increasing function of k. Therefore, the sudden-stop effect is capable of giving rise to a *multiplicity of equilibria*. This is possible because, for example, a smaller k lowers the expected marginal productivity of capital (that is, lowers $\bar{s}$), which induces a lower demand for k. But even in cases where equilibrium is unique, the sudden-stop component implies interesting results. Thus, for instance, assuming $(1 - \theta)K'\Phi' < 1$, we get, by totally differentiating expression (6) with respect to y,

$$\frac{dk}{dy} = \frac{\theta K'}{1 - (1 - \theta)K'\Phi'} > \theta K' > 0 \tag{7}$$

The direct impact of y on k is $\theta K'$ but, by equation (7), the impact is magnified by multiplier $1/[1 - (1 - \theta)K'\Phi'] > 1$.

Interestingly, the direct impact of y on k increases with θ – which, by the last section's analysis is attributed to a larger relative variance of the marginal productivity of capital – while the multiplier is lower as θ rises. The net effect of a rise in θ is ambiguous. To show it, differentiate equation (7) with respect to θ; thus

$$\frac{\partial}{\partial \theta}\left(\frac{dk}{dy}\right) = \frac{K'(1 - K'\Phi')}{[1 - (1 - \theta)K'\Phi']^2} \tag{8}$$

The bracketed expression in the numerator of the right-hand side of expression (8) can be of either sign.

Modelling the demand for emerging markets securities, K

Calvo (1998b) and Calvo and Mendoza (2000) show that as the capital market becomes globalized, the response of investors to news about expected returns (as a proportion of a country's investment) may increase without limit.

It is worth noting that K'/K will also be large if K is 'small' (one way of characterizing emerging markets), and K' is somewhat invariant to K (that is, total investment in emerging markets). Thus, for example, this property would hold in a portfolio model in which returns are normally distributed and the utility function exhibits constant absolute risk aversion, because K is linear in the rate of return ($= s$, in the present notation) and, hence, K' is totally invariant with respect to K.

These examples illustrate the possibility that being small in a global-ized capital market may make K'/K large, magnifying the damage caused by a negative signal coming from the capital market. (For a more detailed discussion see the appendix in Calvo (1999).)

4 Final words

- The key insight of the above analysis is that under asymmetric information, rational but imperfectly informed investors could react very strongly to signals emitted by informed individuals. Those signals, in turn, may be due to factors that are relevant to informed individuals (for example, margin calls) but that bear no relationship to fundamentals in emerging-market economies. Moreover, sudden-stop effects contribute to the existence of multiple equilibria, and may give rise to multiplier effects. These elements help to explain why the Russian shock spread so viru-lently beyond Russia, and still lingers after a long period in which it has become apparent that much of the global turmoil was caused by problems in the capital market itself (for example, margin calls), and owed little or nothing to new problems in emerging-market economies (except Russia).
- The chapter does not discuss how the signal is emitted by the informed. This is an important issue that may be left for another occasion. However, it is worth noting that specialists may send a negative signal even if they do not run down their stock of emerg-ing-markets securities. This is so because emerging markets exhibit current account deficits that need financing. Thus, absence (or diminished presence) of specialists in the auctioning of new emerg-ing-markets securities is likely to be noticed and taken as a negative signal.
- This analysis places special emphasis on *quantity* signals, while much of the traditional finance literature, such as Grossman and Stiglitz (1980) or Wang (1994), has focused on *price* signals. I feel that price signals are less relevant in emerging markets because those markets have a relatively short lifespan and have exhibited sizeable volatility, largely unrelated to 'fundamentals'.[5] However, assuming that the uninformed pay attention to price signals will not in general eliminate the effects highlighted in this chapter. Actually, price signals could aggravate the effects on margin calls, as shown in Genotte and Leland (1990) and, more recently, Kodres and Pritsker (2002).

- The study assumes the existence of one homogeneous emerging-markets security; extensions are straightforward. A simple extension is to assume that there is a variety of securities, indexed by $i = 1, ...,I$. Let us assume that:
  (1) the returns on securities are mutually independent random variables,
  (2) the unconditional distribution for the return on security i is $n(\bar{s}, \sigma^2)$, the same for all i, and
  (3) there is an observable variable associated with each security $y_i = s_i - m$.

  Then, if there exists a large number of securities, uninformed investors could closely estimate m and, in that fashion, approximately pinpoint the value of each s_i.

  However, the assumption of a common m shock in all the y_i equations is hard to justify in a context where there are sizeable fixed information costs. Under those conditions, there will be few investors who are informed about *all* emerging markets. Most of them are likely to specialize on a few of them. Thus, the polar case in which there exists an m-type shock for each y_i, for example $y_i = s_i - m_i$, where m_i are mutually stochastically independent, could be a better approximation. Clearly, increasing the number of markets in this case yields no informational bonus. Actually, Calvo and Mendoza (1999) show examples where incentives to collect information declines with the number of markets, which would worsen the forecast-error problem.

- The above models are static, while sudden-stop effects are essentially dynamic. An unexpected change in the demand for emerging-markets securities causes disruptions in the financial sector because (in a richer, though straightforward, model) it brings about unexpected changes in relative prices. Thus, in a realistic scenario with incomplete financial contracts (in which, for instance, the loan rate of interest is not made contingent on variables such as y), a change in relative prices may cause bankruptcy and, through that channel, bring about a fall in the marginal productivity of capital. However, these effects are likely transitory. As firms are dismantled, new firms will spring to life. Thus, the initial drop in the marginal productivity of capital may be followed by a renaissance in which marginal productivity increases over time and even overshoots its value prior to crisis.

- A deeper analysis, of course, will have to rationalize why loan interest rates are not indexed to observables like y. One answer is that y may be observable but hard to *verify*, as suggested by Townsend (1976). Another is that indexation to y is likely to be a function of the indexation rules adopted in other contracts since, for example, a given firm's financial difficulties probably depend on the financial situation of its clients and suppliers (through the interenterprise-credit channel, for example) – the latter, in turn, being a function of the adopted indexation formulae. The complexity of the problem may be so great that one could possibly invoke bounded-rationality considerations for market incompleteness.

Notes

1   In Calvo (1998a) I have argued that the analysis underlying the sustainability of current account deficits leaves much to be desired, but the topic is not central to this chapter.
2   The economics of margin calls or, more generally, of collaterals are not discussed here.
3   The appendix in Calvo (1999) shows that these phenomena can be captured in terms of a general equilibrium model.
4   The model is isomorphic to that underlying the Lucas supply function in Lucas (1976).
5   However, financial analysts seem to pay a great deal of attention to sovereign bonds prices.

References

Calvo, G. A. (1998a) 'The "Unforgiving" Market and the *Tequilazo*', in J. M. Fanelli and R. Medhora (eds), *Financial Reform in Developing Countries* (London: Macmillan – now Palgrave).
Calvo, G. A. (1998b) 'Varieties of Capital Market Crises', in G. A. Calvo and M. King (eds), *The Debt Burden and its Consequences for Monetary Policy*, ch. 7 (London: Macmillan – now Palgrave).
Calvo, G. A. (1998c) 'Understanding the Russian Virus – with Special Reference to Latin America', paper presented at the Deutsche Bank Conference 'Emerging Markets: Can They Be Crisis Free?' in Washington, DC, 3 October.
Calvo, G. A. (1998d) 'Capital Flows and Capital Market Crises: The Simple Economics of Sudden Stops', *Journal of Applied Economics*, vol. 1, no. 1 (November), pp. 35–54.
Calvo, G. A. (1999) 'Contagion in Emerging Markets: When *Wall Street* is a Carrier' (mimeo online at http://www.bsos.umd.edu/econ/ ciecrp8.pdf.
Calvo, G. A. and E. G. Mendoza (2000) 'Rational Contagion and the Globalization of Securities Markets', *Journal of International Economics*, vol. 51 (June), pp. 79–113.

Cole, H. L. and T. J. Kehoe (1996) 'A Self-Fulfilling Model of Mexico's 1994–95 Debt Crisis', *Journal of International Economics*, vol. 41 (September), pp. 309–30.

Gennotte, G. and H. Leland (1990) 'Market Liquidity, Hedging, and Crashes', *American Economic Review*, vol. 80, no. 5 (December), pp. 999–1021.

Grossman, S. J. and J. E. Stiglitz (1980) 'On the Impossibility of Informationally Efficient Markets', *American Economic Review*, vol. 70 (June), pp. 393–408.

Hausmann, R. and L. Rojas-Suarez (eds) (1996) *Volatile Capital Flows: Taming Their Impact on Latin America* (Washington, DC: Inter-American Development Bank).

Kodres, L. E. and M. Pritsker (2002) 'A Rational Expectations Model of Financial Contagion', *Journal of Finance*, vol. 57 (April), pp. 769–99.

Lucas Jr., R. E. (1976) 'Econometric Policy Evaluation: A Critique', *Carnegie-Rochester Conference Series on Public Policy*, vol. 1.

Obstfeld, M. (1994) 'The Logic of Currency Crises', *Cahiers Economiques et Monétaires*, no. 43, Banque de France.

Townsend, R. M. (1976) 'Optimal Contracts and Competitive Markets with Costly State Verification', *Journal of Economic Theory*, vol. 21 (October), pp. 265–93.

Wang, J. (1994) 'A Model of Competitive Stock Trading Volume', *Journal of Political Economy*, vol. 102, no. 1 (February), pp. 127–68.

Part II
Trade and Trade Agreements

6
Preferential Trade Agreements at the Turn of the Century

T. N. Srinivasan

1 Introduction

I first met Rolf and Ana Maria Mantel at Yale in the early 1960s. I was then teaching at Yale. Both Rolf and Ana Maria were in my graduate econometrics course in the fall of 1964 as auditors, if my memory serves me right. Econometrics in those days consisted mostly of the standard linear regression and simultaneous equation models of the Cowles Commission and the then new tobit models. Analytical developments in theory and econometrics have been dramatic in the past four decades, and Rolf, although he also developed an interest in applied theory and policy, remained a distinguished theorist.

Rolf, of course, was celebrated for the result of this work, so that little need be added about aggregate excess demand functions other than their homogeneity of degree zero in prices and that they satisfy Walras' Law. The November 1999 issue of *Econometrica* contains a paper by Chiappori and Ekeland (1999) that extends Rolf's theorem to market demand functions using mathematical tools not previously used in economics. One might have thought that with Rolf's theorem, much of international trade theory, let alone econometrics of demand, would be wasted. After all, a country's net offer curve is its excess demand curve. If one cannot say much about its shape, one can say even less about trade policy, since policy analysis is no more or no less than comparative statics of equilibria, but fortunately Rolf and Ana Maria wrote several important papers on international trade issues.

First, I discuss the Mantels' contribution to the theory of economic integration of nations. Then, in section 2, I review some recent theoretical research and empirical evidence from the performance of Mercosur and other preferential trading arrangements (PTAs) to argue that the case for preferential trade, as opposed to non-discriminatory and multilateral trade, is exceedingly weak.[1] Further, the record of enforcement of Article XXIV of the General Agreement on Tariffs and Trade (GATT), and now the World Trade Organization (WTO) which permits PTAs to deviate from the core principle of non-discrimination under specified conditions is disappointing. I propose that Article XXIV be replaced by a requirement that any preferences granted under any proposed PTA be extended to all members of the WTO on a most-favoured-nation (MFN) basis within five years of coming into force of such agreement.

Section 3 discusses the role of developing countries in the GATT and in the WTO since its founding in 1995, and their interests in any future multilateral trade negotiations. As it turned out, no such negotiations were launched at the third Ministerial Meeting of the WTO in Seattle, USA.

Rolf and Ana Maria wrote two remarkable papers on the economic integration of nations (Mantel and Martirena-Mantel, 1980; 1982), neither of which received the attention they deserved. The 1980 paper – originally a 1975 paper in Spanish – is a *tour de force*; it analyses not only the welfare impact of integration between two economies as is common in the literature, but also the changes in consumption structure following integration. The analytical framework adopted by the Mantels was one of general equilibrium, without restrictive assumptions about the preferences of different social groups or about production technology (except the standard one of downward-sloping transformation curves). Government was assumed to produce public goods and services using its own resources, technical knowledge and the revenues it obtained from tax-paying social groups and from taxes on foreign trade. The latter paper started with a partial equilibrium geometrical set-up reminiscent of traditional public-finance analysis of dead-weight losses, but in the appendix the analysis is done in terms of the algebra of general equilibrium.

The most interesting feature of both papers is their explicit recognition that the preintegration tariff structure of the two economies considering integration is not arbitrary and historically given as assumed in the traditional Vinerian type of analysis, but the result of a non-cooperative Cournot–Nash tariff game. As such, the Mantels argued that in assessing the effects of integration one should not include the effects arising from the fact that, by definition, in the integration negotiation the authorities of the two economies would bargain rationally in contrast to their non-cooperative behaviour in the preintegration situation. A second feature of the Mantels' analysis is their approach to the welfare of countries which lie outside the integrated group. In their second paper they define an equilibrium *benevolent* union as a customs union, which starting from a pre-union non-cooperative Cournot equilibrium in tariffs among its members, frees trade within the union and establishes a common external tariff leaving the rest of the world unaffected. Thus the benevolent union is the analogue of the union analysed by Kemp and Wan (1976) for the case of historically-given (rather than non-cooperatively determined) pre-union tariffs in member countries. A *belligerent* union is one whose common external tariff is optimally chosen to maximize *union* welfare in the absence of retaliation by non-members.

The Mantels, in Mantel and Martirena-Mantel (1982) dismiss the benevolent customs union altogether writing 'We find no empirical content to the benevolent customs union, carefully designed not to hurt the non-partners of the union.' I feel sure they would agree to rethink this assertion! First, it is not clear how they arrived at the conclusion of a lack of empirical content in a benevolent union, though I must admit that I am sympathetic to their view. Second, while they correctly dismiss the assumption of historically-given, arbitrary initial tariffs in member countries, on the ground that governments set tariffs in their interest and not arbitrarily, by assuming the rest of the world (ROW) remains passive in response to the common external tariff chosen by the union, they do not extend this logic to the ROW.

The Mantels, in Mantel and Martirena-Mantel (1980, p. 352), justify the passive behaviour of ROW (country C in their notation) towards the union of A and B by arguing that 'This is certainly justified whenever countries A and B are small since in that case their action will not affect C at all' or (paraphrasing Chamberlain) the 'influence will be spread over so many other countries that the impact felt by any one of them is negligible and does not lead it to retaliate'. If we take the first argument literally, not only the common external tariff should be zero and the distinction between the two types of unions disappears, but even the pre-union Cournot game in tariffs becomes moot with both countries rationally adopting free trade. The second justification is more plausible but rests on some implicit collective-action problem among the ROW countries. Indeed, the Mantels must have felt uncomfortable with their justifications, as in Mantel and Martirena-Mantel (1980, p. 352) they qualify their analysis to say 'In the event that C does retaliate, our analysis has to be considered as a first approximation. In that case, it will be assumed that C's offer curve corresponds to tariff levels of the pre-integration policy equilibrium. The gains from integration for A and B will then be the gains before C's retaliation to the union'. Thus C's policy-makers are assumed to have been rational before the union of A and B as well as rational in the future after the union, but the analysis covers the interregnum between the formation of the union and the rational response of C.

One further interesting aspect of the Mantels' analysis is that while they do not refer to Article XXIV of GATT which requires, *inter alia*, that substantially all trade among members of a proposed Customs Union be free for the Union to be GATT-compatible, they assume it to be the case in their 1982 paper. However, in their 1980 paper they allow the members of a union to bargain over tariffs to be applied on intra-union trade. This is interesting in that it contrasts the non-cooperative Cournot behaviour of the two integrating countries prior to integration with the rational process of bargaining over post-union tariffs on internal trade. The latter is over the choice of a point on the portion of the contract curve that lies within the bargaining set defined by the initial equilibrium which, by definition, is not on the contract curve and hence not Pareto-optimal. As such, post-union internal trade will not be free, if the free-trade point (by definition on the contract curve) is not in the bargaining set. Even if it is, the bargaining equilibrium need not settle on it. The literature on the requirement of Article XXIV that substantially all internal trade be free has not, I believe, approached internal tariffs of a union from the perspective adopted by the Mantels. Also, whether the extended time frame within which internal tariffs were (or are) to be dismantled in customs unions of the contemporary world, such as the EU, Mercosur or NAFTA, could be rationalized using the Mantel framework is an open question.

Figure 6.1, a slightly amended version of figure 7 of Mantel and Martirena-Mantel (1980), illustrates this point. I want to use it to raise an issue that the Mantels probably condidered but chose not to address. In Figure 6.1, asterisks denote a country with which the home country (denoted without asterisks) is considering integration. I have eliminated, as the Mantels did, the ROW from the figure since it is assumed to behave passively. Trade indifference curves $AA'(A^*A^{*\prime})$ denote the autarky indifference curves, $FF'(F^*F^{*\prime})$ the free trade indifference curves, and $NN'(N^*N^{*\prime})$ the trade indifference curves corresponding to the pre-integration Cournot–Nash tariff equilibrium. The locus of tangencies of indifference curves of home and foreign countries representing Pareto-optimal trades is the contract curve $C_A C_o C_o {}_{\bullet} C_A {}_*$. The free-trade equilibrium FTE is on the contract curve.

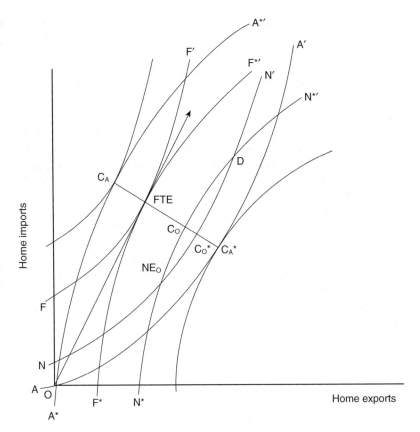

Figure 6.1 Indifference curves illustrating trade between two countries AA′ (A*A*′) = autarky indifference curves, FF′ (F*F*′) = free trade indifference curves; NN′ (N*N*′) = trade indifference curves

As long as countries cannot be forced to trade, viewed from autarky at the origin, the relevant portion of the contract curve is that between the C_A and C_{A^*} on the two trade-indifference curves passing through the autarky point, that is the origin. Starting from the initial Nash equilibrium point NE_o, the bargaining set (that is, the set of trades that makes neither country worse-off relative to NE_o) is the set of points in the lens $NE_oC_oDC^*_oNE_o$. The Mantels argued that a bargaining equilibrium will be some point on the part $C^*C^*_o$ of the contract curve that lies in the lens. As depicted, the free-trade point FTE is not on it, and will not be a potential bargaining equilibrium.

The Mantels were correct in saying that in the post-integration bargaining equilibrium trade need not be free. But the question arises: why did the countries first behave non-cooperatively and then bargain rationally during the integration process? Had they begun their negotiations *ab initio* from their autarky positions and bargained rationally, their bargaining set would have been the lens formed by the two autarky indifference curves and it would have included the free-trade point FTE. The entire contract curve $c_A C_A$ would then be possible bargains. I wonder why the Mantels, having rightly argued that the initial equilibrium should not be viewed as arbitrary, did not push their argument even further to autarky and the initiation of trade between the two countries.

I have dwelt on the Mantels' work on economic integration, not only to celebrate the life and work of Rolf Mantel, but because much of the volume of analytical literature on preferential trade agreements or PTAs since the start of the Uruguay Round of multilateral trade negotiations, has adopted the Mantels' approach that the choice of tariffs by governments be seen as equilibrium outcomes of some well-specified game (one-shot or repeated). Unfortunately, many authors seem unaware of the Mantels' papers, perhaps because they were in Spanish, and the English version of one paper was in a volume published by the Organization of American States.

2   Recent literature on PTAs

The analytical literature is diverse in terms of issues analysed, perspectives adopted and whether a static or dynamic view is taken. Excellent surveys of the literature include Baldwin and Venables (1995), Winters (1998), Anderson and Blackhurst (1993), de Melo and Panagariya (1993), Baldwin, Coles, Sapir and Venables (1998) and Bhagwati, Krishna and Panagariya (1997)). A symposium on 'Regionalism and Development' was also reported in the *World Bank Economic Review* (May 1998), where non-economic benefits of a PTA and economic benefits or losses to member and non-member countries from a PTA were analysed. In 1951, the political objective of the formation of the European Coal and Steel Community was to prevent another world war originating in Europe. In 1957 this became the European Economic Community (EEC) and, following the single market decision of 1992, the European Union (EU). Political and related national security considerations were analysed by Schiff and Winters (1998) and their quoted references. More generally, domestic political economy considerations and their implications for preferential versus multilateral trade liberalization have been explored in several contributions, including Raff (1998a). In particular, whether entering into a PTA with a strong partner is a more credible commitment mechanism than membership of the WTO for pursuing economic reforms by a weak government is an important issue in the context of economic reform in Latin America. In a world where not only international trade in goods and services but also international capital flows are important, whether entering into a PTA enables an economy to attract a more desirable type of capital flow is yet another issue. The implication of membership in a PTA on capital inflows is one of many issues classed as 'deep integration', meaning issues of coordination, if not full harmonization, of domestic policies including competition policy and product safety standards among members. These non-traditional aspects of PTAs are nicely surveyed in Fernandez and Portes (1998).

When a new analytic tool becomes available it is soon applied to a variety of problems, and analysis of PTAs is no exception. The development of the so-called New Trade Theory based on scale economies of production and the resultant imperfectly competitive market structures, as well as the so-called New Economic Geography, based on positive transport costs, agglomeration and scale economies, have both been applied. A nice example of the former is Puga and Venables (1998) in the context of industrial development of less-developed countries (LDCs), and of the latter Ludema (1999) in the context of tax competition for foreign direct investment. The literature spawned by Krugman (1991) on 'Natural Trading Blocs' is illustrative of the implications of transport costs on the benefits and costs of regionalism. The role of PTAs in the competition of footloose foreign capital through tariff protection (inducing tariff-jumping investment) and domestic profit taxation (offering tax holidays and concessions to attract investment) is modelled as sub-game perfect equilibria in Raff (1998b).

In several empirical analyses of the effects of trade liberalization from the Uruguay Round agreement, the tools of applied general equilibrium analysis – static, dynamic, with or without scale economies in production, with or without purely competitive market structure – has been effectively used. But only a few, for example Martin and Winters (1996), have addressed the impact of PTAs. The impact of particular PTAs, such as Chang and Winters (1999) and Yeats (1998) on Mercosur, Krueger (1999) on NAFTA, and the effect of membership in a PTA on bilateral trade of the partners have been examined using cross-sectionally estimated gravity models of trade, including Frankel (1997) and Soloaga and Winters (1999). Most of the exponentially growing numbers of cross-country growth regressions often include measures of openness – Sachs and Warner (1995) – but rarely any variable to capture the impact of PTAs. The latter is taken up in Ben-David (1993) and Vamvakidis (1998).

Finally, I should mention the literature on systemic issues raised by the trend towards regionalism starting from the question raised by Bhagwati (1991): 'Are regional agreements "stepping stones" or "stumbling blocks" on the path towards global free trade?' Bagwell and Staiger (1996a, b, c; 1997a, b; 1999a, b) explored in depth the role played by the cardinal principle of GATT, namely, non-discrimination or the most-favoured-nation principle (MFN), and the rule of reciprocity between countries in the exchange of tariff reductions; for example, in preventing opportunism afforded by future regional or bilateral agreements to erode the benefits to non-members from current multilateral agreements. Others, such as Bond (1999), Levy (1997, 1999) and Syropoulos (1999), also address some of the issues. In Srinivasan (1998a) I discussed some of these contributions in detail.

Without surveying this literature in depth here, let me summarize what I take to be its overall findings. First, there is no support in theory or in empirics for the assertion that most of the non-traditional (political, investment, commitment) benefits of PTAs could not be obtained through the multilateral process. Second, the traditional Vinerian trade-diversion effects of recent regional agreements appear to be significant. For example, in a study that received critical comments, particularly from politicians, Yeats (1998, p. 24) concludes that but for the changes in trade policy introduced under Mercosur transitional arrangements:

> Mercosur's trade patterns would not have changed much and the shift toward apparently uncompetitive capital-intensive intrablock trade would not have occurred. Thus, if the Mercosur countries had achieved an equivalent degree of liberalization on a nondiscriminatory basis, they would have maintained a more efficient import structure, paying less or obtaining better goods, and they would have purchased more from their trading partners outside the block.

Third, notwithstanding the many insights from using models that deviate from the traditional assumptions of pure competition, complete markets and the absence of scale economies and externalities, the case for multilateral trade liberalization remains robust. Fourth, attempts to alleviate discrimination inherent in any regional trade agreements, while taking advantages of intra-regional trade liberalization through some form of 'open regionalism', do not seem promising. The former Director General of the WTO, Renato Ruggeiro, contrasted two interpretations of 'open regionalism'. The first essentially required that any regional preferential trade arrangement be consistent with Article XXIV of GATT 1994 and the understanding on its interpretation incorporated in the UR agreements on Trade in Goods. In the second:

> the gradual elimination of internal barriers to trade within a regional grouping will be implemented at more or less the same rate and on the same timetable as the lowering of barriers towards nonmembers. This would mean that regional liberalization would in practice as well as in law be generally consistent with the m.f.n. principle. (WTO, 1996)

He preferred the second. Yet this interpretation seems odd: after all, if regional liberalization is to be extended *on the same timetable* 'in practice and in law' to non-member countries on an MFN basis, it would be multilateral and not regional. If that is the case, why would any group initiate it on a regional basis in the first place? As such, it would seem that there is no meaningful way regionalism could ever be made consistent with multilateralism, and 'open regionalism' is an oxymoron!

3 Developing countries and the global trading system

The debate on the role of openness to international flows of goods, technology and capital in the development process is as old as economics. After all, Adam Smith praised the virtues of openness and competition in *The Wealth of Nations*. A moment's reflection should convince anyone that the sources of economic development are essentially three: the growth in inputs of production, improvements in the efficiency of allocation of inputs across economic activities, and innovation that creates new products, new uses for existing products leading to increased efficiency of use of inputs.

Being open to trade and investment contributes to each of the sources of growth. By allowing the economy to specialize in those activities in which it has comparative advantage, efficiency of the allocation of domestic resources is enhanced. By being open to capital, labour and other resource flows, an economy may augment relatively scarce domestic resources and use part of its abundant resources elsewhere where they earn a higher return. Clearly, efficiency of resource use in each nation and across the world is enhanced by the freedom of movement of resources. Finally, the fruits of innovation become available everywhere in such an open world. While the potential benefits of openness from the perspective of growth and development and world welfare have been obvious since Adam Smith, if not earlier, appreciation of this potential has been slow. Even now doubts persist. The recent financial crises resulting from volatility of short-term capital flows in some erstwhile rapidly growing and outward-oriented economies of East Asia have revived scepticism about outward-orientation. I would argue that the case for outward orientation in trade and investment remains strong.

Yet until the Tokyo Round of multilateral trade negotiations (MTN), concluded in 1979, most developing countries did not participate effectively in the GATT, although 11 of the 23 signatories to GATT on 30 October 1947 in Geneva were developing countries.[2] In part, this was because early development thinking and policy-making were influenced by the disastrous experience with the global trading and financial system between the two world wars. This experience led to extreme pessimism about the potential of openness to foreign trade and investment in accelerating development, and to the adoption of a development strategy that emphasized import-substituting industrialization. In part it was because GATT was not perceived as relevant to the concerns of developing countries – in fact of the original articles only one, Article XVIII on governmental assistance to development, dealt with problems of developing countries.

In 1958, a decade after the conclusion of the GATT, a panel of experts – Gottfried Haberler, James Meade, Jan Tinbergen and Oswaldo Campos – with Haberler as chairman, published its report. They concluded that barriers in developed countries to the import of products from developing countries contributed significantly to their trade problems. The GATT responded to the Haberler Report by establishing the so-called Committee III on trade measures, restricting LDC exports and initiating a programme for trade expansion by reducing trade barriers. The response of developed countries to Committee III reports, while positive, did not substantially reduce barriers. Indeed, some of the barriers identified by Committee III such as significant tariffs on tropical products, tariff escalation, quantitative restrictions and internal taxes continued until the start of Uruguay Round negotiations. The disappointment with this outcome led 21 developing countries to introduce a resolution in the GATT in 1963 calling for an Action Programme to ban all new tariff and non-tariff barriers, elimination within two years of all GATT-illegal quantitative restrictions, removal of all duties on tropical primary products, elimination of internal taxes on products wholly or mainly produced in developing countries, and adoption of a schedule for the reduction and elimination of tariffs on semi-processed and processed products.

The GATT ministerial meeting of 1963 appointed a committee to draft amendments to the GATT to provide a legal and institutional framework within which GATT-contracting parties could discharge their responsibilities towards developing countries. The proposed amendments were approved in 1964 and became Part IV of the GATT entitled Trade and Development.

Indeed the incorporation of Part IV was in itself a response by GATT to the first meeting of UNCTAD in 1964 under the leadership of its Secretary General, Raul Prebisch, who, with Hans Singer, formulated the Prebisch–Singer hypothesis of the secular decline in the terms of trade of developing countries. At this meeting developing countries formed a solid bloc and voted almost unanimously for recommendations that espoused a managed international market and discriminatory trade arrangements as the best means to close the 'foreign-exchange gap'; that is, the difference between their export earnings and import requirements for sustaining their growth targets. The developed countries were divided, with the French in particular and the EC in general supporting the positions of developing countries, while others, notably the USA, opposed them. Since the developed countries were to take the actions recommended by UNCTAD I, and they were opposed, little happened.

After the incorporation of Part IV in 1964, the next major GATT event from the perspective of developing countries was the grant of a ten-year waiver from the nation MFN clause, with respect to tariff and other preferences favouring trade of developing countries. This so-called Generalized System of Preferences (GSP) was later included under the rubric of the 'enabling clause' of the Tokyo Round that formulated the Differential and More Favourable Treatment of developing countries in the GATT. Under GSP, each developed country could choose the countries to be favoured, the commodities to be covered, the extent of tariff preferences and the period for which the preferences were granted.

The Tokyo Round of MTN was the first of seven rounds in which developing countries participated in strength, but the outcomes were not in their long-term interest, primarily because their demands continued to be driven by the import-substitution ideology. The formal incorporation at the Tokyo Round of their demands for a Differential and More Favourable Treatment, including not being required to reciprocate any tariff 'concessions' by developed countries, triply hurt them: through the direct costs of enabling them to continue their import-substitution strategies; by allowing developed countries to continue their GATT-inconsistent barriers (for example in textiles) against imports from developing countries; and by allowing industrialized countries to keep higher than average MFN tariffs on goods of export interest to LDCs.

The experience of developing countries in the GATT up to the conclusion of the Tokyo Round could be interpreted in two diametrically opposite ways. On the one hand, it could be said that from its inception developing countries had been repeatedly frustrated in getting the GATT to reflect their concerns. Tariffs and other barriers in industrialized countries on their exports were reduced to a smaller extent than those on exports of developed countries in each round of the MTN. Products in which they had a comparative advantage, such as textiles and clothing, were taken out of the GATT disciplines altogether. Agriculture, a sector of great interest to developing countries, was also subjected to a waiver and remained largely outside the GATT framework. 'Concessions' granted to developing countries, such as inclusion of Part IV on Trade and Development and the Tokyo Round enabling clause on special and differential treatment were mostly rhetorical, and others, such as GSP, were always heavily qualified and quantitatively small. In sum, the GATT was indifferent, if not actively hostile, to the interests of developing countries.

The other interpretation is that developing countries, in their relentless but misguided pursuit of import-substitution as the strategy of development, in effect 'opted out' of the GATT. Instead of demanding and receiving 'crumbs from the rich man's table' such as GSP and a permanent status of inferiority under the 'special and more favourable' treatment clause, they could have participated fully, vigorously on equal terms with the developed countries. Had they adopted an outward-oriented development strategy, they could have achieved faster and better growth. The success of East Asia, despite the recent financial crisis, suggests that the second interpretation is closer to the truth.

In the ministerial meeting that launched the Uruguay Round negotiations, developing countries were split into the Group of 10 led by

Brazil and India and the Group of 40 chaired by Colombia and Switzerland which included 20 developing countries. The insistence of developing countries on special and more favourable treatment and their earlier reluctance to agree to the initiation of the round itself did not help Their opposition to the inclusion of non-traditional issues such as Services, TRIPS and TRIMS, and later agreeing to their discussion, with services on a separate track, led to the incorporation in the final agreement of the Uruguay Round of these three into the WTO. In my view this was a mistake that has since opened the door for demands for linkage of trade policy instruments that govern market access to enforce labour and environmental standards. Indeed linkage has come to be protectionism through other means. Had the developing countries not opposed discussing TRIPS at all, but insisted on discussing it in the appropriate forum, namely the WIPO, and insisted on better enforcement of WIPO conventions, it is conceivable that the unfortunate consequence of TRIPS in the WTO would have been avoided.

In the final Uruguay Agreement, developing countries took steps towards a greater acceptance of multilateral disciplines. For example, they increased the percentage of bound tariffs on manufactures other than textiles from 21 to 73 per cent, which brought them closer to the near-universal binding of tariffs on the part of developed countries. The agreement also phased out over 10 years the infamous Multifibre Arrangement, which had been an egregious violation of the principles of GATT. Agricultural trade was basically brought under the same disciplines as applied to trade in manufactures. Indeed the 'tariffication' process in the UR that converted non-tariff border measures into tariffs prior to their reduction was near scandalous: developed and developing countries bound tariffs at levels far higher than the actual or applied tariffs in many cases. While subsidization of manufactured exports is ruled out, the use of agricultural export subsidies was not made inconsistent with WTO rules but only their levels were reduced. The extent of liberalization of agricultural trade was extremely modest.

The General Agreement on Trade in Services is not the analogue of GATT in terms of non-discrimination and national treatment. None the less, it is a step forward. The agreements in telecommunications and financial services are important, yet on the movement of natural persons in which the developing countries have a significant interest, progress towards an agreement has been slow.

The anticipated quantitative gains to developing countries from the trade liberalization achieved in the Uruguay Round (UR) are both modest and unevenly distributed. Almost all estimates suggest that sub-Saharan Africa might in fact lose rather than gain. There are two main reasons for this: first, the industrialized countries (and some developing countries) had liberalized most of their trade prior to the UR agreement and stood to benefit from liberalization of other countries under UR agreement; and second, the dynamic gains to developing countries are likely to be substantial but difficult to quantify. The effects of the UR agreement on new issues such as services, TRIMS and TRIPS, as well as the strengthening of the dispute settlement mechanism (DSM) cannot be quantified.. It is likely that gains, if any, may not outweigh costs by a substantial margin for developing countries. For example, in many LDCs, the domestic financial markets are undeveloped and repressed, and their financial sectors need to be reformed and appropriate laws and regulations enacted and regulatory institutions created or strengthened to enable domestic providers of financial services to survive the opening up of financial markets to foreign competition. The recent financial crises have brought this well-known fact into the open.

The strengthened dispute settlement mechanism (DSM) is undeniably in the interest of all members of the WTO. The provisions in the UR agreement that make available the services of the WTO secretariat, if needed, to enable the developing countries to avail of the DSM are welcome. Yet, realistically speaking, the administrative and information-gathering capabilities of many developing countries may prove inadequate even with the assistance of the WTO secretariat. Besides, even if a developing country is able to present and win its case against a powerful country, if the latter does not comply with the verdict, the weak country has no realistic recourse. Availing itself of a WTO-sanctioned retaliation against the powerful will hurt it more than it would gain. None the less, the experience with the DSM is encouraging even though unilateralism, which the strengthened DSM of the WTO was meant to curb, has not disappeared. The continuing use by the USA of Section 301 of its domestic trade legislation to put countries on a watch-list for their weak enforcement of intellectual property rights, and their recent action against the EU even before the final pronouncement by the Dispute Settlement Body on the extent of damage to the USA of the EU banana import regime, are unfortunate examples of unilateralism.

The third ministerial meeting of the WTO at Seattle, Washington, failed to launch a new round of multilateral negotiations. There are complex issues relating to whether or not this was the opportune time to initiate a new round, and if it were, whether its coverage should be limited or broad and whether a relatively short span of three years should be set for the conclusion of negotiations. The UNCTAD (1999) has raised the 'question of whether it is in the interest of developing countries to enter into negotiations with wealthier trading partners from a position of chronic weakness not only in terms of economic power but also in terms of research, analytical and intellectual support and negotiating skills'.

I find UNCTAD's question somewhat puzzling. First, because of their relative power imbalance as measured by their share in world trade, developing countries cannot prevent the developed countries from negotiating a new trade agreement by simply refusing to participate. After all, as Winham (1989, p. 54, cited in Srinivasan 1998b, p. 35) pointed out in commenting on the differences between some developing countries and others on whether the Uruguay Round should be launched or not:

> It was a brutal but salutary demonstration that power would be served in that nations comprising 5 per cent of world trade were not able to stop a negotiation sought by nations comprising 95 per cent of world trade.

Second and more important, the power imbalance ought to matter less in the WTO than in other multilateral institutions. The reason is that, unlike in the World Bank, the IMF and the UN Security Council, each WTO member has one vote and the convention is that all decisions are by consensus. Thus, developing country members can in principle have a much greater say in WTO decisions than their power, as measured by their share in world trade, would warrant.

What should be on the agenda from the perspective of developing countries? I suggest 10 items not necessarily in order of their importance:

1 As already mentioned, an unfortunate mistake was made in the Uruguay Round in bringing TRIPS into the WTO. There were other fora, notably the World Intellectual Property Organization (WIPO) and also the Berne and Paris Conventions which could have been the natural arena for negotiating agreements on intellectual property and related concerns. Yet it was agreed to bring TRIPS into the WTO and this agreement has opened the door for demands to bring even less trade-related issues such as labour and environmen-

tal standards into the WTO. The TRIPS review should consider taking TRIPS out of the WTO and put it into the WIPO, if necessary after strengthening its enforcement mechanism.

2 There is as yet no agreement on movement of natural persons. The comparative advantage of developing countries in certain labour-intensive services such as construction, nursing and software dictates that a liberal agreement on such movement is essential for their being able to exploit their comparative advantage. This should be concluded at the earliest.

3 Although the interests of agricultural (particularly food) exporters and importers among developing countries do not necessarily coincide, their overall interests are better served if agricultural trade is fully integrated into the WTO. In particular, developing countries should insist on the elimination of export subsidies and the phasing out of interventions in agricultural trade such as through the EU Common Agricultural Policy. The horror show that was the process of tariffication of agricultural supports in the Uruguay Round should not be allowed to apply to the new round in other areas. The disciplines that apply to trade in manufactured goods should be extended to agricultural trade, with tariffs bound at reasonable levels and reduced substantially. Existing non-tariff barriers must be phased out. In particular sanitary and phytosanitary restrictions must not become non-tariff barriers. I commend Argentina for its constructive role as a member of the Cairnes group in the UR negotiations on agriculture. I hope that other major agricultural economies will join the Cairnes group in promoting full liberalization of agricultural trade in the new round.

4 Allowing anti-dumping measures (ADMs) as legitimate WTO instruments encourages their abuse. Unlike safeguard measures, ADMs can be applied to exports from a particular country or even by a particular firm. Sadly many developing countries have also begun to use ADMs. Some have suggested that the use of ADMs be made harder, for example by raising the threshold of injury to domestic industries before ADMs could be invoked, but I would call for the removal of ADMs from the arsenal of permitted trade-policy instruments. In my view, ADMs have no economic rationale; they are the analogues of chemical and biological weapons in the arsenal of trade-policy instruments.

5 Ministers from developing countries should insist that there be no further discussion of labour or environmental standards at the WTO and that the International Labour Organization should be

the forum for negotiations on labour standards. The notion that lower labour standards in a country confers competitive advantage is deceptive. Humanitarian concerns in rich countries about poor working conditions and the use of child labour in less-developed countries are better addressed through other means than by using trade sanctions. The demand for the inclusion of a 'social clause' in the WTO is just protectionism through other means. The United Nations Environmental Programme could be the negotiating forum for environmental issues. Ministers should also propose that the Committee on Trade and Environment at the WTO be wound up.

6 Peaks in tariffs and escalation in tariffs by stages of processing that restrict exports of developing countries to the industrialized world should be eliminated.

7 As suggested earlier, Article XXIV of GATT should be replaced by the requirement that all preferences granted to partners of existing or proposed future preferential trading agreements, such as free trade or customs-union agreements, regional or otherwise in geographic coverage, should be extended to all members of the WTO on a MFN basis within a specified 15–10-year period of the coming into force of such agreements.

8 It seems premature, at least from the perspective of developing countries, to negotiate and conclude a Multilateral Agreement on Investment and related issues such as competition policies. An agreement to make current policies transparent should be the first step.

9 Although the experience with the DSM is encouraging, it has serious flaws that need correction (see Hoekman and Mavroidis, 1999).

10 The legitimate concern of the community of trading nations for accelerating the economic and social development of the least developed and less dynamic countries should be channelled into providing them the resources, knowledge and technology to promote faster growth and reap the benefits of integration within the global economy. Offering them preferential access to world markets will not only create a sense of complacency on the part of rich counties of having done enough, but also, more seriously and deleteriously, enable the rich countries to persist in maintaining trade barriers detrimental to developing countries. Indeed, by demanding and receiving a special and differential treatment in the GATT, and agreeing to the creation of the Generalized System

of Preferences which are exceptions to the GATT's fundamental principle of non-discrimination, developing countries allowed the industrialized countries to get away with their own GATT-inconsistent trading arrangements such as the Multifibre Arrangement. Developing countries have much to gain by participating fully and as equal partners with developed countries in a liberal world trading system.

Notes

1   The phrase 'free trade' in regional PTAs, such as the North American Free Trade Agreement or the European Free Trade Area, is misleading. It masks the fact of discrimination against non-members by invoking free trade!

2   See Srinivasan (1998b) for a history of developing countries in the GATT since its inception in 1947, and its being subsumed into the WTO in 1995.

References

Anderson, K. and R. Blackhurst (eds) (1993) *Regional Integration in the Global Trading System* (London: Harvester Wheatsheaf).

Bagwell, K. and R. W. Staiger (1996a) 'Preferential Agreements and the Multilateral Trading System', Columbia University, NY (mimeo).

Bagwell, K. and R. W. Staiger (1996b) 'Reciprocal Trade Liberalization', NBER working paper no. 5488, Cambridge MA.

Bagwell, K. and R. W. Staiger (1996c) 'Regionalism and Multilateral Tariff Cooperation', Columbia University NY (mimeo).

Bagwell, K. and R. W. Staiger (1997a) 'Multilateral Tariff Cooperation during the Formation of Regional Free Trade Areas', *International Economic Review*, vol. 38, no. 2, pp. 271–319.

Bagwell, K. and R. W. Staiger (1997b) 'Multilateral Tariff Cooperation during the Formation of Customs Unions', *Journal of International Economics*, vol. 42, nos 1/2, pp. 91–123.

Bagwell, K. and R. W. Staiger (1999a) 'Multilateral Trade Negotiations, Bilateral Opportunism and the Rules of GATT', Department of Economics, Columbia University, NY (mimeo).

Bagwell, K. and R. W. Staiger (1999b) 'An Economic Theory of GATT', *American Economic Review*, vol. 89, no. 1 (March), pp. 215–48.

Baldwin, R. and A. Venables (1995) 'Regional Economic Integration', in G. Grossman and K. Rogoff (eds), *Handbook of International Economics*, Vol. III (Amsterdam NL: North-Holland).

Baldwin, R., D. Cole, A. Sapir and A. Venables (eds) (1998) *Regional Integration* (Cambridge: Cambridge University Press).

Ben-David, D. (1993) 'Equalizing Exchange: Trade Liberalization and Income Convergence', *Quarterly Journal of Economics*, vol. 108, no. 3, pp. 653–79.

Bhagwati, J. (1991) *The World Trading System at Risk* (Princeton: Princeton University Press).

Bhagwati, J., P. Krishna and A. Panagariya (1997) *Analyzing Preferential Trading Agreements: Alternative Approaches* (Cambridge MA: MIT Press).

Bond, E. (1999) 'Multilateralism, Regionalism, and the Sustainability of Natural Trading Blocs', Department of Economics, Pennsylvania State University (mimeo).

Chang, W. and A. Winters (1999) 'How Regional Blocs Affect Excluded Countries: The Price Effects of MERCOSUR', discussion paper no. 2179, Centre for Economic Policy Research, London.

Chiappori, P. A. and I. Ekeland (1999) 'Aggregation and Market Demand: An Exterior Differential Calculus Viewpoint', *Econometrica*, vol. 67, no. 6, pp. 1435–57.

de Melo, J. and A. Panagariya (eds) (1993) *New Dimensions in Regional Integration* (Cambridge: Cambridge University Press).

Fernandez, R. and J. Portes (1998) 'Returns to Regionalism: An Analysis of Nontraditional Gains from Regional Trade Agreements', *World Bank Economic Review*, vol. 12, no. 2, pp. 197–220.

Frankel, J. (1997) *Regional Trading Blocs in the World Economic System* (Washington, DC: Institute for International Economics).

Hoekman, B. and P. C. Mavroidis (1999) 'Enforcing Multilateral Commitments: Dispute Settlement and Developing Countries', paper given at Conference on Developing Countries and the Millennium Round, 20–1 September 1999, Geneva.

Kemp, M. and H. Wan (1976) 'An Elementary Proposition Concerning the Formation of Customs Unions', *Journal of International Economics*, vol. 6, pp. 95–7.

Krueger, A. (1999) 'Rules of Origin as Protectionist Devices', in J. Melvin, J. Moore and R. Reisman (eds), *International Trade Theory: Essays in Honor of John Chipman* (New York: Routledge).

Krugman, P. (1991) 'Is Bilateralism Bad?', in E. Helpman and A. Razin (eds), *International Trade and Trade Policy* (Cambridge, MA: MIT Press).

Levy, P. (1997) 'A Political Economic Analysis of Free Trade Agreements', *American Economic Review*, vol. 87, no. 4, pp. 506–19.

Levy, P. (1999) 'Asymmetric Information and Inference from Free Trade Agreements', Department of Economics, Yale University (mimeo).

Ludema, R. (1999) 'Why are Preferential Trade Agreements Regional?', Department of Economics, Georgetown University, Washington, DC (mimeo).

Mantel, R. and A. Martirena-Mantel (1980) 'Economic Integration, Income Distribution and Consumption: A New Rationale for Economic Integration' (ch. 13) in R. Ferber (ed.), *Consumption and Income Distribution in Latin America*, an ECIEL book for the Organization of American States, Washington, DC.

Mantel, R. and A. Martirena-Mantel (1982) 'On the Measurement of the Social Benefits of a Customs Union', *Anales de la Asociación Argentina de Economía Política*, Universidad Nacional de La Plata (in Spanish).

Martin, W. and L. A. Winters (eds) (1996) *The Uruguay Round and the Developing Countries* (Cambridge: Cambridge University Press).

Puga, D. and A. Venables (1998) 'Trading Arrangements and Industrial Development', *World Bank Economic Review*, vol. 12, no. 2, pp. 221–50.

Raff, H. (1998a) 'Politics and the New Regionalism', Department of Economics, Indiana University (mimeo).

Raff, H. (1998b) 'Preferential Trade Agreements and Tax Competition for Footloose Firms', Department of Economics, Indiana University (mimeo).

Sachs, J. D. and A. Warner (1995) 'Economic Reforms and the Process of Global Integration', *Brookings Papers on Economic Activity*, pp. 1–118.

Schiff, M. and L. A. Winters (1998) 'Dynamics and Politics in Regional Integration Arrangements: An Introduction', *World Bank Economic Review*, vol. 12, no. 2, pp. 177–96.

Soloaga, I. and L. A. Winters (1999) 'Regionalism in the Nineties: What Effect on Trade?', discussion paper no. 2183, Centre for Economic Policy Research, London.

Srinivasan, T. N. (1998a) 'Regionalism and the World Trade Organization: Is Non-Discrimination Passé?', in A. O. Krueger (ed.), *The World Trade Organization as an International Institution* (Chicago: The University of Chicago Press), pp. 329–49.

Srinivasan, T. N. (1998b) *Developing Countries and the Multilateral Trading System: From the GATT (1947) to the Uruguay Round and the Future Beyond* (Boulder, Colorado: Westview Press).

Syropoulos, C. (1999) 'Customs Unions and Comparative Advantage', *Oxford Economic Papers*, no. 51, pp. 239–66.

UNCTAD (1999) *Trade and Development Report, 1999* (New York and Geneva: United Nations).

Vamvakidis, A. (1998) 'Regional Integration and Economic Growth', *World Bank Economic Review*, vol. 12, no. 2, pp. 251–70.

Winham, G. (1989) 'The Prenegotiation Phase of the Uruguay Round', in J. Gross Stein (ed.), *Getting to the Table* (Baltimore and London: Johns Hopkins University Press), pp. 44–67.

Winters, L. A. (1998) 'Regionalism and Multilateralism', in R. Baldwin, D. Cole, A. Sapir and A. Venables (eds), *Regional Integration* (Cambridge: Cambridge University Press).

WTO (1996) 'The Road Ahead: International Trade Policy in the Era of the WTO', the Fourth Annual Sylvia Ostry Lecture, Ottawa, WTO Press/49, 29 May 1996.

Yeats, A. (1998) 'Does Mercosur's Trade Performance Raise Concerns about the Effects of Regional Trade Arrangements?', *World Bank Economic Review*, vol. 12, no. 1, pp. 1–28.

7
The Role of Sub-regional Agreements in Latin American Economic Integration

Victor L. Urquidi

1 Introduction

In this chapter, we contend that in today's context of globalization, Latin American economic regional integration is no longer feasible on a broad scale. Wherever possible, integration should rely on strong sub-regional agreements, with the less-industrialized countries being aided to become the suppliers of intermediate products to the leading members of the sub-regional groups. As outlined in Urquidi (1998a, b) on which this chapter draws heavily, this would require investment and long-term financing by the latter to the supplier countries, and cooperation to upgrade technology, training and management, and assistance for middle and higher education. The UN Economic Commission for Latin America and the Caribbean (ECLAC) and other UN agencies, as well as the Inter-American Development Bank (IDB) and sub-regional financial institutions would be given a special role, working through sub-regional committees and sub-committees, and working groups.

The remainder of this chapter is treated under the following headings: section 2, early postwar economic integration agreements; section 3, the creation of Mercosur; section 4, sub-regional trade and investment requirements; and section 5, sub-regional hubs with extensions through subcontracting.

2 Earlier postwar economic integration agreements

The idea of deriving benefits from free trade or trade liberalization was fairly common in the early nineteenth century among policy-makers in the Latin American region,[1] doubtless influenced by leading

115

thinkers, academics and political leaders in the region. Nevertheless, no free-trade or even partial or sub-regional agreement in the modern sense was signed before 1958. Briefly in the 1830s, a five-country sub-region in Central America formed a federation of 'provinces', and El Salvador and Honduras subscribed to a bilateral trade agreement in 1918. Then in the early 1950s the idea of integration was revived. In 1951, within the framework of ECLAC and inspired by European moves towards freer trade, an Economic Cooperation Committee of the Central American Isthmus (thus open to Panama) was set up at ministerial level, to prepare studies, guidelines and recommendations for a customs union and economic integration treaty. A draft agreement was ready for signature by June 1958.This agreement was, perhaps, too cautious on trade liberalization, which was limited to just a 'positive list' of commodities. The integration programme, however, was ambitious from the start, focusing on the integration of Central American economies, and included transportation, energy, agriculture and a special régime for 'integration industries', public administration, technological innovation and even population policy.

All this depended on a political will that did not really exist, and which faced domestic difficulties and external pressure. In 1960, a second treaty was signed. This was the reverse of the earlier one: trade was to be liberalized in general under a common-market scheme, except for a limited list of products which would gradually be added through protocols. The GATT, of which only Nicaragua had been a member, assented to these agreements under Article XXIV provisions. Intra-Central American trade increased by leaps and bounds, until the Honduras–El Salvador armed conflict of 1968 resulted in a sharp drop. Integration as such – visualized by the ECLAC secretariat as 'a common development policy' – was limited, although some aspects and institutions remained in place after 1968; in particular, the planned 'industrial integration' was opposed by both local and outside interests, although many foreign firms benefited from intra-regional tariff reductions.

Economic integration on a broader geographic basis, mainly trade liberalization, was also advocated – chiefly by the ECLA secretariat. By 1960, following the Treaty of Montevideo, 10 South American republics and Mexico had joined the Latin American Free-Trade Agreement (LAFTA). This complied formally with Article XXIV of GATT, although in practice liberalization was slow. LAFTA was seen largely as a 'multilateralization' of earlier bilateral agreements, which would be implemented over 12 years. It was a new departure, but was not regarded as a strong instrument for economic integration; some attention was paid to the conditions under which the weaker member countries operated, and a means was included for negotiations among business enterprises. LAFTA was not a success, and by the late 1970s it became apparent that the spirit of integration had faded. LAFTA had become a preferential trade agreement, so new negotiations were proposed to salvage its original purpose. This led to the second Treaty of Montevideo in 1980, which established the Latin American Integration Association (ALADI). Little came of this agreement – which I described as a 'feeble-trade' agreement – though it still exists. Vacchino (1991) gives a detailed account of the ALADI, while Urquidi (1993), Herrera (1991), Almeida (1991) and Salgado (1991) discuss the issues at length.[2]

The Andean Pact (Treaty of Cartagena, 1966), which had in its conception a political motivation from governments in the Christian democratic or social democratic tradition, was rather ambitious in that it went beyond trade liberalization and attempted planned regional development of certain industrial activities (with some resemblance to the Central American original integration idea), and eventually an 'economic union'. Its initial members were Colombia, Ecuador, Peru, Chile and Bolivia, and later Venezuela. It established a strong secretariat in Lima, with quasi-supranational powers. When it negotiated a common treatment of direct foreign investment, Chile withdrew. Bolivia and Ecuador were supposed to receive special treatment. The Andean Pact in effect represented a weakening of LAFTA, with which negotiations were not successful, although all its members retained their membership. Intra-Andean Pact trade increased, and a clearing house régime for payments compensation and an investment fund were established. However, the agreement's aims and requirements were not always adhered to – the term *incumplimiento* became the 'common currency'. Eventually, the financial crises and debt payment problems of the early 1980s and changes in the political underpinnings were the main causes of the Pact's failure.

A number of Caribbean countries and Guyana created CARIFTA – in 1973 transformed into CARICOM, a 17-country sub-regional free-trade agreement area. CARICOM aimed at establishing a customs union (see Urquidi and Vega, 1991, pp. 27–65). Although intra-trade accounted for less than 10 per cent of total trade, some integration and cooperative arrangements took place in areas other than commodity trade.

3 The creation of Mercosur

In 1986, Argentina and Brazil created Mercosur, a new programme for economic integration and cooperation. This was intended to become a full common market, and remains the most significant sub-regional trade and integration agreement in the Latin American region today, for the following reasons:

1 it is based on a fairly intensive preexisting reciprocal trade between Argentina and Brazil, partly complementary in nature;
2 both countries have a fairly high per capita product, in the range of US$4,500 to 6,000;
3 these countries have an important industrial base, together with a rich and varied agriculture sector, which ensures the development of a solid domestic market;
4 they have the most advanced R&D programmes in the Latin American region;
5 they have a solid well-established entrepreneurial sector, both domestic and international;
6 in addition to good overland connections, they possess a 'natural' infrastructure in their ocean and coastal navigation routes, with natural ports in the estuaries and bays, and had an important international shipping fleet;
7 their external trade is well-diversified in terms of foreign markets, in addition to the European and US markets, there are some direct connections to African and Asian markets; and
8 above all, they have shown the political will to proceed with sub-regional integration, unlike the other sub-regional integration schemes in the region.

From the start, both countries envisaged a series of supplementary agreements to deal with technological innovation, front-line information industries, biotechnology, entrepreneurial cooperation in key industries, such as motor vehicles and capital goods, and, most important, adequate funding for new enterprises. In 1991, Uruguay and Paraguay were incorporated and more recently Chile and Bolivia have signed a special agreement with Mercosur

4 Sub-regional trade and investment requirements

Except for Mercosur intra-trade, general intra-Latin American trade, covered by various minor multilateral agreements, has not been significant. This means, essentially, that mere liberalization of trade, including the partial elimination of non-tariff barriers, is insufficient. The same applies to the many bilateral trade agreements. And yet the notion of full-scale Latin American (and Caribbean) integration continues, at least in the common rhetoric of governments and political groups, with frequent reference to historical roots which are no longer relevant. The Latin American region today is far from homogeneous, if it ever was. Following the oil crises of the early 1970s, the ensuing external debt crises of the late 1970s and early 1980s, and the financial crises of the 1990s, a solid, homogeneous 'Latin American economy' has all but vanished. Although it is still fashionable in financial circles and the media, as well in the statistics of certain international agencies, to treat data for 'Latin America' as a whole by aggregating GDP and trade figures (sometimes including or excluding certain countries without much data consistency), in reality the Latin American region consists of a series of sub-regions. A few stand out, namely the Mercosur region, the Ecuador–Colombia–Venezuela subregion (with some Caribbean connections), and the Central American sub-region (although differences in development among the five countries have become sharper). Panama stands on its own, given its peculiar economy based on the Canal; the Guyanas have their own links and allegiances; Haiti and the Dominican Republic are not necessarily suited to mutual integration; and Cuba remains a special case, outside these arrangements.

Above all, Mexico has turned its back on the rest of the Latin American region. Its economy is increasingly integrated with that of the USA, which since the mid-1940s has been its traditional trading market and source of finance and investment. Meanwhile, economic integration with Canada under NAFTA is being undertaken on a lesser scale. It should be recalled that Mexico was never fully accepted into LAFTA, was turned down by the Andean Pact, and was later also turned down by Mercosur, while its attempts to forge economic links with Central America have been erratic. In effect, Mexico belongs to a sort of 'Merconorte'!

In recent years, the notion of a Hemispheric Free-Trade Area from Alaska to Patagonia, animated by a vague unilateral declaration by President Bush in 1990, has gained ground. It is difficult to imagine that it could ever become an effective agreement in the light of the many sub-regional agreements. It is even more difficult to imagine that a successful Mercosur will suddenly merge with a number of unsuccessful sub-regional arrangements, or with the NAFTA pact, including Canada and the USA (plus Alaska and Puerto Rico). There are surely better ways to assist in the development of the Latin American and Caribbean region, and some ideas are offered below.

5 Future integration: clusters, sub-regional hubs and subcontracted extensions

The first requirement, of course, is to abandon any idea that a 'Latin American' economy exists, and to consign all nineteenth-century historic documents to museums. Next, a general declaration by all heads of state is needed to the effect that development – sustainable development, that is – is a matter for each country or sub-regional group of countries to work out for themselves in terms of institutions and political possibilities. It should be recalled that most countries in the Latin American and Caribbean region are not only not industrialized, but rely for their exports on a short list of basic commodities, mostly minerals, cereals and other food products, fibres or 'sun and sea'. These typically face fluctuating and internationally competitive markets. Most of these countries have hardly reached the stage of semi-processed export products, and even the larger, semi-industrialized ones still have a strong natural resource export component. Indeed, only six countries in the region have achieved any significant degree of industrialization and institutional development in the modern sense: Argentina, Brazil, Chile, Colombia, Venezuela and Mexico. Moreover, in today's globalized economy, where Latin American and Caribbean territories are wide open to international business (real and financial), it is totally illusory to aim at full regional economic integration – it is essentially unrealistic.

Rapid technological innovation and instant financial transfers have eroded the decision-making capacity of formerly autonomous regional groupings and individual countries. In addition, the burden of external indebtedness – the interest burden rather than aggregate debt – has seriously weakened the domestic savings potential.

Mercosur demonstrates the case for limited sub-regional integration, which depends on complementarity as well as competitiveness and is underpinned by a sound industrial and technological base. But this is not a matter of trade barriers alone; what is needed is reciprocal real investment, preferably joint investment to create trade, not the other way around. If this is a valid proposition, it has important implications and possibilities for those economies that have been left behind in terms of development and technology. Through this investment, these countries might gradually become suppliers of intermediate products to industrial centres in more advanced economies, in the sub-regions and in the Latin American region as a whole. It should be possible through cooperative arrangements to create clusters of suppliers. Thus, an obvious possibility would be for countries such as Ecuador, Colombia, Bolivia, Paraguay, Uruguay and Chile to become suppliers of products to Argentina and Brazil, with wherever possible transversal arrangements and investments to ensure market security for these initiatives. Just as in an industrial centre in a developed country 'vertical' industrial integration is abandoned, and parts and other supplies, including services, are obtained from other domestic regions and other countries, Mercosur could be instrumental in developing clusters of suppliers. In effect, if such clusters were appropriately financed and met modern technological and environmental requirements, both Mercosur centres and supply clusters would benefit. Provided the suppliers are competitive, they do not need to subscribe to any basic sub-regional agreements, but only to gain most-favoured-nation treatment, enabling competition to work to the advantage of all trading partners. Initially, these supply patterns might be merely subcontractors adding little value, but in time they might develop into more integrated links with the major industries in the sub-regions or in the region as a whole.

This is not to argue for a 'closed' sub-region with satellites, but to envisage the possibility of horizontal integration of the type that exists between industries in highly industrialized countries. It is not a closed territorial matter either. There is no reason to assume that Mexican, Costa Rican or Venezuelan suppliers of intermediate products could not penetrate Mercosur, or that suppliers in Uruguay or Chile could not penetrate the industrial networks of Venezuela or Mexico. If the Latin American region continues to consider itself an exclusive region, it may fail to derive any advantage from future external benefits to be obtained from the proliferation of knowledge and technology.

Nevertheless, one must recognize Mexico's painful and complex integration of its main industrial activities into the North American, that is, US and Canadian markets. Further, Central American countries will continue gravitating towards the US economy. Because of its oil surpluses, Venezuela might stand on its own, but, nevertheless, supplier-based integration with Mercosur seems more likely than with other possible sub-regions. Intra-trade will increasingly depend on reciprocal arrangements negotiated by large corporations, based on high-tech investment, including management and marketing. This will lead to a large component of intra-firm trade in intermediate and semi-manufactured products, rather than increasing trade from a reduction in tariff barriers.

Future patterns of trade and investment will not necessarily be reformed without the addition of a fundamental ingredient, that is, the means to enable the lesser economies of the Latin American region to acquire the necessary skills and management abilities. This requires a similar strategy to that adopted by the European Union (EU) towards its less-developed members. Unfortunately, left to market forces, the strategy would soon flounder, leading to greater concentration and technological and management support. This could mean a new role for Mercosur, and for other multilateral agencies including the IDB and the UN ECLAC. Until recently ECLAC has been mainly concerned with overall development strategy, and the intricacies of modern industrial development. It has also generally treated economic integration (with some exceptions, as in Central America) as part of its overall mission. Since this is clearly not attainable, it would be reasonable for ECLAC to redefine its functions and put greater emphasis on technical cooperation with countries that have potential as suppliers to the more advanced industrial areas of the region. ECLAC might learn from the UN Economic Commission for Asia and the Pacific, and the early experience of the UN Economic Commission for Europe, both of which worked through committees and sub-committees dealing with policy, practical matters and technological cooperation – instead of indulging in endless meaningless meetings and summits of the ministries of finance in the region.

These committees, sub-committees and working groups should be organized on a sub-regional rather than regional basis. ECLAC might help to bridge the gap between Mercosur and smaller supplier economies, by guiding them, together with UN system agencies and Mercosur itself, towards becoming active participants in sub-regional arrangements. ECLAC could have a similar role mediating between the non-Mercosur countries and their related zones of influence, in order to enable these to become suppliers as well as consumers. Needless to say, ECLAC should also devote itself to the improvement of transport systems and other infrastructure.

It may not be possible in the Latin American region to adopt the notion of 'convergence' current in the EU. The basic dissimilarity of countries in the Latin American region cannot readily be corrected by adopting common macroeconomic policy indicators. The sustainable development issues of economies in the Latin American region have deep roots in the social and political structures created during European (mostly Spanish) colonization. Institutional rigidities prevail. This is not to say that new trends deriving from increasing globalization and competitiveness cannot be introduced – this already occurs in small areas of these societies. But it would be a grave error to emphasize the latter without modernizing social structures to enhance the democratic process. One of the major tasks facing the Latin American region is to get rid of myths connected with so-called similarities, common stances and periods of past glory. What is needed is a serious appreciation of the global prospects, the role of knowledge and technology, and the power from concentrating financial resources at a few centres. At the same time, the heavy burden of inadequate education and training, the lack of legal and institutional security, poor infrastructure, and the stifling burden of past external indebtedness must be addressed. A special effort is needed to stress the diversity of conditions in the geographical area mistakenly called 'Latin America', some of whose sub-regions are rich in natural resources, but subject to predatory exploitation. It will be increasingly important not only to single out different sub-regions, but also to show how disparities within them and between the various sub-regions could be reduced. Population growth is a major problem in the light of macro policies that tend to dismiss the unemployment effect of many industrial developments. Policies that favour small-and medium-sized industries, and the upgrading of basic commodities in rural areas, have hardly begun to be defined or implemented. Training to supplement lacunae in the educational system is only marginally available.

Looking ahead, it is clear that most countries in the Latin American region will need to redefine their objectives in the context of the global society. This has important implications for effective political participation, for solving long-term structural problems and the construction of solid domestic markets. The role of sub-regional integration schemes will be vital, and the supporting role of the international community, including the UN and other multilateral agencies, will be of major importance. A whole century of 'development' ended with little positive benefit. Let us hope the new century will unleash new ideas and proposals to establish sustainable development and equitable social conditions.

Notes

1   I refer to the 'Latin American region' in the sense of the area covered by the UN ECLAC, rather than to 'Latin America' as such, which I regard as a myth.
2   I have written a personal account of these early efforts in Urquidi (1998c).

124 Trade and Trade Agreements

References

Almeida, R. (1991) 'Reflexiones acerca de la integración latinoamericana' (Thoughts on Latin American Integration), in V. L. Urquidi and G. Vega Cánovas (eds), *op. cit.*

Herrera, F. (1991) 'Hacia una América Latino integrada' in V. L. Urquidi and G. Vega Cánovas (eds), *op. cit.*

Salgado, G. (1991) 'La crisis de la integración', in V. L. Urquidi and G. Vega Cánovas (eds) *op. cit.*

Urquidi, V. L. (1993) 'Free-trade Experience in Latin America and the Caribbean', *Annals of the American Academy for Social Sciences*, no. 526, (March), pp. 58–67.

Urquidi, V. L. (1998a) 'Requisites for Effective Latin American Participation in a Global Society', paper presented at the Latin American Studies Association (LASA) XXI International Congress, Chicago.

Urquidi, V. L. (1998b) 'Hacia una perspectiva para la CEPALC en el siglo XXI', paper written on the occasion of UN-ECLAC 50th Anniversary Meeting, Santiago (Spanish only).

Urquidi, V. L. (1998c) 'Incidents of Integration in Central America and Panama', *Revista de la CEPAL* (ECLA Review) October.

Urquidi, V. L. and Vega Cánovas, G. (eds) (1991) 'Unas y otras integraciones: seminario sobre integraciones regionales y subregionales', El Colegio de México y Fondo de Cultura Econónmica, Serie Lecturas no. 72 (Spanish only).

Vacchino, J. M. (1991) 'ALALC–ALADI: Experiencias y Perspectivas', in V. L. Urquidi and G. V. Cánovovas (eds), *op. cit.*

8
International Specialization and Trade Regimes in Argentina: 1960–99

*Luis Miotti, Carlos Quenan and Carlos Winograd**

1 Introduction

During the 1990s, particularly in the early years, Argentinian exports soared. Between 1990 and 1996, exports increased by 11 per cent a year on average, rising from US$12 billion to US$25 billion. In 1998–99 an adverse external shock led to a temporary decline in exports by value. This rise in exports during a period of monetary stabilization and deep economic restructuring (trade liberalization cum massive privatization) generated controversy. What was the source of this development? Was the pattern of export growth sustainable? Which dynamic sectors explained this performance? Was there any process of primary export deepening that might induce low growth, and constrain the economy? How important was Mercosur and the 'Brazil effect'? This chapter attempts to answer these questions by studying changes in Argentina's pattern of trade, tracing the historic perspective in order to isolate fundamental long-term trends from the frequent, abrupt short-run changes. We have, therefore, studied developments in the performance over 40 years, focusing on changes in Argentina's comparative advantage. Section 2 provides an overview of trade performance; section 3 discusses alternative trade regimes, while section 4 suggests some conclusions.[1]

* This chapter is a shorter version of Miotti, Quenan and Winograd (2000) which presents a more detailed analysis and explains the methodology for the empirical analysis of changes in comparative advantage. The evaluation of comparative advantage is based on sectoral indicators' contribution to the trade balance (Lafay, 1987 and Guerrieri, 1994). All data are from from the Comparative Trade Performance Data Base (CTP-DATA) developed by the authors (Quenan, Miotti and Winograd, 1994) for Latin American countries on the basis of the OECD Trade Data Base, Stan-OECD, CHELEM and Comtrade (United Nations).

2 Trade performance since 1960

Over the past 40 years, the Argentine economy exhibited a high degree of instability, with wide swings in economic policy.[2] Within this eventful history, four distinct phases in the trade regime can be distinguished. Until the mid-1970s the level of protection remained high with widespread backing for import-substitution strategies (ISS). However, the exhaustion of ISS and rising macroeconomic instability led to growing criticism of economic policy. Trade liberalization could not be sustained during the deep economic crisis of the early 1980s. Macroeconomic volatility and the Latin American debt crisis led to a partial reversal in trade liberalization. In the 1990s, widespread rapid change in economic policy took place: price stabilization, massive privatization, financial deregulation, the removal of barriers to foreign trade and the build-up of Mercosur. This led to fundamental changes in the economic environment.

Exports and imports: an overview

The evolution of the trade balance shown in Figure 8.1 reveals distinct phases in the pattern of growth of both exports and imports. Exports progressed slowly until the early 1970s, followed by more dynamic behaviour in the second half of that decade. In the 1980s, exports more or less stagnated. In the 1990s, renewed dynamism was reinforced as Argentina's share of world exports recovered after a long period of decline. However, despite the recent period of rapid growth, the increase in total exports from 1960 was markedly lower than that of world trade. The country's share of world exports, around 2 per cent in the 1950s, was only 0.5 per cent in 1996 as shown in Table 8.1.

The pattern of import growth also shows abrupt change: slow increase in the 1960s, when the economy grew, but the trade regime was one of extreme protection and deepening ISS. The level of import openness fell from 30 per cent of GDP in 1913 to 8 per cent in 1950 and 6 per cent in 1970. Then trade liberalization, coupled with currency appreciation and a consumption boom, led to explosive and unsustainable import growth in the second half of the 1970s. A balance of payments cum debt crisis in 1981–82 triggered a reversal of earlier trade reforms. Higher protection and economic stagnation resulted in slow import growth during the volatile 1980s, while in the 1990s trade liberalization and increasing domestic demand were associated with a rapid rise in imports.

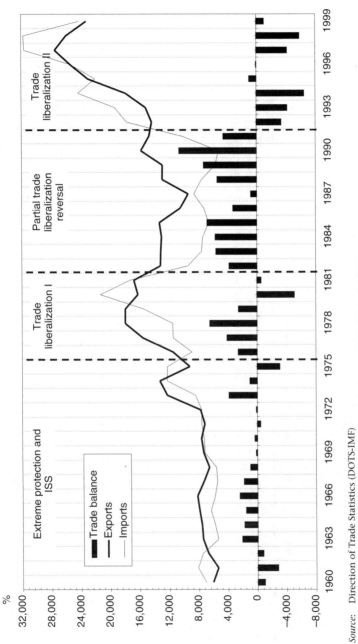

Source: Direction of Trade Statistics (DOTS-IMF)

Figure 8.1 Argentine exports, imports and trade balance 1960–99 (m$ 1999)

Table 8.1 Argentine trade 1960–99 (average annual percentage change)

	Exports		Imports		World exports		Export share
	Nominal value	Real value	Nominal value	Real value	Nominal value	Real value	(% of world exports)
1960–64	6.5	6.1	−0.8	−1.2	7.3	6.9	0.88
1965–69	3.4	0.8	6.9	4.2	10.6	6.5	0.73
1970–74	10.3	1.1	17.0	7.9	19.7	13.1	0.55
1975–79	19.9	11.3	19.6	11.0	16.2	7.7	0.46
1980–84	1.3	−1.4	−18.3	−21.1	4.8	−0.5	0.44
1985–89	7.3	3.4	−0.7	−0.7	11.9	8.0	0.35
1990–94	10.6	7.5	31.9	31.9	7.9	4.8	0.36
1995–99	2.5	0.2	4.6	4.6	2.7	0.5	0.45

Source: DOTS/IMF and WTO

Changes in the level of imports, strongly correlated with economic fluctuations, explain most movements in the trade balance. Until the 1990s, the response to balance of payments problems was typically a sharp contraction in imports, with slight export growth. In the past 40 years, structural change and policy reversals have influenced the Argentinian trade pattern. The degree of concentration in imports has decreased significantly since the mid-1980s, and is now similar to the OECD level in the late 1990s. Although exports were diversified, they remained more concentrated than in OECD countries, as shown in Table 8.2.

The structure of exports shows a declining share of primary products and an increasing share of industrial exports.[3] Primary products fell from 55 per cent in the early 1960s to 33 per cent in the 1990s, while the increase in industrial exports is mainly explained by a sharp rise in the share of manufacturing, from 5 to 28 per cent as shown in Table 8.3. Natural resource industrial goods maintained a stable share of 40 per cent over the period. However, their composition changed, with a sharp reduction in the exports of meat on account of EEC protectionist policies in the early 1970s. In the 1980s the decline in beef exports was offset by the rise in exports of vegetable oils (particularly soya beans) petroleum and natural gas.

Primary products and natural-resource-intensive industrial goods accounted for 95 per cent of total exports in 1960 and 72 per cent in the early 1990s. However, considering the growth in fuel exports (including processed goods) since the early 1980s, we observe a stronger trend in the fall of the share of traditional (agricultural) primary goods, from 93 to 55 per cent. Argentina has been an oil producer for decades, but only recently became an exporting country following rapidly rising output, linked to the deregulation of the sector, price liberalization and the privatization of the largest company, YPF. Within the long-term trend of decreasing primary exports, a short-term increase in trade can be observed in the 1990s when the increase in the degree of industrialization of exports was interrupted. Exports of primary goods are likely to expand in the future, as several big-scale mining projects come on stream.

The rise in the share of manufacturing exports was particularly strong in two sub-periods, the first half of the 1970s and the late 1980s, due to the contribution of labour-intensive goods produced in large-scale plants whose exports expanded despite chronic macroeconomic instability, as shown in Figure 8.2. Industrial exports grew fast in the 1990s, based mainly on sectors that enjoyed subsidies in the last phase

Table 8.2 Concentration of Argentine trade, 1960–99 (%)

	1962–65	1966–70	1971–75	1976–80	1981–85	1986–90	1991–95	1996–99
Argentina								
Exports	31.2	28.9	28.0	21.6	24.5	21.8	20.0	18.9
Imports	18.9	16.6	18.2	17.4	18.3	13.5	12.3	12.1
OECD								
Exports	9.9	10.3	10.3	10.4	11.0	11.6	11.7	n.a.
Imports	10.1	10.3	14.3	18.2	18.0	12.1	12.1	n.a.

Source: CTP-Data

Table 8.3   Argentine exports by sector, 1962–99 (%)

Sets of products	1962–65	1966–70	1971–75	1976–80	1981–85	1986–90	1991–95	1996–99
Primary products	56.6	49.5	45.1	46.0	49.0	31.1	33.6	33.9
Agriculture	56.1	49.1	44.7	45.7	48.5	30.3	28.7	24.8
Mining	0.3	0.4	0.3	0.3	0.2	0.3	0.1	1.2
Energy (fuels)	0.2	0.0	0.0	0.0	0.2	0.5	4.7	7.9
Industrial products	43.3	50.5	54.8	53.9	50.9	68.9	66.2	65.1
Natural resources-intensive	38.2	41.1	36.5	33.8	34.8	45.8	41.4	36.6
Agriculture	37.4	40.3	36.0	32.0	27.7	37.6	34.3	31.3
Mining	0.2	0.2	0.2	0.7	1.4	3.5	1.8	1.6
Energy (refining & other)	0.5	0.6	0.3	1.1	5.7	4.7	5.3	3.8
Manufacturing	5.1	9.4	18.3	20.2	16.2	23.1	24.8	28.4
Labour-intensive	0.1	0.4	1.1	2.6	0.8	1.7	2.2	1.6
Economies of scale-intensive	4.0	6.0	10.5	11.2	10.6	15.4	15.5	19.4
Specialized suppliers (machinery & capital goods)	0.4	1.1	3.8	4.1	2.6	3.5	4.3	4.1
Science-based (R&D-intensive)	0.7	1.9	2.9	2.3	2.2	2.6	2.9	3.3
Residuals	0.1	0.1	0.1	0.1	0.1	0.1	0.1	1.0

Source: CTP-Data

of the ISS (industrial commodities such as steel and aluminium) and the automotive industry as a result of Mercosur.

Export growth: endowments, market dynamism, technology and trade regimes

This section considers the relative sectoral contribution. Export performance is viewed from complementary perspectives, highlighting the resource endowments ('Hecksher–Ohlin'), the expansion of markets ('neo-Keynesian') and the technological content ('Schumpeterian' view).[4] We examined export trends taking account of the changes in trade regimes.

Export performance oscillated sharply. In the first period of extreme protection, exports increased slowly at 2 per cent a year. Despite strong currency appreciation between 1976 and 1981 – a period of trade liberalization – exports rose to over 10 per cent a year. The balance-of-payments crisis in the early 1980s triggered protectionist policies, and led to a long phase of persistent macroeconomic instability, ending in the hyperinflation of 1989–90 leading to a fall in GDP per head. Export performance worsened as the rate of growth fell to 6 per cent as shown in Table 8.4a. During the 1990s, successful monetary stabilization and a new round of trade liberalization (TL2) were associated with renewed export dynamism at nearly 10 per cent a year. We noted not only sharp fluctuations in export growth, but also a cyclical pattern in the institutional environment, particularly the trade regimes. Successive phases of protection and trade liberalization were separated by crises triggering regime shifts. At first glance, one might be tempted to establish a direct link between trade liberalization and export dynamism. In the recent controversies on the role of trade regimes in export performance and economic growth, this result would support the favourable view on the positive (negative) impact of openness (protection). However, detailed study of the pattern of export growth suggests a more cautious conclusion.

In the first phase, 1962–75, of protection and slow total export growth we note the relatively strong performance of manufacturing exports. These started from negligible levels, but showed significant dynamism, accounting for 74 per cent of total export growth in the period (Table 8.4a). Thus, if the extreme ISS shows the negative effect of trade distortions on natural-resource-intensive sectors, we also see the positive impact of *learning by doing* and infant industry effects *à la* List–Rosenstein Rodan–Prebisch, more recently revisited by Krugman (1995). These ambiguous results are reinforced by examining the

133

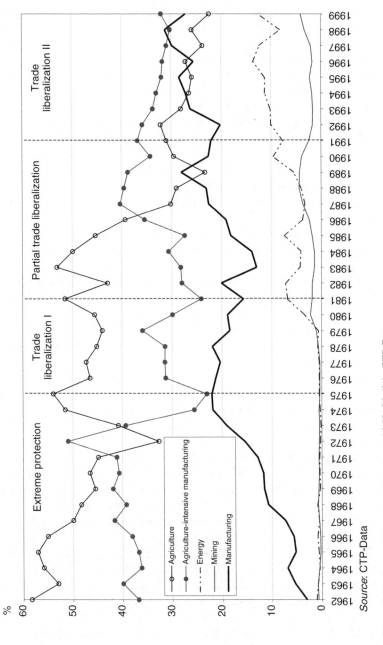

Figure 8.2 Argentine export structure, 1962–99 (%), CTP Data

Source: CTP-Data

degree of dynamism in world markets for Argentine exports, and analysing the technological intensity of exported goods. Sales to highly dynamic markets showed a strong increase as shown in Table 8.4, whereas the major contribution to sluggish total export growth came from these groups of goods. The more dynamic sectors in this period were also those with a relatively high technological content (medium-high and medium-low, shown in Table 8.4c).

The second period (1976–81) of trade liberalization and rapid export growth (TL1), shows that the major contribution came from natural-resource-intensive goods (primary and natural-resource-intensive industry), which accounted for 92 per cent of total export growth. Manufacturing exports (particularly capital goods) were weak, suggesting a strong negative impact from the abrupt import-opening cum severe currency overvaluation (Table 8.4a). In this period the favourable effect of import liberalization through more productive technologies does not show in rising manufacturing exports, and seems to be offset by massive competitive pressures. The soya bean boom is the distinctive development of the later 1970s. The sectors with positive export performance during these years were mainly in markets with relatively low dynamism or in regression (Table 8.4b), or with low technological intensity (Table 8.4c).

The third phase, during the 1980s, was one of trade reform reversal and sluggish export growth, not unlike the 1960s, and showed a relatively better performance by manufacturing. This sector accounted for a large share of export growth (Table 8.4a). Again, the exports of natural-resource-intensive industries (for example, soya bean oil) increased greatly. Petroleum and natural gas exports also gained in importance. Despite extreme macroeconomic instability, the persistent contraction of the domestic market contributed to an export drive. Increasing exports were a survival strategy, especially for sectors with economies of scale (manufactured commodities such as steel and aluminium). As in the first phase of a protectionist regime, exports increased mainly in relatively dynamic world markets (Tables 8.4b). However, contrary to the 1960s, export growth had a low technological intensity.

In the fourth period (the 1990s), export growth showed a comparatively balanced pattern. As in the previous liberalization phase during the 1970s, the primary sector showed strong growth, but now a major contribution came from of oil and gas, which rose by 32 per cent (Table 8.4). Contrary to the 1970s episode of failed trade reform, manufacturing exports grew rapidly. We note the positive behaviour of

Table 8.4a Argentine export performance by sector: Hecksher–Ohlin view (% change)

	Average rate of growth* (% per year)				Contribution to total export growth			
	1962–75	1976–81	1982–90	1991–99	1962–75	1976–81	1982–90	1991–99
Primary Products	1.0	9.0	-8.9	8.2	40.5	48.8	374.3	35.5
Agriculture	1.1	8.9	-9.2	4.4	41.9	48.6	393.2	7.3
Mining	1.5	18.1	-1.0	40.6	0.1	0.3	1.7	7.0
Energy (Fuels)	-29.1	-78.2	97.9	31.7	-1.4	-0.1	-20.5	21.2
Industrial Products	5.2	10.9	3.9	7.4	59.3	51.2	-274.2	59.0
Natural resource-intensive	1.4	15.2	3.5	4.8	-14.6	43.3	-180.8	22.3
Agriculture	1.5	10.6	3.8	6.0	-14.4	25.5	-133.1	27.3
Mining	3.5	81.3	14.0	1.8	-0.5	3.3	-31.0	-2.5
Energy (Refining & others)	-3.7	73.4	-2.9	-1.3	0.3	14.5	-16.7	-2.5
Manufacturing	18.6	4.6	5.0	11.9	74.0	7.9	-93.3	36.7
Labour intensive	36.3	21.7	9.5	6.5	3.2	2.1	-2.5	0.7
Economies of scale-intensive	14.8	6.4	5.9	12.8	33.6	7.7	-85.2	21.9
Specialized suppliers	32.8	-4.3	3.9	9.9	24.5	-2.4	-8.1	6.6
Science-based	20.9	3.4	-0.1	12.3	12.6	0.6	2.4	7.5
Total exports	3.2	9.9	-1.2	7.9	100.0	100.0	100.0	100.0

Table 8.4b Dynamism of export performance: neo-Keynesian view (% change)

	Average rate of growth* (% per year)				Contribution to total export growth			
	1967–75	1976–81	1982–90	1991–97	1962–75	1976–81	1982–90	1991–99
Highly dynamic	32.1	37.8	3.2	10.4	33.5	5.5	4.9	6.3
Dynamic	9.3	4.5	1.2	20.5	51.6	–27.3	69.0	50.9
Medium dynamism	14.3	2.9	3.9	7.5	22.1	11.9	–65.3	–1.9
Low dynamism	3.3	–2.9	7.6	5.7	–8.3	15.3	–256.4	28.2
In regression	1.2	7.1	–8.4	7.5	1.1	94.7	347.8	16.4
Total exports	8.1	9.9	–1.2	8.6	100.0	100.0	100.0	100.0

Table 8.4c Technological intensity of exports: Schumpeterian view (% change)

	Average rate of growth* (% per year)				Contribution to total export growth			
	1962–75	1976–81	1982–90	1991–99	1962–75	1976–81	1982–90	1991–99
High intensity	20.2	1.8	–3.5	11.4	18.6	0.3	–2.6	6.7
Medium-high intensity	12.9	4.1	7.1	16.7	41.5	3.1	16.1	44.0
Medium-low intensity	19.5	17.9	–2.4	3.8	41.3	31.5	4.3	7.3
Low intensity	2.9	11.3	5.3	5.7	–1.4	65.0	82.2	42.0
Total industrial exports	5.2	10.9	3.9	7.4	100.0	100.0	100.0	100.0

* % of growth in constant 1999 US$
Source: . CTP-DATA

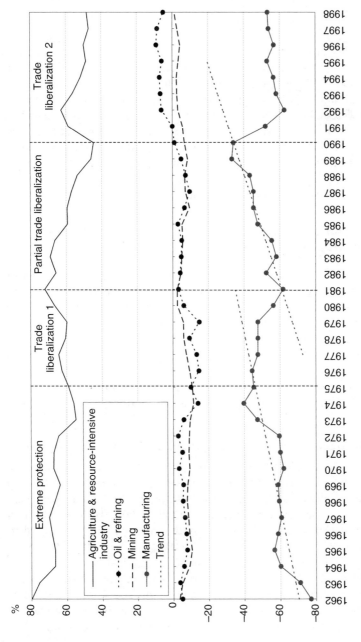

Figure 8.3 Revealed comparative advantage (RCA)

the economies-of-scale-intensive goods, the recovery of exports of capital goods and R&D-intensive sectors.

The analysis of the relative contributions to total export growth, which takes into account the initial size of the exporting sectors, shows an evenly distributed effect of agriculture-based sectors (primary and industry), manufacturing and oil and gas (Table 8.4a). Manufacturing contributed 37 per cent to export growth compared to 8 per cent in the TL1 period), with a particularly strong contribution from the economies-of-scale-intensive goods. In this phase, sales to highly dynamic import markets had a major role, again in contrast to the late 1970s (Table 8.4b). The technological intensity of industrial exports also showed a marked contrast with the behaviour of the export pattern during TL1: goods with high technological intensity had a relatively more dynamic performance in the recent period (Table 8.4c).

3 Specialization and trade regimes: import substitution versus trade liberalization

This section complements the previous discussion of export performance by studying the evolution of revealed comparative advantage (RCA) under the different trade regimes. RCA takes into account not only the sectoral export behaviour, but also the dynamics of imports, leading to a measure of specialization on the basis of sectoral trade balances. The RCA may contain biases as an indicator of trade trends in an economy with wide swings in the volume of exports. Therefore, we will try to detect long-term *structural* change, as opposed to short-run variations due to transitory fluctuations in output and real exchange rates.

Global trade specialization: long-term trends and the short run

The long-term perspective shows that primary goods have a major role in Argentina's pattern of specialization. Revealed comparative advantage (RCA), as measured by the sectoral contribution to the trade balance, is positive not only for primary goods, but also for industrial goods intensive in natural resources (Table 8.5a). Indeed, the manufacturing sector shows a persistent comparative disadvantage over the entire 40 years.

The analysis of specialization and import-market dynamism (Table 8.5b) reveals a stable degree of comparative disadvantage in growing sectors, a slow improvement in goods of intermediate dynamism and a strong increase (decrease) of the revealed comparative advantage (RCA) in sectors of slow dynamism (regression). Also,

Argentina has enjoyed an advantage in goods with low technological intensity and a structural disadvantage in higher technological intensity goods (Table 8.5c). Within these general trends in long-term specialization, important changes can be identified. In particular, we noted a considerable decrease in the comparative advantage of the *traditional* primary agricultural sector, and the emergence of a strongly rising RCA of the primary energy sector (oil and natural gas), due to the expansion of production of these goods in the 1990s. In the natural-resource-intensive agriculture-based sectors, exports of beef declined, while other goods, such as vegetable oils (corn, soybean and sunflower) had strong growth. Refined fuels show a fluctuating RCA, with an increase in comparative advantage until the early 1990s and a subsequent relative decline. The same pattern can be observed in the case of mining, although this sector can be expected to become an important exporter as large-scale projects reach maturity.

The analysis of RCA in manufacturing shows a decrease in the structural comparative disadvantage of this sector until the late 1980s, and a subsequent reversion of this trend in the 1990s (Table 8.5a). The improvement in the RCA of manufacturing between 1960 and 1990 has its sources in the positive behaviour of the economies of scale-intensive (ESI) goods, the capital goods and a relatively weaker change in the labour-intensive industrial sector, as opposed to the persistent deterioration of the RCA in the R&D sector. The increase in the comparative disadvantage of manufacturing in the 1990s was widespread among groups of goods, with the exception of ESI. This decrease of the RCAs of the manufacturing sector coupled with the recent increase in the comparative advantage of the primary goods seems to support the hypothesis that the economy was again becoming specialized in primary goods. However, as we have shown in the study of export growth (section 3), and contrary to the fairly smooth behaviour of the RCA in the traditional agricultural sector (primary and industry), manufacturing performance changed sharply where repeated breaks in trend overlapped with changes in the trade regime (Figure 8.3). During phases of high protection, the comparative disadvantage of this sector decreases, while phases of rapid trade liberalization reinforce the traditional trade specialization and the RCAs of manufacturing (in particular of capital goods and R&D) deteriorate.

The first period of trade liberalization – TL1 in the late 1970s – shows both a sharp rise in imports of consumer goods, but also a rapid increase in capital goods due to competitive pressures, economic

Table 8.5a By sector (Hecksher-Ohlin Revisited)

	1962–75	1976–81	1982–90	1990–98	1990	1991	1992	1993	1994	1995	1996	1997	1998
Primary Products	29.5	28.9	17.5	27.4	8.6	20.3	29.3	27.1	28.0	27.6	31.7	27.1	28.0
Agriculture	37.1	38.9	28.8	24.1	18.1	26.1	28.9	24.9	22.9	22.5	24.1	20.2	22.8
Mining	−2.8	−3.5	−5.1	−1.5	−6.2	−4.0	−1.9	−1.4	−1.2	−1.7	−1.5	−0.9	0.7
Energy (Fuels)	−4.8	−9.5	−6.2	4.8	−3.3	−1.8	2.3	3.6	6.3	6.8	9.0	7.7	4.6
Industrial Products	−29.2	−25.5	−17.0	−26.9	−7.8	−19.4	−28.7	−26.6	−27.7	−26.9	−31.0	−26.9	−27.8
Natural resource-intensive	29.0	25.4	29.1	28.9	26.3	32.7	33.9	31.5	28.8	26.1	25.7	26.8	25.4
Agriculture	36.3	28.3	29.5	29.2	24.7	32.6	31.2	29.4	29.0	28.6	28.5	27.8	26.7
Mining	−5.8	−2.2	−1.5	−1.7	−0.6	−1.7	−1.3	−1.2	−1.1	−1.7	−2.9	−1.9	−1.9
Energy (Refining & others)	−1.5	−0.7	1.0	1.3	2.2	1.8	4.0	3.2	0.9	−0.7	0.1	0.9	0.6
Manufacturing	−58.3	−50.9	−46.1	−55.7	−34.2	−52.1	−62.6	−58.0	−56.6	−53.0	−56.7	−53.7	−53.2
Labour intensive	0.4	1.2	0.7	−0.8	0.8	−0.5	−2.1	−1.2	0.3	−0.4	−0.6	−0.6	−1.2
Economies of scale-intensive	−32.4	−23.5	−19.2	−21.8	−12.1	−21.3	−27.2	−23.3	−22.9	−18.6	−22.3	−20.0	−18.9
Specialized suppliers (machinery & capital goods)	−19.4	−17.7	−14.6	−17.3	−12.5	−14.8	−16.0	−16.6	−16.4	−18.9	−19.5	−17.7	−18.3
Science-based (R&D intensive)	−6.8	−10.8	−13.0	−15.9	−10.4	−15.5	−17.3	−17.0	−17.5	−15.1	−14.4	−15.4	−14.8
Residuals	−0.3	−0.4	−0.5	−0.5	−0.8	−0.9	−0.6	−0.5	−0.3	−0.7	−0.7	−0.2	−0.2

Table 8.5b By world market dynamics (neo-Keynesian view)

	1967–75	1976–81	1982–90	1990–97	1990	1991	1992	1993	1994	1995	1996	1997	1998
Highly dynamic	−15.0	−18.1	−10.4	−15.8	−11.8	−15.9	−13.6	−15.1	−16.0	−16.7	−17.1	−16.5	n.a.
Dynamic	20.7	1.5	−15.2	−4.9	−15.1	−6.9	−5.8	−4.8	−2.0	−2.9	−6.7	−5.5	n.a.
Medium dynamism	−22.0	−1.0	−4.1	−14.4	−2.2	−14.9	−17.7	−15.0	−17.2	−10.5	−11.5	−13.9	n.a.
Low dynamism	9.4	−8.0	6.9	17.9	13.6	22.3	21.7	18.4	17.9	14.3	15.2	15.6	n.a.
In regression	6.9	25.7	22.8	17.3	15.5	15.4	15.4	16.5	17.3	15.8	20.1	20.2	n.a.

Table 8.5c By technological intensity (Schumpeterian view)

	1962–75	1976–81	1982–90	1990–98	1990	1991	1992	1993	1994	1995	1996	1997	1998
High intensity	−5.3	−9.0	−9.8	−12.5	−6.4	−11.4	−14.4	−14.1	−14.3	−11.4	−10.7	−12.2	−11.9
Medium-high intensity	−17.9	−16.6	−24.1	−24.6	−23.9	−26.2	−24.4	−24.5	−24.5	−24.1	−27.9	−22.9	−21.9
Medium-low intensity	−23.4	−20.1	−10.3	−13.1	−4.2	−10.0	−12.8	−11.8	−12.6	−14.8	−15.3	−13.4	−13.9
Low intensity	17.4	20.2	27.1	23.3	26.7	28.1	22.9	23.8	23.7	23.4	23.0	21.6	19.9
Industrial Products	−29.2	−25.6	−17.0	−26.9	−7.8	−19.4	−28.7	−26.6	−27.7	−26.9	−31.0	−26.9	−27.8

Source: CTP-Data.

restructuring and a fall in the price of imported machinery (lower tariffs and currency appreciation). The revealed comparative advantage (RCA) of manufacturing fell, but productivity increased significantly. This contributed to the improvement of the RCA in the protectionist phase of the 1980s.

During the TL2 in the 1990s, the intra-regime trend changed after 1993; manufacturing RCA improved and the energy sector (primary and refining) showed a rising comparative advantage. However, the RCA of the traditional agricultural sector declined (Figure 8.3). Conclusions from this break in the trade pattern should be treated with caution as the number of observations were limited. Changes in the trend of manufacturing RCAs were caused by relatively few sectors (Table 8.6). The changing path in the pattern of international trade in manufacturing can be explained by a various factors:

1 Despite the strong increase in exports of capital goods (section 3) the revealed comparative disadvantage in the trade of these goods increased. This resulted from the fast rise in investment, which led to a surge in imports. A long period of chronic instability, high inflation and erratic output performance handicapped the expected return on investment in the 1980s, and thus reduced the demand for capital goods. By contrast, in the 1990s, monetary stability, a consumption boom and massive privatizations (whereas investment had been repressed in a number of state firms) produced a sharp change in the number of profitable projects. Trade liberalization, the elimination of *national preference* laws for certain capital goods and a real currency appreciation induced a decrease in the relative price of capital goods, reinforced by a decline in international and domestic real interest rates.

2 The R&D sector exhibited special features. In spite of having the highest export growth rate (excluding oil and gas) in the 1990s, it still suffered increasing comparative disadvantage. Massive investment by privatized telecom firms largely accounted for the pattern of trade in the R&D sector. Following major restructuring, obsolete capital stock had been renewed between 1990 and 1992, and the revealed comparative disadvantage of the sector diminished.

3 The RCA trend in manufacturing of labour-intensive goods, such as textiles, also changed significantly. After a first phase of increasing comparative disadvantage, the RCA improved after 1993. The restructuring policy with rapid trade liberalization cum currency appreciation resulted in competitive pressure and led to a surge in

net imports. In the second phase, restructuring and strong productivity gains explain the relative improvement in RCA.

4 The behaviour of economies-of-scale-intensive goods, and in particular of the automotive sector, had a major influence in the change of the RCAs of manufacturing. Again, there was comparative disadvantage in the initial phase of TL2 (1990–92), followed by a second period of decreasing disadvantage from 1993. Despite the general process of trade liberalization, the automotive sector enjoyed a specific transitory trade-protection regime in the framework of the Mercosur agreement. A system of administered trade was introduced whereby intra-regional exchanges had to be balanced (over time), and extra-regional imports into Argentina were subject to quantity restrictions. This sector, an extremely dynamic component in Mercosur, would benefit from further analysis of intra-industry trade with Brazil.

Mercosur has had a significant impact on Argentina's trade structure (Miotti, Quenan and Winograd, 1997, 1998). The analysis of the bilateral trade specialization with Brazil shows that Argentina's comparative advantage in the production of primary commodities increased, largely the result of increased oil exports. Intra-industry trade also increased as a result of the rise in intra-firm trade (mostly by multinational auto companies). Sales to Brazil also enjoyed a rising share of a set of goods with a relatively high degree of technological complexity.

Can the 'Brazil effect' explain the growth of exports in the 1990s? Table 8.7 confirms that sales to Brazil accounted for half of the total growth of Argentine exports in recent years. This contribution to total export growth was similar to that observed during the 1980s. On the other hand, if the LC1 and LC2 phases of trade liberalization are compared, LC1 shows no evidence of a 'Brazil effect'. In the recent phase, rising sales to other Mercosur countries comprised increased exports of traditional and non-traditional raw materials and manufactured goods (particularly goods intensive in economies of scale).

4 Conclusions

Raw materials continue to play an important role in Argentine trade specialization. The country has enjoyed persistent comparative advantage in industrial goods intensive in natural resources, whereas the

Table 8.6 Manufacturing: contribution by sector (%)

Sector	Revealed comparative advantage			Change	Change	1990–92		1992–95-8	
	1990	1992	Av. 1995/8	1990–92	1992–95/8	Increase	Decrease	Increase	Decrease
Manufacturing	−34.16	−62.60	−54.17	−28.44	8.43	9.88	−38.32	19.91	−11.48
Labour intensive	0.85	−2.13	−0.70	−2.97	1.43	0.11	−3.08	1.55	−0.13
Economies of scale-intensive	−12.09	−27.24	−19.94	−15.15	7.29	6.14	21.29	11.61	−4.32
Specialized suppliers	−12.52	−15.97	−18.62	−3.46	−2.65	1.84	−5.30	2.38	−5.03
Science-based	−10.40	−17.26	−14.90	−6.86	2.36	1.79	−8.65	4.37	−2.01
Main changes									
Textiles	0.00	−2.19	−1.33	−2.20	0.85		−2.20	0.91	−0.05
Wearing apparel	0.49	−1.50	−0.37	−1.99	1.13		−1.99	1.15	−0.01
Household equipment	−0.16	−1.40	−0.95	−1.24	0.45		−1.24	0.45	
TV and radio receivers and sound recorders	−0.72	−3.03	−0.77	−2.31	2.25		−2.31	2.29	
Steel pipes	1.43	2.06	−0.68	0.63	−2.74	0.63			−0.68
Iron & steel	0.70	−2.34	1.81	−3.04	4.15	0.20	−3.24	2.23	−0.42
Machinery	−5.22	−7.87	−8.43	−2.65	−0.55	0.54	3.20	1.66	−2.10
Tyres	−0.06	−0.66	−0.31	−0.60	0.35		−0.60	0.35	
Automotive	−2.18	−10.22	−4.77	−8.04	5.48		8.04	5.55	−0.11
Telecom equipment	−1.51	−4.24	−4.11	−2.74	0.13		2.74	0.13	
Office & computing machinery	−1.27	−2.75	−3.46	−1.48	−0.71		−1.48	0.15	−0.86
Subtotal				−25.66	10.79	1.37	−27.03	14.74	−4.24
Net change						−25.66		10.50	
Total change in manufacturing						−28.44		8.43	
Contribution to Total change						90.2%		124.6%	

Source: CTP-Data

Table 8.7 The Brazil effect: exports to Brazil – percentage of total export growth

	Total export growth		Exports to Brazil growth		'Brazil-effect'	
	1990–97	1997–99	1990–97	1997–99	1990–97	1997–99
Primary products	12.4	-7.8	23.4	-15.1	39.9	49.3
Agriculture	8.1	-9.2	16.5	-10.6	40.5	50.9
Mining	22.8	119.4	5.0	81.5	6.5	-3.2
Energy (fuels)	45.7	-11.7	172.7	-28.5	40.5	0.2
Industrial products	10.8	-6.7	31.0	-17.6	53.2	37.3
Natural resource-intensive	7.7	-3.6	21.0	-7.6	26.2	52.4
Agriculture	9.9	-4.8	18.5	-9.4	16.2	36.1
Mining	-0.8	-4.5	8.1	2.2	-91.3	85.0
Energy (refining & others)	-0.6	6.9	38.5	-4.6	-783.3	-29.1
Manufacturing	15.9	-10.7	36.1	-20.9	74.7	30.9
Labour intensive	12.6	-18.4	48.0	-46.0	46.0	5.3
Economies of scale-intensive	16.1	-13.5	40.7	-22.9	84.4	21.8
Specialized suppliers (machinery & capital goods)	17.0	-8.7	26.4	-17.5	67.2	64.7
Science-based (R&D intensive)	16.0	7.6	21.2	5.2	33.6	-48.2
Residuals	65.6	21.8	29.6	-43.7	1.3	-0.5
Total	11.5	-6.5	28.3	-16.8	47.7	43.0

Source: CTP-Data

performance of exports of other manufactured goods led to a decrease in the comparative disadvantage over the 40-year period.

Trade specialization has been studied from three complementary perspectives. The first was the Hecksher–Ohlin–Samuelson (HOS) view based on factor endowments. The second, the Schumpeterian approach, evaluated the profile of trade specialization considering the level of technological development. The third approach, the neo-Keynesian, analysed international specialization on the basis of the dynamism of international markets.

This analytical methodology has helped to identify important changes in the evolution of Argentina's specialization. In particular, we found a slight weakening of Argentina's comparative advantage in agriculture and a strengthening of the energy sector's comparative advantage. The prospects of the mining sector indicate a rising comparative advantage in the future. As for manufacturing, following a fall in structural comparative disadvantage during the 1980s, the trend appears to have shifted in the opposite direction in the 1990s.

From the viewpoint of technology content, Argentina has shown comparative advantage in non-intensive, that is in higher-technology goods. Seen from a neo-Keynesian perspective, the comparative disadvantage of the dynamic sectors has remained stable, while, in the long term, products of intermediate dynamism have become more competitive.

This study has also discussed whether the shift in Argentine trade policy, from trade protection to trade liberalization, affected the pattern of specialization. During phases of high protection (1962–75 and 1982–90) the comparative disadvantage of the manufacturing sector declined. In periods of trade liberalization, comparative advantage rose in most of the primary sectors, while manufacturing sectors suffered from increased foreign competition. Nevertheless, during the liberalization of the 1990s the trend seemed to change: after 1993, manufacturing's comparative advantage began to rise. Initially, the sharp rise in imports of final goods was reflected in a strong increase in the comparative disadvantage in manufacturing, which was partially reversed later on due to gains in productivity. In any case, these movements should be interpreted with caution, since they could be the consequence of short-run effects.

Greater regional integration also influenced Argentine trade patterns; exports to Brazil, for example, increased rapidly in the 1990s. However, the 'Brazil effect' was not the only reason for the growth in export volumes or the higher degree of diversification of exported goods. Sales to Brazil accounted for 50 per cent of the change in exports; thus they have played an important but by no means exclusive role.[5] Rising exports to Brazil were associated with a structural shift in their composition. The manufacturing sector, which represented 25 per cent of total sales in the early 1980s, had risen to over 40 per cent of all exports to Brazil by 1996. During the 1990s there was a large increase in energy exports from Argentina to Brazil, and manufactured products intensive in economies of scale and equipment goods. Before the 1980s, Argentina's sales to Brazil were biased (compared with exports to third countries) towards traditional raw materials; today, the opposite is the case.

Notes

1 For an historical perspective on Argentina see Diaz Alejandro (1970), Mallon and Sourrouille (1975), Winograd (1988), Miotti (1991) and Véganzones and Winograd (1997, 1998).

2 The empirical analysis is based in the sectoral classification of goods. In the case of manufactured goods, we also consider the source of *competitiveness*, as in Pavitt (1984).

3 For a Schumpeterian perspective and neo-Keynesian approach on the gains from trade see Dosi, Pavitt and Soete (1988) and Guerrieri (1994). For a theoretical review of the literature, Grossman and Helpman (1991), Baldwin (1992), Falvey (1994), Smith (1994), Grossman and Rogoff (1995), Rodrik (1988) and Krugman (1995). For a review on the empirics of trade theory see Leamer and Levinsohn (1995).

4 For a detailed analysis of the impact of regional integration and trade with Brazil see Miotti, Quenan and Winograd (1997, 2000) and Quenan, Miotti and Winograd (1994).

References

Baldwin, R. (1992) 'Measurable Dynamic Gains from Trade', *Journal of Political Economy*, vol. 100(1), pp. 162–74.

Diaz Alejandro, C. F. (1970) *Essays on the Economic History of the Republic of Argentina* (New Haven: Yale University Press).

Dosi, G., K. Pavitt and L. Soete (1988) *The Economics of Technical Change and International Trade* (Brighton: Wheatsheaf).

Falvey, R. (1994) 'The Theory of International Trade', in D. Greenaway and L. A. Winters (eds), *Surveys in International Trade* (Oxford: Basil Blackwell).

Grossman, G. and E. Helpman (1991) *Innovation and Growth in the Global Economy* (Cambridge, MA: MIT Press).

Grossman, G. and R. Rogoff (1995) *Handbook of International Economics* (Amsterdam, NL: North-Holland).

Guerrieri, P. (1994) 'International Competitiveness, Trade Integration and Technological Interdependence', in C. Bradford Jr. (ed.), *The New Paradigm of*

Systemic Competitiveness: Toward More Integrated Policies in Latin America (Paris: OECD).

Krugman, P. (1995) 'Increasing Returns, Imperfect Competitions and the Positive Theory of International Trade', in G. Grossman and R. Rogoff (eds), *Handbook of International Economics* (Amsterdam: North-Holland).

Lafay, G. (1987) 'Avantage Comparatif et Compétitivité' (Comparative Advantage and Competition), Economie Prospective Internationale, no. 29 (1st qtr), CEPII, Paris.

Leamer, E. and J. Levinsohn (1995) 'International Trade Theory: The Evidence', in G. Grossman and R. Rogoff (eds), *Handbook of International Economics* (Amsterdam: North-Holland).

Mallon, R. and J. V. Sourrouille (1975) *La Politica Economica en una Sociedad Conflictiva: El Caso Argentino* (Economic Policy in a Society in Conflict: The Case of Argentina (Buenos Aires: Amorrortu).

Miotti, L. (1991) 'Accumulation, Régulation et Crises en Argentine (1860–1990') (Accumulation, Regulation and Crises in Argentina), Université de Paris VII, Paris (PhD thesis).

Miotti, L., C. Quenan and C. Winograd (1997) 'Economic Restructuring, Trade Regimes and Specialization: Is Argentina Deepening a Primary Exporter Pattern?', Delta, Paris (mimeo).

Miotti, L., C. Quenan and C. Winograd (1998) 'Spécialisation internationale et intégration régionale: l'Argentine et le Mercosur' (International Specialization and Regional Integration: Argentina and Mercosur), *Economie Internationale*, no. 74 (2nd qtr), Paris, pp. 89–120.

Miotti, L., C. Quenan and C. Winograd (2000) 'Trade Specialization and Trade Regimes in Argentina, Empirics in the Long Term' University of Paris–Evry (mimeo).

Pavitt, K. (1984) 'Sectoral Patterns of Technical Change: Toward a Taxonomy and Theory', *Research Policy*, vol. 13.

Quenan, C., L. Miotti and C. Winograd (1994) 'Especialización Internacional, Competitividad y Oportunidades de Comercio: América Latina y la Unión Europea' (International Specialization, Competition and Commercial Opportunities: Latin America and the European Union), SELA–EEC, Caracas.

Rodrik, D. (1988) 'Imperfect Competition, Scale Economies and Trade Policy in Developing Countries', in R. Baldwin (ed.), *Trade Policy Issues and Empirical Analysis* (Chicago: University of Chicago Press).

Smith, A. (1994) 'Imperfect Competition and International Trade', in D. Greenaway and L. A. Winters (eds), *Surveys in International Trade* (Oxford: Basil Blackwell).

Véganzones, M. A. and C. Winograd (1997) *Argentina in the 20th Century: An Account of Long Awaited Growth* (Paris: OECD).

Véganzones, M. A. and C. Winograd (1998) 'Human Capital, Trade Openness and Convergence', *Labour*, vol. 12(2), pp. 305–52.

Winograd, C. (1987) 'Exchange Rate, Anchored Disinflation and Macroeconomic Stability', University of Oxford (mimeo).

Winograd C. (1988) 'Essais sur les politiques de stabilization macroé-conomiques' (Attempts at Macroeconomic Stabilization Policies) PhD thesis, DELTA-Ecole des Hautes Etudes en Sciences Sociales, Paris.

9
Testing the Short- and Long-Run Exchange-Rate Effects on the Trade Balance: The Case of Colombia

*Hernán C. Rincón**

1 Introduction

The primary objective of this chapter is to examine the role of the exchange rate in determining short- and long-run trade-balance behaviour for Colombia in a model which includes money and income. That is, the aim is to examine whether the trade balance is affected by the exchange rate, and whether hypotheses such as the Bickerdike, Robinson Metzler model (BRM), the Marshall–Lerner conditions, or J-curve type of hypotheses hold for current data. In addition, to test the empirical relevance of the *absorption* and *monetary* approaches for these data.

Studying the relationship between the trade balance and the exchange rate is especially important for developing economies with poorly developed capital markets where trade flows drive balance-of-payments accounts. In addition, exchange-rate behaviour, whether determined by exogenous or endogenous shocks or by policy, has been a common, yet controversial, policy issue in many countries. Economic authorities in developing countries have repeatedly resorted to nominal devaluation as a means not only to correct external imbalances and/or *misalignments* of the real exchange rate, to increase competitiveness and revenues, but also as a key element of adjustment programmes, and/or to respond to pressures from interest groups such as exporters. The decision to devalue has fequently been taken even if devaluation might cause inflationary spirals, domestic market

* I am grateful to Professors David Bullock, Soyoung Kim, Gerald Nelson and Zhijie Xiao for their valuable comments. Also, I thank Luis E. Arango, Javier Gómez, Enrique Ospina and Carlos E. Posada from the Banco de la República for their comments and suggestions.

distortions, disruptive effects on growth and undesirable redistributive effects.

Conventional wisdom says that a nominal devaluation improves the trade balance. This conjecture is rooted in a static and partial equilibrium approach to the balance of payments known as the elasticity approach (Bickerdike, 1920; Robinson, 1947; Metzler, 1948). The model, commonly known as the BRM model, has been recognized in the literature as providing a sufficient condition (the BRM condition) for a trade-balance improvement when the exchange rate is devalued. The hypothesis that devaluation improves the trade balance has been rooted in a particular solution of the BRM condition, known as the Marshall–Lerner condition (Marshall, 1923; Lerner, 1944).

Empirically, the evidence has been inconsistent in both rejecting and supporting the BRM or Marshall–Lerner conditions. In the vast number of cases where these conditions have been deduced, drawing primarily on data from developed countries and using simple OLS on single equation models, the testing procedure has relied on direct estimation of elasticities (see Artus and McGuirk, 1981; Artus and Knight, 1984; Krugman and Baldwin, 1987; Krugman, 1991). It is well-known that estimated elasticities suffer problems ranging from measurability to identification. As a consequence, the evidence is suspect. Moreover, the results derived from most of the studies are based on *spurious* results. The findings have been contradictory, depending on whether data from developed and developing countries are used (see Cooper, 1971; Kamin, 1988; Edwards, 1989; Paredes, 1989; Rose and Yellen, 1989; Rose, 1990, 1991; Gylfason and Radetzki, 1991; Pritchett, 1991; Bahmani-Oskooee and Alse, 1994).

Historical data for developed and developing countries have shown that devaluation may cause a negative effect on the trade balance in the short run, but an improvement in the long run; that is, the trade balance followed a time path which looked like the letter 'J'. The main explanation for this *J-curve* has been that, while the exchange rate adjusts instantaneously, there is a time-lag as consumers and producers adjust to changes in relative prices (Junz and Rhomberg, 1973; Magee, 1973; Meade, 1988). In terms of elasticity, domestically, there is a high export supply elasticity and a low short-run import demand elasticity. Moreover, recent literature, which has used dynamic-general equilibrium models, has found that the trade balance is negatively correlated with current and future movements in the terms of trade (measured by the real exchange rate), but positively correlated with past movements (Backus, Kehoe and Kydland, 1994).

Section 2 discusses the theory of the three main balance-of-payments views: elasticity; absorption; monetary. Section 3 develops the econometric framework, presents the data and tests for stationarity and order of integration of the relevant series. Section 4 tests the relevant hypotheses, discusses the estimations and comments on the results. Finally, section 5 summarizes the main findings, comments on the limitations, and suggests directions for future research.

2 The theory

This section develops the Bickerdike–Robinson–Metzler (BRM) model, its theoretical implications and discusses the *absorption* and the 'modern' *monetary* approaches.

The BRM model and the BRM and Marshall–Lerner conditions

The BRM model, or imperfect substitutes model, is a partial equilibrium version of a standard two-country (domestic and foreign), two-goods (export and imports) model.[1] The effects of exchange-rate changes are analysed in terms of separate markets for imports and exports, and the equations that define the model are given as follows.[2] The domestic demand for imports is a function of the nominal price of imports measured in domestic currency:

$$M^d = M^d (P_m) \qquad (1)$$

Observe that P_m is nothing but $P_m = EP_m^*$, where E is the nominal exchange rate (the domestic currency price of foreign exchange) and P_m^* is the foreign currency price (level) of domestic imports (* refers to the analogous foreign variable). The foreign demand for imports (domestic exports) can be similarly defined as

$$M^{d*} = M^{d*} (P_x^*) \qquad (2)$$

where M^{d*} is the quantity of foreign imports and P_x^* is the foreign currency price (level) of domestic exports. Analogous to the definition above, P_x^* is $P_x^* = P_x/E$, where P_x is the domestic currency price (level) of exports.

Similarly, the export supply functions are defined depending only on nominal prices. The domestic and foreign export supply functions are defined as

$$X^s = X^s (P_x) \qquad (3)$$
$$X^{s*} = X^{s*} (P_m^*) \qquad (4)$$

where X^s and X^{s*} are the quantity of domestic and foreign supplies of exports, respectively. The market equilibrium conditions for exports and imports are then

$$M^d = X^{s*} \tag{5}$$
$$M^{d*} = X^s \tag{6}$$

Given equations (1) to (4), the domestic trade balance, in domestic currency, is

$$B = P_x X^s - P_m M^d \tag{7}$$

Now, the question is, does devaluation of the domestic currency improve the trade balance as defined by equation (7)? The answer is not as obvious as one might think. A sufficient condition for trade-balance improvement and for stability of the foreign exchange market under the model, is provided by the *BRM condition*. Differentiating equation (7) and putting the results in elasticity form, a general algebraic condition is derived. This condition relates the response of the trade balance to exchange-rate changes and the domestic and foreign price elasticities of imports and exports:

$$\frac{dB}{dE} = P_x X^s \left[\frac{(1+\varepsilon)\eta^*}{\left(\varepsilon + \eta^*\right)} \right] - P_m M^d \left[\frac{(1-\eta)\varepsilon^*}{\varepsilon^* + \eta} \right] \tag{8}$$

where η and ε denote the price elasticities (in absolute values) of domestic demand for imports and supply of exports. Analogously, η^* and ε^* denote the respective foreign price elasticities. As can be shown, if $B = 0$ (initial equilibrium), then $dB/dE > 0$ if and only if

$$\frac{\eta\eta^*\left(1+\varepsilon+\varepsilon^*\right)-\varepsilon\varepsilon^*\left(1-\eta-\eta^*\right)}{\left(\varepsilon+\eta^*\right)\left(\varepsilon^*+\eta\right)} > 0 \tag{9}$$

Another result that can be derived from condition (9) is the so-called *Marshall–Lerner condition* (ML condition), which comes from letting $\varepsilon \to \infty$ and $\varepsilon^* \to \infty$. This assumption implies that the left-hand side of condition (9) becomes $\eta^* + \eta - 1$. Thus, for a trade balance improvement when a country's currency devalues, $\eta^* + \eta > 1$ must hold. Or, in the standard presentation of the ML condition, $|\eta + \eta^*| > 1$.

The question that is relevant for the purposes of this chapter is whether or not the BRM or ML condition empirically holds for a developing country such as Colombia. As discussed above, at least as derived from theory, it does not seem to. The Colombian economy might be better characterized by a *small-country* case ($\varepsilon^* = \eta^* = \infty$). Thus, a devaluation might or might not improve the trade balance (in domestic currency).[3]

The absorption approach (AA) and the monetary approach (MA)

The AA (Harberger, 1950; Meade, 1951; Alexander, 1952) shifted the focus of economic analysis to the balance of payments, and solved some of the original criticisms of the EA. The core of this approach is the proposition that any improvement in the trade balance requires an increase of income over total domestic expenditures.[4] A devaluation reduces the relative prices of domestic goods in domestic currency, which produces two direct effects. First, there is a substitution effect that causes a shift in the composition of demand from foreign goods towards domestic goods; that is, the exchange-rate change causes an *expenditure-substituting* effect. Assuming unemployment, domestic production increases. Second, there is an income effect which would increase absorption, and then reduce the trade balance. The AA argues that, in general, a country's devaluation causes a deterioration in its terms of trade, and thus a deterioration in its national income. The presumption is that a devaluation will result in a decrease in the price of exports measured in foreign currency. In all, the final net effect of a devaluation on the trade balance will depend on the combined substitution and income effects. As predicted by the AA, the trade balance will improve, but it would be smaller (because of the income effect on absorption) than that predicted by the BRM model.

The MA (Hahn, 1959; Mundell, 1968, 1971; Pearce, 1961; Polak, 1957; Prais, 1961) also shifted the focus of economic analysis to the balance of payments and sought to solve some of the criticisms of the EA and AA. The core of the monetary approach is the claim, discussed by Frenkel and Johnson (1977, p. 21) that 'the balance of payments is essentially a monetary phenomenon'.[5] That is, under the MA any excess demand for goods, services and assets resulting in a deficit of the balance of payments, reflects an excess supply or demand of the stock of money. Accordingly, the balance of payments behaviour should be analysed from the point of view of the supply and demand of money. The fundamental implication of this claim is that to analyse what happens in the (overall) balance of payments one should concentrate on the analysis of what happens with the central bank's balance of foreign reserves. What does the MA say about the nominal (or real) effects of devaluation? Unlike the EA and AA, the monetary approach says little about the underlying behavioural relationships. Moreover, it says little about the effects of exchange-rate changes and the transmission mechanisms on those relationships. The role of the exchange rate is reduced to its temporary effects on the money supply. The relevant question for our purposes is: what is the 'temporary', or short-run, effect of devaluation under the MA? In the short run, this approach predicts that an increase in prices, caused by a nominal devaluation, may reduce the real money stock, and then improve the trade balance.

3 The econometric framework

Below we develop testable hypotheses from the theoretical models presented in section 2 and use an econometric technique to distinguish among those hypotheses.

The econometric procedure and the regression model

The econometric procedure used here is the version of analysing multivariate cointegrated systems originally developed by Johansen (1988), then expanded and applied in Johansen and Juselius (1990, 1992). It consists of a full-information maximum-likelihood estimation of a system characterized by r cointegrating vectors.

The reduced formulation of the statistical model is given by the vector $z_t = (TB, REER, M1, RGDP)'_t$, where TB is a trade balance measurement, $REER$ is a real exchange-rate index, $M1$ is a money stock, and $RGDP$ is the real gross domestic product (GDP). This vector is thought to capture the effects of the exchange rate on the trade balance in a model that puts together (*nets*) the elasticity, absorption and monetary approaches to the balance of payments. I am not aware of any literature that has included income and money in trade-balance estimations or has used the current econometric procedure on the issue being analysed.[6]

It is useful to summarize the hypotheses about the exchange-rate trade balance and income- and money-trade balance relationships developed in section 2. For the EA, devaluation improves the trade balance by changing the relative prices between domestically and foreign-sourced goods. In the AA, an exchange-rate change can only affect the trade balance if it induces an increase in income greater than the increase in total domestic expenditure (absorption). Thus, both relative prices and income are primary determinants of trade-balance behaviour. The MA asserts that exchange-rate changes have only temporary effects. Hence, there should be no long-run equilibrium relationship between the trade balance and the exchange rate.

With respect to the income variable, what is expected is a negative/positive under the absorption/monetary approach. From the point of view of the MA, according to Hallwood and MacDonald (1994, p. 148) 'if ... [an] economy is growing over time ... it will *ceteris paribus* run a ... [trade balance] surplus'. The reason is the implicit assumption that income growth raises expenditure by less than output, therefore improving the trade balance.

As for the money variable, under the AA the money supply is an exogenous variable; it is a policy instrument. Thus, the monetary authorities offset, or sterilize (through open market operations) the impact on the domestic money stock of foreign-exchange market intervention.[7] It follows that there should be no effect of the money stock on the balance of payments (or on expenditure). On the other hand, the MA argues that in a fixed exchange-rate regime the money supply is endogenously determined by the interaction of the supply and demand of the money stock. Assuming the domestic credit is exogenously determined and equal to a constant, the nominal money stock change equals the change of foreign reserves. Hence, it is equal to the trade balance surplus or deficit. This would imply a zero coefficient for the money variable in the trade balance equilibrium equation, that is, the trade balance explains the money stock, and not vice versa. Notice, however, that under this framework feedback effects of the change in the real money stock can be present. In this case, an exogenous increase in the real money stock worsens the trade balance through an increase in expenditure.

The data – and a graphical inspection

The data-set consists of quarterly time-series data for Colombia from the first quarter 1979 to the fourth quarter 1995. The time series includes observed values of exports, imports, a real effective exchange-rate index (*REER*), narrow money (*M1*), the RGDP, consumer price index (*CPI*), and an index of the world price of coffee and of oil.[8] The data sources are the *Revista del Banco de la República* (Bogotá, Colombia) and the *International Financial Statistics*, IMF (CD Rom). The measure of trade balance (*TB*), which is used in the estimations, is represented by the ratio of exports to imports. This ratio, or its inverse, has also been used in similar settings by Haynes and Stone (1982), Bahmani-Oskooee

(1991) and Bahmani-Oskooee and Alse (1994). All nominal time series are deflated using the CPI. Additionally, all series are logged (natural logs). This is indicated by preceding the name of the variable with *L*.

Figure 9.1 plots the observed trade balance, the real effective exchange rate, the real money stock and the real GDP. The data reveal the following empirical regularities:

1 The trade balance and the real exchange rate seem to behave as a non-stationary series, specifically, as random walks. The real exchange rate seems to go through sustained periods of appreciation, depreciation, and again appreciation without a tendency to revert to a long-run mean.
2 The trade balance moved from deep deficits to elevated surpluses, and then to deep deficits again, with no tendency to revert to an equilibrium or to a specific value.
3 The real money stock and real GDP exhibit some form of seasonality. They also seem to contain linear trends. This implies that these series might have a stochastic time-variant mean;
4 The trade balance and real exchange rate, and the real money stock and real GDP, seem to share co-movements. For example, the trade balance appears to closely mimic the real exchange-rate movements. The real money stock and the real GDP seem to be similarly timed;
5 All variables seem to display a high degree of persistency. For instance, a high depreciation at the middle of the 1980s lasted almost six years.

The unit-root tests

To cross-check the results several tests were computed: the augmented Dickey–Fuller test (ADF), the Schmidt–Phillips test (SP), the Dickey and Pantula *sequential* procedure (DP procedure), and the HEGY seasonal unit-root test (Hylleberg, Engle, Granger and Yoo, 1990), later expanded by Ghysels and Noh (1994).

Table 9.1 reports the results. The null hypothesis of unit root cannot be rejected at the 5 per cent level of significance for all variables when the ADF test is used. Using the SP test, however, the null hypothesis is rejected in the cases of the money and income series, contradicting the results of the ADF test. To test for the presence of more than one unit root, in all variables where the unit-root hypothesis was rejected by one of the tests, two types of tests were implemented. One was the 'standard' unit-root test in the series' first differences, and the other was the DP procedure; only the former is reported in Table 9.1, and it

157

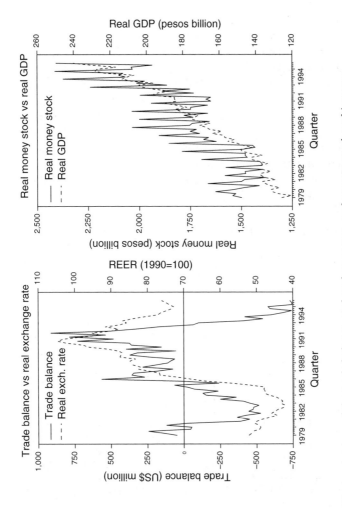

Figure 9.1 Observed values of the trade balance, real exchange rate, real money stock and income

shows that the null hypothesis is rejected for all variables, which actually indicates that they seem to behave as $I(1)$ processes. When the DP procedure was computed the money stock has two unit roots and real GDP effectively one. The findings of more than one unit root in the money stock seemed to be related with seasonal unit roots. To test for this possibility, the HEGY test was used (not reported here).[9] It was found that, effectively, for the case where the DP procedure indicated the presence of more than one unit root, the HEGY test corroborated them. The money stock, in fact, seems to have unit roots at zero and biannual frequencies.

According to the tests and the initial graphical conjectures, it seems that all series are integrated of order one, at least at zero frequency. Since the variable *LMI* behaves as an $I(2)$ process, a procedure suggested by Hylleberg, Engle, Granger and Yoo (1990) and Ilmakunnas (1990) was followed. When the exercise was implemented in the series, it continued showing a behaviour between $I(1)$ and $I(2)$ processes. The choice was to consider *LMI* as a unit-root process, which is a standard result in the literature.

4 Hypotheses testing and estimations

This section tests the hypotheses about the relationship between the exchange rate and the trade balance discussed in section 2, and

Table 9.1   Unit-root tests

Variable[1] [2]		ADF test (level)	Q(12)[3]	ADF test (first difference)	Q(12)	SP test
LTB_t	$\tau_\mu=$	−2.20	11.33 (0.41)	−10.42*	10.59 (0.48)	−
$LREER_t$	$\tau_\mu=$	−1.06	12.60 (0.25)	−4.52*	12.13 (0.35)	−
LMI_t	$\tau_\tau=$	−3.22	12.93 (0.07)	3.47*	9.45 (0.31)	−7.37*
$LRGDP_t$	$\tau_\tau=$	−3.27	7.72 (0.05)	−3.45*	12.24 (0.09)	−4.84*

Notes: [1]*LTB* is the log of the trade balance measurement, *LREER* is the log of the real exchange-rate index, *LMI* is the log of real money stock (real M1), and *LRGDP* is the log of the real GDP. [2]The τ_μ test is the τ-test for a regression equation that includes an intercept or drift term and the τ_τ test is the τ-test for a regression equation that includes both a drift and a linear time trend. The asymptotically critical values for τ_μ and τ_τ are −2.89 and −3.45 respectively. The critical value for the SP's $\bar{\tau}$ test is −3.06. [3]Q(12) is the Ljung-Box statistic. Its marginal significance level (or *p*-value) is in brackets.

estimates the statistical model under the specification defined in section 3, that is, under $z_t = (LTB,LREER,LMI,LRGDP)_t$.[10]

Specification and misspecification tests

These tests were used primarily to choose an 'appropriate' lag structure and to identify the deterministic components to be included in the model. They followed the methodology suggested by Johansen (1992). Then, multivariate and univariate specification and misspecification tests were implemented (serial correlation, normality, and heteroskedasticity). To complement the formal tests, the actual and fitted values for each equation and the *correlogram* of the residuals were plotted (the results are not reported here). All the tests indicated that the performance of the VECM representation of the actual data was generally satisfactory.

Finding the rank of matrix Π

Table 9.2 shows the tests of the rank of matrix Π. The first column represents the estimated eigenvalues λ_i. The null hypothesis of $r = 0$ (no cointegration) is rejected in favour of $r = 1$ by both tests at the 10 per cent level. The null hypothesis of $r = 1$ (or $r \leq 1$ using the λ_{Trace} test) in favour of $r = 2$ is not rejected by both tests. The null hypotheses of $r = 2, 3$ (or $r \leq 2, r \leq 3$ using the λ_{Trace} test) in favour of $r = 3, 4$ are not rejected by both tests. Thus, Table 9.2 indicates the presence of just one cointegrating relationship among the trade balance, real exchange rate, real money stock and real income.

In order to improve the statistical specification of the model, tests of exclusion from the cointegration space and tests of weak exogeneity were carried out (they are not reported here). The tests showed that none of the variables should be excluded. Also, they indicated that the trade balance and the real GDP were effectively endogenous and the real exchange rate and money stock were *weakly exogenous*. Notice that the fact that the real GDP is endogenous and the money stock is exogenous seems to agree with the absorption view, and contradict the monetary argument, which states that income is endogenous while money is exogenous to the model.

The estimations under $r = 1$

Since $r = 1$, the problem of identification of the cointegration space need not emerge. Thus, one can make direct inference from both the long-run and short-run estimates. If only one cointegrating relationship exists, it is *just identified* (Johansen and Juselius, 1994). The

Table 9.2   Tests of cointegration rank

λ_i (i = 1,2,3,4)	Ho	Ha	λ_{max}	ACV (10%)	Ho	Ha	λ_{Trace}	ACV (10%)
0.65	r = 0	r = 1	45.47*	18.03	r = 0	r > 0	71.10*	49.92
0.27	r = 1	r = 2	13.59	14.09	r ≤ 1	r > 1	25.63	31.88
0.19	r = 2	r = 3	9.19	10.29	r ≤ 2	r > 2	12.04	17.79
0.06	r = 3	r = 4	2.85	7.50	r ≤ 3	r > 3	2.85	7.50

Note: The test statistics have a small sample correction as suggested by Reinsel and Ahn (1992). It consists of using the factor $(T - kp)$ instead of the sample size T in the calculation of the tests. ACV stands for asymptotical critical values. * denotes significant at the 10 per cent level.

estimated equation of the conditional model in error-correction form for the trade balance is (the value of the *t*-test is in brackets):

$$\Delta LTB_t = -0.28\Delta LTB_{t-1} - 0.26\Delta LTB_{t-2} - 1.12\Delta LRGDP_{t-1} + 1.33\Delta LRGDP_{t-2} +$$
$$- (2.41) \qquad (-2.36) \qquad (-1.05) \qquad (1.16)$$
$$0.95\Delta LREER_t + 0.22\Delta LREER_{t-1} + 0.53\Delta LREER_{t-2} + 0.55\Delta LMI_t +$$
$$(1.74) \qquad (.37) \qquad (.95) \qquad (1.80)$$
$$0.88\Delta LMI_{t-1} + 0.54\Delta LMI_{t-2} + (-0.06)[1.82LTB_{t-3} +$$
$$(2.47) \qquad (1.62) \qquad (-2.22)$$
$$6.38LRGDP_{t-3} + 1.99LREER_{t-3} - 14.11LMI_{t-3} + 62.8].$$

Statistics: $ARCH(3)$ = 4.71; normality = 0.12; serial correlation: $LM(12)$ = 8.2 (*p-value* = .77); Ramsey RESET test: $LR(3)$ = 2.8 (*p-value* = .42)

The short-run estimates indicate that the significant coefficients are those for the dependent variable (at lags 1 and 2 at the 95 per cent level of significance), the real exchange rate (contemporaneously at the 10 per cent level), and the real money stock (contemporaneously at the 10 per cent level, and at lag 1 at the 5 per cent level). Income results are insignificant in the short run. Thus, the short-run estimates indicate that the trade balance responds positively and contemporaneously to real devaluation and positively to variations of the money stock. The first result presents evidence against the J-curve type of hypothesis. The latter result implies that the 'impact' and lagged effect of an increase in the real money stock is an improvement in the trade balance. This could happen, following the monetarist arguments, if there is a rapid increase in prices that offsets the increase in the nominal money stock. People would have a shortfall in real money balances, which will result in hoarding (agents want to restore their real money balances) and in a trade balance improvement. The speed of adjustment coefficient is negative and significant. According to the estimates, a short-run trade balance disequilibrium is corrected to a speed of 7 per cent per quarter.

Now solving the equation above for the long-run relationship one has (observe that in equilibrium the Δs equal zero):

$$LTB + (6.38/-1.82)LRGDP + (1.99/-1.82)LREER + (-14.11/-1.82)LM1 + (62.84/-1.82) = 0$$

After solving for LTB, one gets the estimated long-run equation for the trade balance:

$$LTB = 34.34 + 3.49LRGDP + 1.09LREER - 7.71LM1$$

This equation represents the estimated long-run relationship between the trade balance, the real exchange rate, money and income. The equation reveals that the estimated long-run exchange-rate elasticity has a positive sign. Accordingly, a (real) devaluation will lead to an improvement in the (real) trade balance. The estimated coefficient says that for a 1 per cent increase in the real exchange rate, keeping other variables constant, the real trade balance on average increases by about 1 per cent.[11] Thus, the empirical evidence shows that the BRM or ML conditions seem to hold in the case of Colombia.[12] The positive sign of the estimated coefficient for the income variable is consistent with what the monetary view would say; income has a positive relationship with the trade balance. Notice, however, that the presence of the money stock in the long-run equation is inconsistent with what the monetary approach would predict for the long-run relationship between trade balance and money. Indeed, one would expect an inverse causality. The trade balance explains the money stock, not vice versa. This result is consistent with that approach only where feedback effects were present.[13]

5 Conclusions

We have examined empirically the role of the exchange rate in determining the short-and long-run behaviour of the Colombian trade balance under alternative approaches to the balance of payments. The major findings are that the variable specification of the statistical model showed that the exchange rate does play a role in determining the short-run and long-run equilibrium behaviour of the Colombian trade balance. Therefore, the trade balance cannot be treated as exogenous with respect to the exchange rate. These findings constitute evidence against the literature claiming that no direct relationship between the trade balance and the exchange rate exists and the monetary view which claims that the exchange rate has only temporary effects. The estimations reported one cointegrating relationship between the trade balance, exchange rate, money and income. That is, a long-run equilibrium relationship between those variables existed. The results also showed that the BRM or ML conditions were supported by the data, which implied that (real) devaluation improved the equilibrium trade balance. Moreover, the positive effect of exchange-rate devaluation on the trade balance seemed enhanced if accompanied by a reduction in the stock of money and an increase in income. With respect to the short-run estimates, estimations revealed a significant positive short-run relationship between the trade balance and the exchange rate. This is considered evidence against the J-curve hypothesis.

The findings with respect to income and money variables did not fully reject or accept hypotheses from the absorption or monetary approaches, either for the short or the long run. What was generally found, however, was that money stock and income were important determinants of the long-run trade-balance behaviour. From the point of view of trade-balance modelling, these results suggest that a model that seeks to explain the long-run behaviour of the trade balance should include at least the exchange rate, money and income.

The main limitation of this study was that capital markets were not considered. Several directions for future research are suggested. One direction, the natural one, is to include capital in the analysis. Another direction is to use the current technique or alternative econometric techniques, for example impulse response functions to analyse the short-run effects more thoroughly. This should shed light on why we found opposite results to those hypothesized by the J-curve or S-curve. Finally, econometric methodology should be applied to a sample of developing countries.

Notes

1 Two basic assumptions underlie this model. First, there is perfect competition in the world market. Second, both countries are 'large' countries. The model says nothing explicitly with respect to the equilibrium of the domes-

tic market, non-traded goods, and monetary or financial assets; these markets are relegated to the background.

2 The current presentation of the model draws heavily on the analysis of Dornbusch (1975). Some of the conditions arising from it, in addition to the general BRM condition, are discussed in Vanek (1962), Magee (1975) and Lindert and Kindleberger (1982).

3 Different arguments, such as Dornbusch (1987), Krugman (1987) and Krugman and Baldwin (1987), using partial equilibrium studies, claim the ML condition may not hold, prevented by market failures such as elasticity pessimism, hysteresis, pricing to market behaviour, or uncertainty.

4 Note two points: (1) as with EA, in AA the current account is reduced to the trade balance and countries are 'large' countries; (2) unlike the EA, money and income are introduced.

5 The term 'balance of payments' is understood by this approach to be all those items that are *below the line*; those items constitute what is called the *money account*.

6 Rincon (1995) uses current econometric methodology and tests for the ML condition and J-curve applied to Colombian data; only the real exchange rate and trade balance is included in the VECM system.

7 For example, a country with a trade-balance surplus (buying foreign exchange and hence expanding the money supply) may sterilize the extra money supply by open-market sales of bonds that balance the money supply. From the monetarist point of view, this policy is only feasible in the short run.

8 The latter two variables will be included as dummy-type variables in the statistical system to capture exogenous shocks which may affect the statistical properties of the system.

9 Ghysels, Lee and Noh (1994) show that the ADF test can be used to test the null of a unit root at the zero frequency, even in the presence of unit roots at other seasonal frequencies.

10 The implicit assumption, which was tested, is that the trade balance is homogeneous of degree zero with respect to all the individual components of the real exchange-rate index, that is, with respect to prices (domestic and foreign) and the nominal exchange rate.

11 To double-check this result, a proportionality (homogeneity) restriction on the trade and exchange-rate coefficients was tested. The likelihood ratio test could not reject the null. The rest of the coefficients did not change when the restriction was imposed, except for the estimate of α, now 0.063.

12 Similar results were found by Rincón (1995) using quarterly data for 1970 to 1994.

13 The significance of the money variable in the cointegrating vector was separately examined. The null hypothesis was rejected using the standard level of significance.

References

Alexander, S. S. (1952) 'Effects of a Devaluation on a Trade Balance', International Monetary Fund Staff Papers, no. 2, pp. 263–78.

Artus, J. R. and A. K. McGuirk (1981) 'A Revised Version of the Multilateral Exchange Rate Model', International Monetary Fund Staff Papers, no. 28, pp. 275–309.

Artus, J. R. and M. D. Knight (1984) 'Issues in the Assessment of the Exchange Rates of Industrial Countries', Occasional Paper 29, International Monetary Fund.

Backus, D. K., P. J. Kehoe and F. Kydland (1994) 'Dynamics of the Trade Balance and the Terms of Trade: The J-Curve?', *American Economic Review*, vol. 84, no. 1, pp. 84–103.

Bahmani-Oskooee, M. (1991) 'Is There a Long-Run Relation Between the Trade Balance and the Real Effective Exchange Rate of LDCs?', *Economics Letters*, pp. 403–7.

Bahmani-Oskooee, M. and J. Alse (1994) 'Short-Run versus Long-Run Effects of Devaluation: Error-Correction Modeling and Cointegration', *Eastern Economic Journal*, vol. 20, no. 4, pp. 453–64.

Bickerdike, C. F. (1920) 'The Instability of Foreign Exchanges', *Economic Journal*, March, pp. 118–22.

Cooper, R. N. (1971) 'Currency Devaluation in Developing Countries', *Essays in International Finance*, no. 86, Princeton University.

Dornbusch, R. (1975) 'Exchange Rates and Fiscal Policy in a Popular Model of International Trade', *American Economic Review*, vol. 65, pp. 859–71.

Dornbusch, R. (1987) 'Purchasing Power Parity', in J. Eatwell, M. Milgate and P. Newman (eds), *The New Palgrave Dictionary of Economics* (London: Macmillan), vol. 3, pp. 1075–85.

Edwards, S. (1989) 'Real Exchange Rates, Devaluation, and Adjustment: Exchange Rate Policy in Developing Countries' (Cambridge, MA: MIT Press).

Frenkel, J. A. and H. G. Johnson (1977) 'The Monetary Approach to the Balance of Payments', in J. A. Frenkel and H. G. Johnson (eds), *The Monetary Approach to the Balance of Payments* (London: Affen & Unwin).

Ghysels, E., H. S. Lee and J. Noh (1994) 'Testing for Unit Roots in Seasonal Time Series: Some Theoretical Extensions and a Monte Carlo Investigation', *Journal of Econometrics*, vol. 62, pp. 415–44.

Gylfason, T. and M. Radetzki (1991) 'Does Devaluation Make Sense in the Least Developed Countries?', *Economic Development and Cultural Change*, vol. 40(1), pp. 1–25.

Hahn, F. H. (1959) 'The Balance of Payments in a Monetary Economy', *Review of Economic Studies*, vol. 26, pp. 110–25.

Hallwood, C. P. and R. MacDonald (1994) *International Money and Finance*, 2nd edn (Oxford: Basil Blackwell).

Harberger, A. C. (1950) 'Currency Depreciation, Income, and the Balance of Trade', *Journal of Political Economy*, vol. 58, pp. 47–60.

Haynes, S. E. and J. A. Stone (1982) 'Impact of the Terms of Trade on the US Trade Balance: A Reexamination', *Review of Economics and Statistics*, vol. 64, pp. 702–6.

Hylleberg, S., R. F. Engle, C. W. Granger and B. S. Yoo (1990) 'Seasonal Integration and Cointegration', *Journal of Econometrics*, vol. 44, pp. 215–38.

Ilmakunnas, P. (1990) 'Testing the Order of Differencing in Quarterly Data: An Illustration of the Testing Sequence', *Oxford Bulletin of Economics and Statistics*, vol. 52, no.1, pp. 79–88.

Johansen, S. (1988) 'Statistical Analysis of Cointegration Vectors', *Journal of Economic Dynamics and Control*, vol. 12, pp. 231–54.

Johansen, S. (1992) 'Cointegration in Partial Systems and the Efficiency of Single-Equation Analysis', *Journal of Econometrics*, vol. 52, no. 3, pp. 389–402.

Johansen, S. and K. Juselius (1990) 'Maximum Likelihood Estimation and Inference on Cointegration with Applications to the Demand for Money', *Oxford Bulletin of Economics and Statistics*, vol. 52, pp. 169–210.

Johansen, S. and K. Juselius (1992) 'Testing Structural Hypotheses in a Multivariate Cointegration Analysis of the PPP and the UIP for UK', *Journal of Econometrics*, vol. 53, pp. 211–44.

Johansen, S. and K. Juselius (1994) 'Identification of the Long-Run and the Short-Run Structure: An Application to the ISLM Model', *Journal of Econometrics*, vol. 63, pp. 7–36.

Junz, H. B. and R. R. Romberg (1973) 'Price Competitiveness in Export Trade among Industrial Countries', *American Economic Review*, vol. 63, pp. 412–18.

Kamin, S. B. (1988) 'Devaluation, External Balance, and Macroeconomic Perfomance: A Look at the Numbers', *Princeton Studies in International Finance*, no. 62, Princeton University.

Krugman, P. R. (1987) 'Pricing to Market when the Exchange Rate Changes', in S. Arndt and J. D. Richardson (eds), *Real-financial Linkages Among Open Economies* (Cambridge, MA: MIT Press).

Krugman, P. R. (1991) 'Has the Adjustment Process Worked?', *Policy Analyses in International Economics*, no. 34, IIE.

Krugman, P. R. and R. E. Baldwin (1987) 'The Persistence of the US Trade Deficit', *Brookings Papers on Economic Activity*, vol. 1, pp. 1–43.

Lerner, A. P. (1944) The Economics of Control: Principles of Welfare Economics (New York: Macmillan).

Lindert, P. H. and C. P Kindleberger (1982) *International Economics*, Irwin Series in Economics (Homewood, IL: Richard D. Irwin).

Magee, S. (1973) 'Currency Contracts, Pass-through, and Devaluation', *Brookings Papers on Economic Activity*, no. 1, pp. 303–23.

Magee, S. (1975) 'Prices, Incomes and Foreign Trade', in P. B. Kenen (ed.), *International Trade and Finance: Frontiers for Research* (Cambridge: Cambridge University Press).

Marshall, A. (1923) *Money, Credit and Commerce* (London: Macmillan).

Meade, E. E. (1988) 'Exchange Rates, Adjustment, and the J-Curve', *Federal Reserve Bulletin*, vol. 74, no. 10, pp. 633–44.

Meade, J. E. (1951) *The Balance of Payments* (Oxford: Oxford University Press).

Metzler, L. (1948) *A Survey of Contemporary Economics*, Vol. I (Homewood, IL: Richard D. Irwin).

Mundell, R. A. (1968) *International Economics* (London: Macmillan).

Mundell, R. A. (1971) *Monetary Theory* (Pacific Palisades, CA: Goodyear).

Paredes, C. E. (1989) 'Exchange Rates, the Real Exchange Rate and Export Perfomance in Latin America', *Brookings Discussion Papers in International Economics*, no. 77.

Pearce, I. F. (1961) 'The Problem of the Balance of Payments', *International Economic Review*, vol. 2, pp. 1–28.

Polak, J. J. (1957) 'Monetary Analysis on Income Formation and Payments Problems', *IMF Staff Papers*, no. 6, pp. 1–50.

Prais, S. J. (1961) 'Some Mathematical Notes on the Quantity Theory of Money in a Small Open Economy', IMF Staff Papers no. 2, pp. 212–26.

Pritchett, L. (1991) *The Real Exchange Rate and the Trade Surplus: An Empirical Analysis for Non-oil Exporting LDCs* (Washington, DC: World Bank).

Reinsel, G. C. and S. K. Ahn (1992) 'Vector Autorregressive Models with Unit Roots and Reduced Rank Structure: Estimation, Likelihood Ratio Tests, and Forecasting', *Journal of Time Series Analysis*, vol. 13, pp. 353–75.

Rincón, C. H. (1995) 'Exchange Rates in a Popular Model of International Trade, Again: The Case of a Small Open Economy', University of Illinois at Urbana-Champaign (mimeo).

Robinson, J. (1947) *Essays in the Theory of Employment* (Oxford: Basil Blackwell).

Rose, A. K. (1990) 'Exchange Rates and the Trade Balance: Some Evidence from Developing Countries', *Economic Letters*, vol. 34, pp. 271–5.

Rose, A. K. (1991) 'The Role of Exchange Rates in a Popular Model of International Trade: Does the "Marshall–Lerner" Condition Hold?', *Journal of International Economics*, vol. 30, pp. 301–16.

Rose, A. K. and J. L. Yellen (1989) 'Is There a J-curve?', *Journal of Monetary Economics*, vol. 24, pp. 53–68.

Vanek, J. (1962) *International Trade: Theory and Economic Policy* (Homewood, IL: Richard D. Irwin).

10
External Shocks, Relative Prices and Sectoral Reallocation in a Small Open Economy: Evidence from Mexico

Talan İşcan

1 Introduction

In a small open economy external disturbances such as currency devaluations and terms-of-trade shocks seem to have a significant impact on real output. For instance, the Mexican peso crisis of December 1994 resulted in a severe economic recession: in the first quarter 1995, the Mexican gross domestic product (GDP) declined at a rate equal to 10 per cent a year. In 1997, currency devaluations in various Asian countries reduced real aggregate output. These observations appear to agree with the empirical evidence on the recessionary consequences of devaluation in developing countries noted by Edwards (1989) and Yotopoulos (1996); Mendoza (1995) found that relatively large terms-of-trade disturbances had a significant impact on aggregate output and investment levels in developing countries.

Despite wide empirical evidence on the income effects of the real exchange rate and terms-of-trade shocks, surprisingly little is known about the response of individual sectors to relative price changes. Yet, these disturbances also impact on the reallocation of resources across sectors either through substitution or relative price effects. Recent theoretical literature has emphasized the importance of relative prices in adjusting to external disturbances. Gavin (1990), for example, using an intertemporal general equilibrium model, argued that the adjustment of sectoral output to relative price changes resulting from a terms-of-trade disturbance profoundly affects relative supplies of tradable and non-tradable goods, as well as current account dynamics.[1] A similar issue arises in the context of exchange-rate devaluation. In principle, devaluation leads to the reallocation of resources from non-tradable sectors to tradable sectors by inducing a change in their relative prices. This may alleviate balance-of-payments constraints which typically cause the devaluation in the first place. But the issue remains: to what extent have the real exchange-rate and terms-of-trade disturbances been conducive to an (efficient) reallocation of resources in developing countries? This chapter investigates this using cross-section time-series data from Mexico over the period 1970 to 1993, a country whose recent history is marked by large swings in its terms of trade (primarily due to changes in world oil prices) and in the value of its currency.

Given that the data are highly disaggregated, this analysis attempts to provide a framework to isolate relative price effects on sectoral output levels. We specify and estimate reduced-form sectoral output regression equations which relate output to a range of sector-specific and aggregate variables. Using the panel structure of the data, we examine to what extent the real exchange rate and terms-of-trade shocks were conducive to reallocating output between tradable and non-tradable goods sectors.

Several findings emerge from the analysis. First, formal tests show a considerable diversity both within and across tradable and non-tradable sectors given their estimated responses to external shocks. Thus we specify and estimate a random coefficient regression model which accommodates parameter heterogeneity across sectors and enables us to estimate the average effect of relative prices on sectoral output. Second, in Mexico, both the terms-of-trade shocks and the real exchange-rate movements were found to have significant sectoral output effects; the improvement in terms of trade was associated with relative expansion in non-tradables output, and a depreciation of the Mexican peso had a contractionary output effect in non-tradables.

Theoretical studies on the consequences of external shocks have identified elasticity of substitution in consumption between traded and non-traded goods as a key parameter in determining sectoral reallocation of output in response to these shocks. The estimates from the reduced-form regression models may suggest that, in the case of Mexico, this elasticity is below unity.

The rest of the chapter is organized as follows. Section 2 provides an overview of the theoretical literature; section 3 specifies a sectoral output model, and discusses the econometric issues that arise in the context of this dynamic heterogeneous panel; section 4 presents the results of the econometric estimation; and section 5 summarizes the results.

2 Theory and existing evidence

First, we review the literature on the consequences of terms-of-trade and real exchange-rate movements.

The terms-of-trade effect

Numerous studies in international macroeconomics have investigated the impact of exogenous terms-of-trade shocks on aggregate income and output. Recently, a number of studies that go beyond a single aggregate good framework and that distinguish between tradable and non-tradable goods have emphasized the role of intratemporal as well as intertemporal considerations in adjusting to such shocks. In an intertemporal setting, the response of sectoral output levels to terms-of-trade shocks is determined primarily by the intratemporal elasticity of substitution in consumption between tradable and non-tradable goods.

Gavin (1990) and Backus, Kehoe and Kydland (1995, p. 85) showed that if the elasticity of substitution in consumption between tradables and non-tradables is below unity, a permanent improvement in the terms of trade will induce both a shift in factors of production into the non-tradable sector and a current account surplus. In this case, the improvement in the terms of trade leads to an increase in demand for non-traded goods because the elasticity of substitution is low, and to a current account surplus because the income effect dominates the substitution effect. If, on the other hand, the elasticity of substitution is above unity, a permanent improvement in the terms of trade will induce both a movement of the factors of production into the tradable sector and a current account deficit. In this case, the substitution effect dominates the income effect, and consequently the relative price of non-tradable goods declines.[2] Therefore, once income effects are controlled for, these studies identify elasticity of intratemporal substitution in consumption as the central parameter in determining sectoral reallocation in an open economy faced with a terms-of-trade shock.[3]

The real exchange-rate effect

Most theoretical discussion on the impact of the real exchange rate on sectoral reallocation relates to a menu of adjustment policy choices that can be implemented in the face of external imbalances or balance-of-payments problems. Within these policy alternatives, one of the most effective adjustment tools is a devaluation of the domestic currency, especially when nominal wages and prices are sticky (Agénor and Flood, 1995, pp. 236–7). By increasing the relative price of tradable goods, a devaluation helps switch resources from non-tradable goods to tradable goods sectors, and reduces domestic demand for imports.[4]

However, these policies have long been criticized on the grounds that, in an attempt to switch resources from non-tradable to tradable sectors, devaluations curtail domestic consumption relative to domestic income, and may cause aggregate income to contract. The 'structuralist' critique, for instance, argues that a devaluation can lead to a redistribution of income which may in turn generate contractionary aggregate demand effects despite the possible improvements in net exports. According to the three most well-known proposals, a devaluation may redistribute income:

1 from high-propensity consumers of domestic product to low-propensity consumers due to increased profits from rising exports and import-competing sectors (Diaz-Alejandro, 1963);
2 from private sector to the government which collects ad valorem taxes but abstains from spending the additional revenues (Krugman and Taylor, 1978); and,
3 from nationals of the devaluating country to foreigners who transfer their income abroad (Barbone and Rivera-Batiz, 1987).

If the supply-side effects of devaluations are not strong enough to counter the contraction in aggregate demand induced by these redistributive consequences, the adjustment process may culminate in declining aggregate income. Edwards (1993) notes that precisely because of these perceived adverse income effects, some developing country policy-makers have been reluctant to devalue.

Some economists have indicated that costs associated with sectoral reallocation of factors of production can significantly reduce the effectiveness of adjustment to relative price changes. For instance, Diamond (1980), and Dixit and Rob (1994) argued that, due to fixed adjustment costs, reallocation of output may be tenuously related to relative price movements. These adjustment costs may range from real costs of reallocating labour to personal costs of dislocation. In addition, some skills may be sector-specific, and may not be easily transferred across sectors without substantial retraining costs. As a result of these adjustment and reallocation costs, relative price movements induced by a devaluation (or any relative price shock) may not immediately generate the desired resource mobility.

Of course, whether devaluations have contractionary consequences, and whether they are effective policy tools in adjusting to balance-of-payments problems, are ultimately empirical questions. With regard to the first issue, the existing literature concluded that devaluations are contractionary in the short run; see, for instance, Barbone and Rivera-Batiz (1987), Edwards (1986) and Gylfasson and Schmid (1983). However, the impact of devaluation, in particular, and relative price changes, in general, on sectoral reallocation of output remains a largely neglected issue.

3 Econometric specification and data

The model

To explore the consequences of the terms-of-trade and the real exchange-rate movements on the sectoral allocation of resources, a reduced-form sectoral output equation is specified. Because the data-set is disaggregated, the empirical model is intended to accommodate a range of sectoral characteristics that determine output. Therefore, rather than deriving it from 'first principles', we specify a dynamic sectoral-output regression model, and motivate its ingredients by intertemporal considerations. In particular, the model specifies that the logarithm of sectoral output (y) is determined by sector-specific and aggregate effects. In order to gauge the effects of (unobserved) productivity shocks, we include the current and lagged values of the logarithm of average productivity of labour (a) in the regression equation. To capture the persistence in output induced by gradual adjustment, the logarithm of the lagged sectoral output is also included as an explanatory variable in the specification (Blanchard and Fischer, 1989, ch. 2).

The effects of relative price changes on sectoral output are captured by the current and lagged values of the logarithm of the real exchange rate (s), and the terms of trade (q). Since sectoral output in Mexico also depends on government spending, we incorporated the ratio of total government expenditure to gross domestic product (*GOV*) in the regression model to account for fiscal policy shifts.[5] Also a time trend (t) is included.

All these considerations lead to the following dynamic sectoral output equation:

$$y_{it} = \lambda_i\, y_{i(t-1)} + \gamma_{1i}\, a_{it} + \gamma_{2i}\, a_{i(t-1)} + \beta_{1i}\, s_t + \beta_{2i}\, s_{t-1} + \alpha_{1i}\, q_t$$
$$+ \alpha_{2i}\, q_{t-1} + \delta_{1i}\, GOV_t + \delta_{2i}\, t + f_i + \varepsilon_{it} \tag{1}$$

where $i = 1, \ldots, 17$, labels the sectors, $t = 1971, \ldots, 1993$, labels time periods, f_i is the intercept term, and ε_{it} is the error term. Any (unobserved) aggregate shocks, and sector-specific errors that vary over time are included in the error term. Note that the coefficient vector $\theta_i = [\lambda_i, \gamma_{1i}, \gamma_{2i}, \beta_{1i}, \beta_{2i}, \alpha_{1i}, \alpha_{2i}, \delta_{1i}, \delta_{2i}, f_i]'$ is allowed to vary across sectors. We assumed that the vector of coefficient parameters is random with $E(\theta_i) = \bar{\theta}$, and that the regressors are not correlated with the coefficients.

At this point, it is important to emphasize that the above specification does not rule out the possibility that movements in the real exchange rate depend on the changes in aggregate domestic output. The model specifies the exchange rate as exogenous with respect to sectoral output levels because (i) models of exchange-rate determination are known to have low explanatory power, and (ii) since the number of cross-sectional units available is relatively 'large', the impact of individual sectors on the exchange rate is unlikely to be significant. Therefore, no attempt is made in the study to jointly explain exchange-rate movements and sectoral output levels. In view of this, the proposed framework is intended and best suited for the analysis of the consequences of real exchange-rate movements and devaluations, but not for an analysis of their causes.

Econometric issues

In the above specification we are interested in summarizing the response of sectoral outputs to external disturbances by some 'average' of the main parameters of interest. One common approach in estimating these parameters involves pooling the cross-section time-series data by imposing common slopes, allowing for fixed or random intercepts, and estimating 'stacked' regressions. However, following Robertson and Symons (1992), in dynamic panels if the parameters differ randomly and the regressors are serially correlated, the pooled estimates are not consistent. This inconsistency is distinct from the one found in dynamic panels with fixed effects, and with a large number of cross-sections (N) and small number of time-series observations (T) (Nickell, 1981). In this case, imposing common slopes when there is parameter heterogeneity across sectors leads to inconsistent estimates, even if we allow $T \rightarrow \infty$. The problem arises from the fact that ignoring heterogeneity when the regressors are serially correlated results in serial correlation in the error terms which does not disappear even when T is large. One of the estimators that yields consistent estimates of average effects is known as (weighted) mean group estimator (Pesaran and Smith, 1995). This GLS estimator involves running separate regressions for each group and averaging the coefficient estimates over groups using the weights proposed by Swamy (1970).

In the context of the dynamic sectoral output model specified in equation (1), it would be unduly strong to assume that *a priori* the response of individual sectors to relative prices changes will be identical. As suggested by economic theory, tradables and non-tradables are likely to respond differently to changes in intratemporal relative prices. In this case, the random coefficient regression model, which allows individual sector's output responses to differ across sectors while maintaining the assumption of interdependency, is an appropriate modelling choice. Therefore, given the theoretical and econometric considerations, the mean coefficient vector θ and its asymptotic variance–covariance matrix are estimated using Swamy's (1970) estimators.

The data

The data on sectoral output and sectoral gross domestic product (GDP) deflators come from the national income accounts of Mexico and are available from the Instituto Nacional de Estadística, Geografía e Informática (INEGI). Recently, OECD has started publishing these data entitled *National Accounts: Detailed Tables*, vol. II. The data covering the period from 1970 to 1980 are revised figures based on the post-1980 national accounts reclassification. There are 17 sectors included in the sample covering the period 1970 to 1993.

Sectoral average productivity of labour is calculated by the ratio of real output to employees in each sector. *GOV* is the ratio of government final expenditure to GDP multiplied by 100. Government final expenditure came from IMF, *International Financial Statistics (IFS) Yearbook 1992* for 1970–80, and OECD *National Accounts: Detailed Tables*, vol. II for 1981 to 1993. The real exchange rate is the nominal (old) Mexican peso/US$ exchange rate (*IFS Yearbook*, line wf), divided by the ratio of US CPI inflation to Mexican CPI inflation (*IFS Yearbook*, line 64). The real exchange-rate index is obtained by normalizing the real exchange rate of each year by that of 1970. The terms-of-trade index is defined as the unit price of exports relative to imports, and the data are from OECD, *National Accounts: Main Aggregates*, vol. I.

The sectors in the data set are grouped into tradable and non-tradable goods sectors. The definition of tradable and non-tradables closely follows Kravis, Heston and Summers (1982). The tradable goods sector includes agriculture, mining and nine manufacturing industries; non-tradables include construction, electricity, gas and water, wholesale and retail trade, restaurants and hotels, transport, storage and communications, finance, insurance and real estate, and private and government services.[6]

4 Estimation results

Baseline specification

The estimates of regression model (1) are shown in Table 10.1. The formal test of the hypothesis that the coefficient vectors θ are fixed and that the sectoral responses are homogeneous is also conducted. If this homogeneity assumption is rejected, then the data cannot be pooled to estimate the average effects of regressors on the dependent variable. The H_θ statistic, which has a chi-squared distribution with $k(N - 1)$ degrees of freedom, where k is the number of coefficients estimated for each cross-section, reported in Table 10.1, rejects the null hypothesis that the same fixed coefficient vector applies to all the sectors at the 1 per cent level. This suggests that there is significant parameter heterogeneity in terms of the response of sectors to relative price changes. Therefore, the random coefficient regression model is appropriate.[7]

Estimates of the mean coefficient vector $\bar{\theta}$ are presented in 10.1(a). The panel estimates based on all the sectors suggest that relative price effects on sectoral output are highly significant. Specifically, a decline in the real value of the Mexican peso (an increase in the real exchange rate) has on average a negative effect on sectoral output. However, given the positive coefficient on the lagged real exchange rate, some of the short-run contractionary effects of currency devaluations on output appear to be temporary. This result is consistent with the findings of earlier studies, such as Edwards (1986).

Terms-of-trade effects are also significant. In particular, an improvement in it is associated with an increase in sectoral output, but this effect appears to be reversed in the short run as indicated by the negative coefficient estimate on the lagged terms of trade.

Do tradable and non-tradable goods sectors differ significantly in terms of their responses to relative price shocks? Table 10.1 shows the estimation results of equation (1) for tradables and non-tradables separately. Although the response of both sectors to relative price movements appears similar, two observations need highlighting. First, in both cases the H_θ test statistic rejects at the 1 per cent level the hypothesis of parameter homogeneity within these sectors. Therefore, even after splitting the sample into tradables and non-tradables, a significant parameter heterogeneity still remains. It appears that the average responses of tradable and non-tradable output to relative price changes

Table 10.1 Estimates of the sectoral output equations (dependent variable: log output it – sample period, 1971–93)

Variable	All sectors	Tradables	Non-tradables
10.1a			
Real exchange rate t	**−.0318 (.0123)	−.0275 (.0162)	−.0314 (.0198)
Real exchange rate $t-1$	*.0287 (.0149)	*.0359 (.0195)	.0202 (.0241)
Terms of trade t	***.0690 (.0261)	*.0678 (.0331)	*.0833 (.0427)
Terms of trade $t-1$	***−.0813 (.0219)	**−.0999 (.0294)	*−.0560 (.0286)
Log output $i(t-1)$	***.8900 (.0509)	***.8872 (.0637)	***.8283 (.0872)
Log productivity it	***.5398 (.1404)	***.6547 (.1545)	.3010 (.2623)
Log productivity $i(t-1)$	***−.3949 (.1311)	**−.4662 (.1853)	−.1802 (.179)
Gov. spending t	.0034 (.0030)	.0033 (.0032)	.0037 (.0066)
Time trend	−.0011 (.0012)	−.0019 (.0014)	.0007 (.0017)
Constant	**.6297 (.2686)	*.6392 (.3348)	*.9745 (.4578)
H_θ (d.f.)	372.07 (160)	141.61 (100)	132.66 (50)
10.1b			
Terms of trade t	**.0638 (.0235)	*.0553 (.0262)	*.0970 (.0447)
Terms of trade $t-1$	***−.0856 (.0222)	***−.1049 (.0295)	*−.0569 (.0280)
Log output $i(t-1)$	***.8713 (.0482)	***.8813 (.0617)	***.8090 (.0813)
Log productivity it	***.5622 (.1299)	***.6677 (.1525)	.3483 (.2168)
Log productivity $i(t-1)$	**−.3730 (.1328)	**−.4327 (.1860)	−.1986 (.1624)

Table 10.1 Continued

Variable	All sectors	Tradables	Non-tradables
Gov. spending t	.0027 (.0025)	.0020 (.0027)	.0034 (.0051)
Time trend	−.0008 (.0012)	−.0021 (.0013)	.0019 (.0018)
Constant	***.7552 (.2628)	*.7051 (.3317)	*1.1051 (.4583)
H_θ (d.f.)	63.03 (128)	136.93 (80)	131.66 (40)
No of cross sections	17	11	6

Notes: In panel (10.1a) estimated equations are of the form given in equation (1). In panel (10.1b) estimated equations are of the form given in equation (1) with the restrictions $\beta 1i = \beta 2i = 0$ imposed. Estimates of coefficients and standard errors are obtained using Swamy estimators. The H_θ statistic has a X_2 distribution with $k(N-1)$ degrees of freedom under the null hypothesis of parameter homogeneity across sectors. Standard errors are reported in parentheses. Coefficient estimate is significant at the 1 (***), 5 (**) or 10 (*) per cent level based on an F-test as described by Swamy (1970, p. 318)

are determined by parameters that vary significantly within these sectors.

The second observation pertains to the variation of the estimated parameters across tradable and non-tradable goods. Theoretically, the relative response of tradables and non-tradables to relative price movements depends on the elasticity of substitution in consumption between tradable and non-tradable goods and on the extent to which this elasticity differs from unity. The estimates suggest that the real exchange-rate depreciation is associated with relatively less contractionary output effects on tradables, and the terms-of-trade improvements are associated with relatively more expansionary output effects on non-tradables – although coefficient estimates are not always statistically significant at conventional levels. If one wishes to attribute a structural interpretation to these parameter estimates, given the predictions of Gavin's (1990) models and Backus, Kehoe and Kydland (1995), the elasticity of substitution appears to be less than one in Mexico. Put differently, in the event of an improvement in the terms of trade, the income effect appears to dominate the substitution effect, and therefore the factors of production tend to move into the non-tradables.

One pertinent question is to what extent declining terms of trade are causing the real exchange rate movements. If, for instance, devaluations are endogenous responses to adverse terms-of-trade movements, the regression equation (1) would incorrectly attribute the effects of these adverse shocks to the real exchange rate. Given that the terms of trade and real exchange rate data exhibit moderate correlation ($-.36$), the regression model may be susceptible to confusing currency and terms-of-trade movements.

In order to analyse this issue more formally, Table 10.1(b) reports the estimation results of the regression model (1) after imposing the restrictions $\beta_{1i} = \beta_{2i} = 0$. The estimation results vindicate the previous observations. An increase in the terms of trade is still associated with a relatively more expansionary effect on the non-tradables. The coefficient estimates on the current and lagged terms of trade are similar to those reported in Table 10.1(a).

Alternative specifications

Devaluations

In the theoretical literature, significant attention has been paid to the consequences of devaluations on output. This emphasis appears to be based on the premise that devaluations induce asymmetric income and substitution effects that are not matched by currency appreciations. If there is asymmetry in response to exchange-rate movements, then the proposed specification in equation (1) may be inadequate to capture all the relative price effects, because it treats both currency appreciations and depreciations symmetrically.

Another important issue that arises in studying the effects of relative prices in Mexico is the persuasive impact of currency devaluations on output. In the period under consideration there were three large peso devaluations that took place in September 1976, February 1982 and June 1985, and at least the last two devaluations were associated with severe recessions.[8]

To check the robustness of the regression model (1) to possible devaluation effects, the model is augmented by introducing devaluation dummies, and specifying them as (unit) shocks to sectoral output levels. The specification also includes two lags of each devaluation to capture the persistence of their initial impact on sectoral output. In particular, the categorical variables $D(j, t)$ for $j = 0, 1, 2$ are assigned the following values: $D(0, 1976) = .4$, $D(0, 1982) = 1.1$, and $D(0, 1985) = 0.7$, and zero otherwise; $D(1, t) = 1.2$ when $t = 1977$, or 1983, or 1986, and zero otherwise; and $D(2, t) = 1.2$ when $t = 1978$, or 1984, or 1987, and zero otherwise. These choices were made in order to control for the timing of a devaluation within a given year.

The results reported in Table 10.2 indicate that nominal devaluations are indeed followed by declining sectoral output. However, the response of tradable and non-tradable goods sectors to devaluations seem to differ, and the contractionary effects of devaluations on tradable output are estimated to be relatively smaller and short-lived. In non-tradables, a currency devaluation is associated with lower output even after two years of its occurrence. This suggests that the differential real-exchange-rate effect on tradables and non-tradables found earlier (p. 174 ff) applies to currency depreciations as well as appreciations. These findings are consistent with the regression results reported in previous studies such as İşcan (1997). It should be emphasized that introduction of devaluation dummies significantly reduces the efficiency of the coefficient estimates of the model although without altering the main conclusions.

Trade liberalization

Two of the sources of relative price changes analysed are exogenous terms of trade and real exchange-rate movements. We also introduced nominal devaluations, which can be viewed as endogenous policy responses to balance-of-payments crises, and argued that they may

Table 10.2 Estimates of the sectoral output equations with devaluation effects (dependent variable: log output $_{it}$, sample period: 1971–93)

Variable	All sectors	Tradables	Non-tradables
Real exchange rate t	.0190 (.0131)	.0120 (.0178)	.0271 (.0217)
Real exchange rate $t-1$	.0150 (.0132)	.0222 (.0189)	.0067 (.0166)
Terms of trade t	.0357 (.0238)	.0290 (.0344)	.0526 (.0282)
Terms of trade $t-1$	-.0163 (.0218)	-.0425 (.0300)	.0103 (.0315)
Devaluation	***-.0168 (.0056)	-.0107 (.0069)	*-.0235 (.0094)
Devaluation $t-1$	***-.0220 (.0059)	**-.0192 (.0073)	*-.0245 (.0110)
Devaluation $t-2$	-.0045 (.0033)	-.0024 (.0049)	*-.0059 (.0030)
Log output $i(t-1)$	***.9112 (.0460)	***.8828 (.0613)	***.9019 (.0690)
Log productivity it	***.4763 (.1271)	***.6000 (.1549)	.2579 (.2067)
Log productivity $i(t-1)$	**-.3066 (.1249)	*-.3684 (.1745)	-.1441 (.1582)
Gov. spending t	.0041 (.0026)	.0034 (.0034)	.0050 (.0045)
Time trend t	-.0011 (.0012)	-.0019 (.0015)	.0007 (.0017)
Constant	**.5294 (.2439)	*.6817 (.3181)	.5807 (.3754)
H ($d.f.$)	462.94 (208)	161.54 (130)	198.96 (65)
No. of cross sections	17	11	6

Notes: (1) Estimated equations are of the form given in equation (1) with the devaluation dummies, described in the text, added. (2) Estimates of coefficients and standard errors are obtained using Swamy estimators. The H statistic has a X^2 distribution with $k(N-1)$ degrees of freedom under the null hypothesis of parameter homogeneity across sectors. Standard errors are reported in parentheses. (3) Coefficient estimate is significant at the 1 (***), 5 (**) or 10 (*) per cent level based on an F-test as described by Swamy (1970, p. 318)

have significant relative price effects. Arguably another important source of relative price changes originating from the external sector in Mexico is the shifts in the trade-policy regime. Economic theory suggests these policy changes may also impact on the reallocation of resources across sectors. Since one of the salient features of the recent Mexican economic history is contended to be the trade liberalization programme implemented after 1985 (Aspe, 1993), it remains to be seen if this policy change had any impact on the findings.

One way to gauge the liberalization-induced change in relative prices and exposure to foreign trade is to incorporate some measure of trade protection into the analysis. Following Tybout and Westbrook (1995) and İşcan (1998), we used the changes in the effective rates of protection (*ERP*) on tradables between end-1987 and the 1978–81 average – the earliest period for which sectoral protection data were available.[9] In particular, the regression model (1) is augmented by introducing ERP_{it}, which takes zero for $t < 1988$, and the value of change in the sectoral effective rate of protection for $t \geq 1988$. Given the lack of data on protection measures prior to 1978, the coefficient estimates on ERP_{it} should be viewed as the impact of trade liberalization policies on sectoral output, not overall trade policy.

Table 10.3 reports the augmented regression model results for tradables only, which are similar to earlier estimates. The comparison of Table 10.1(a), with Table 10.3 column (1) reveals that the inclusion of a trade liberalization variable does not alter the conclusions regarding the relative impact of the terms of trade and the real exchange-rate movements. Table 10.3 columns (2) and (3) also show alternative specifications for tradables. These results are consistent with our previous findings. Specifically, devaluations are still associated with adverse short-term real output effects, but the contractionary effects of devaluations disappear two years following the devaluation.

The regression analysis attempts to summarize the *average* response of tradables and non-tradables to relative price movements. In order for the coefficient estimates to be valid for group averages, the coefficient parameters of individual sectors should not be correlated with the regressors. In other words, the sectoral response to the real exchange rate and terms-of-trade movements should not be correlated with other observable characteristics of individual sectors. In this regard an important sector-specific issue is the degree of openness to international trade. Although there are a range of such measures, one commonly used variable is the share of exports in sectoral value-added adopted by Harrison (1996).

Table 10.3 Estimates of tradables output equation with effective rates of protection (Dependent variable: log output$_{it}$; sample period: 1971–93, 11 sectors)

Variable	1	2	3
Real exchange rate t	−.0271 (.0188)		.0112 (.0168)
Real exchange rate $t-1$	*.0379 (.0183)		.0257 (.0181)
Terms of trade t		*.0579 (.0275)	.0304 (.0341)
Terms of trade $t-1$	***−.1005 (.0317)	***−.1047 (.0319)	−.0470 (.0305)
Devaluation t			−.0107 (.0067)
Devaluation $t-1$			**−.0189 (.0067)
Devaluation $t-2$			−.0035 (.0056)
Log output $i(t-1)$	***.8857 (.0811)	***.8716 (.0783)	***.8757 (.0728)
Log productivity $_{it}$	***.6858 (.1693)	***.6872 (.1626)	***.6704 (.1629)
Log productivity $_i(t-1)$	**−.5350 (.2234)	*−.4618 (.2243)	**−.4405 (.1954)
Government spending t	.0042 (.0036)	.0028 (.0034)	.0037 (.0035)
Effective protection t	.0002 (.0004)	.0001 (.0003)	.0003 (.0003)
Time trend	−.0018 (.0019)	−.0021 (.0018)	−.0020 (.0019)
Constant	.6317 (.4355)	.7475 (.4193)	*.7222 (.3936)
H θ (d.f.)	188.87 (110)	157.71 (90)	205.26 (140)

Notes: (1) Estimates of coefficients and standard errors are obtained by using Swamy estimators. (2) The H_θ statistic has a χ^2 distribution with $k(N-1)$ degrees of freedom under the null hypothesis of parameter homogeneity across sectors. (3) Standard errors are reported in parentheses. (4) Coefficient estimate is significant at the 1 (***), 5 (**), or 10 (*) per cent level based on an *F*-test as described by Swamy (1970, p. 318)

To see whether the sectoral response to relative price disturbances is related to trade variables, following Kadiyala and Oberhelman (1978) we computed the response predictions for each individual sector using the baseline specification in equation (1).[10] The period averages of the share of exports of sectoral output were not systematically correlated with the response predictions of the terms-of-trade and real exchange variables, and are not reported here. It can, therefore, be concluded that the estimated average response of tradables and non-tradables to relative prices captures important features of these sectors (such as preferences), and are not simply reflections of their degree of exposure to foreign trade and competition.

5 Conclusion

This chapter has examined the effects on sectoral real output of the terms of trade and real exchange rate movements in Mexico, and provided new evidence on their differential impacts on the tradable and non-tradable goods sectors. The results of the study can be summarized as follows. First, the terms-of-trade shocks were shown to have significant sectoral output reallocation effects in Mexico. An improvement in the Mexican terms of trade is associated with a relatively more expansionary output effect in non-tradables. In most models this situation corresponds to the case in which the elasticity of intratemporal substitution in consumption between tradables and non-tradables is below unity suggesting that the income effect dominates the substitution effect.

Second, real exchange-rate movements are found to have significant relative output effects. A depreciation of the Mexican peso is associated with relatively greater contractionary output effects in non-tradables. We also controlled for the impact of three large devaluations on sectoral output, and found that their contractionary impact on output was a short-run adjustment phenomenon. Following a devaluation, output tends to decline relatively more in non-tradable goods sectors. These findings may suggest that in Mexico devaluations have been an effective policy tool in combatting current account problems through changing relative prices.

One should, however, be cautious in extending these findings to other contexts, because sectoral responses depend on preference parameters, such as the elasticity of substitution between tradables and non-tradables, and these parameters may vary significantly across countries and over time periods. Nevertheless our results are indicative of the significance in developing countries of external relative price shocks in reallocating output across sectors.

The results also suggest that although the tradable versus non-tradable distinction is a useful construct in framing a theory and organizing data, there exists significant diversity within these sectors – at least given their response to external shocks. The formal tests conducted in the study show that there is considerable parameter heterogeneity across sectors, and that estimating average responses by pooling data would be inappropriate.

Although the study has explored some previously neglected issues in the empirical literature, the framework had several limitations. In particular, the estimated correlations between the (current and lagged) real exchange rate and sectoral output levels do not by themselves make a strong case for a causal relationship from changes in the exchange rate to output.

Another aspect of this framework is that it is based on reduced-form regression equations, which are only indicative of covariations between sectoral output levels and relative prices. Although these reduced-form regression equations are useful in making inferences about the statistical significance of the estimated relationships, they are not informative about their economic significance. The exploration of this issue requires a structural open-economy model which is left for future research.

Notes

1 Bruno and Sachs (1982) analyse the income effects of terms-of-trade shocks in the context of energy prices.
2 Stockman and Tesar (1995, p. 178) show how empirical estimates of this elasticity of substitution found in the literature seem to vary widely across countries.
3 Some of the earlier literature pioneered by Obstfeld (1982) and Svensson and Razin (1983) emphasized the difference between permanent and temporary terms-of-trade shocks in order to isolate the income effects associated with these shocks. Since the primary focus of this chapter is on relative price effects, and since our time-series data are too short to confidently discriminate between permanent and temporary shocks, we do not attempt to make such a distinction here. Also, the findings of Mendoza (1995) suggest that it is unlikely that this would have a significant effect on our results.
4 See also Sachs and Larrain (1993, pp. 682–83), and Clement *et al.* (1996) on devaluation-based adjustment.
5 Monetary aggregates are not considered because of their endogeneity.
6 The Kravis, Heston and Summers classification treated retail services as traded, but we included them in the non-traded because we could not

separate them from restaurant and hotel services, and most of the value-added in this sector is derived from non-traded inputs.

7 A number of diagnostic tests were also performed before the panel was estimated. Artificial regression techniques (cf. Davidson and MacKinnon, 1993, ch. 10) did not indicate any evidence of first-order autocorrelation for sectoral output equations.

8 The September 1976 devaluation was the first for 22 years, and marked the end of a fixed exchange-rate regime. Between September and October 1976 the peso was devalued by around 100 per cent. The temporary withdrawal in February 1982 of the Banco de Mexico from intervention in the foreign-exchange market amounted to a devaluation, first of 30 per cent and then 19 per cent, directly precipitated by the inability of firms to meet foreign debt obligaitons. In August 1982 a two-tier exchange-rate system was imposed. In June 1982 the Banco de Mexico resumed its interventionist policies. The third devaluation occurred in July 1985; initially of 17 per cent, further depreciations continued in 1986 – equal to 180 per cent between September 1985–86.

9 These data were compiled by Ten Kate and Venturini (1989). Since their estimates are at a higher level of disaggregation, they are aggregated into 11 tradables sectors using 1985 sectoral GDP as weights.

10 Response predictions are the individual mean response vectors in a random coefficient regression model, and the Swamy estimator can be viewed as the mean of these individual coefficient vectors.

References

Agénor, P. R. and R. P. Flood (1995) 'Macroeconomic Policy, Speculative Attacks, and Balance of Payments Crises', in F. Van Der Ploeg (ed.), *Handbook of International Macroeconomics* (Oxford: Basil Blackwell).

Aspe, P. A. (1993) *Economic Transformation the Mexican Way* (Cambridge, MA: MIT Press).

Backus, D. K., P. J. Kehoe and F. E. Kydland (1995) 'Relative Price Movements in Dynamic General Equilibrium Models of International Trade', in F. Van Der Ploeg (ed.), *Handbook of International Macroeconomics* (Oxford: Basil Blackwell).

Barbone, L. and F. Rivera-Batiz (1987) 'Foreign Capital and the Contractionary Impact of Currency Devaluation, with Application to Jamaica', *Journal of Development Economics*, vol. 26, pp. 1–15.

Blanchard, O. J. and S. Fischer (1989) *Lectures on Macroeconomics* (Cambridge. MA: MIT Press).

Bruno, M. and J. Sachs (1982) 'Energy and Resource Allocation: A Dynamic Model of the "Dutch Disease" ', *Review of Economic Studies*, vol.,49, pp. 845–59.

Clément, J. A. P. with J. Mueller, S. Cossé and J. LeDem (1996) 'Aftermath of the CFA Franc Devaluation', International Monetary Fund Occasional Paper, no. 138.

Davidson, R. and J. G. MacKinnon (1993) *Estimation and Inference in Econometrics* (Oxford: Oxford University Press).

Diamond, P. (1980) 'Protection, Trade Adjustment Assistance, and Income Distribution', in J. Bhagwati (ed.), *Import Competition and Policy Response* (Chicago: University of Chicago Press, for NBER).

Diaz-Alejandro, C. (1963) 'A Note on the Impact of Devaluation and the Redistributive Effect', *Journal of Political Economy*, vol. 71, pp. 577–80.

Dixit, A. K. and R. Rob (1994) 'Switching Costs and Sectoral Adjustments in General Equilibrium with Uninsured Risk', *Journal of Economic Theory*, vol. 62, pp. 48–69.

Edwards, S. (1986) 'Are Devaluations Contractionary?', *Review of Economics and Statistics*, vol. 68, pp. 501–8.

Edwards, S. (1989) *Real Exchange Rates, Devaluation and Adjustment* (Cambridge MA.: MIT Press).

Edwards, S. (1993) 'Openness, Trade Liberalization, and Growth in Developing Countries', *Journal of Economic Literature*, vol. 31, pp. 1358–93.

Gavin, M. (1990) 'Structural Adjustment to a Terms of Trade Disturbance: The Role of Relative Prices', *Journal of International Economics*, vol. 28, pp. 217–43.

Gylfason, T. and M. Schmid (1983) 'Does Devaluation Cause Stagflation?', *Canadian Journal of Economics and Political Science*, vol. 16, pp. 641–54.

Harrison, A. (1996) 'Openness and Growth: A Time Series, Cross-country Analysis for Developing Countries', *Journal of Development Economics*, vol. 48, pp. 419–47.

International Monetary Fund (1995) *International Capital Markets: Developments, Prospects, and Policy Issues* (Washington, DC: IMF).

İşcan, T. (1997) 'Devaluations and Aggregate Output Fluctuations: A Random Coefficient Regression Model for Mexico', *Applied Economics*, vol. 29, pp. 1575–84.

İşcan, T. (1998) 'Trade Liberalization and Productivity: A Panel Study of the Mexican Manufacturing Industry', *Journal of Development Studies*, vol. 34, pp. 123–48.

Kadiyala, K. R. and D. Oberhelman. (1978) 'Response Predictions in Regression on Panel Data', *Communications in Statistics*, November, pp. 92–7.

Kravis, I., A. Heston and R. Summers. (1982) *World Product and Income: International Comparisons and Real GDP* (Baltimore, MD: Johns Hopkins University Press).

Krugman, P. and L. Taylor (1978) 'Contractionary Effects of Devaluation', *Journal of International Economics*, vol. 8, pp. 445–56.

Mendoza, E. G. (1995) 'The Terms of Trade, the Real Exchange Rate, and Economic Fluctuations', *International Economic Review*, vol. 36, pp. 101–37.

Nickell, S. (1981) 'Biases in Dynamic Models with Fixed Effects', *Econometrica*, vol. 49, pp. 1417–26.

Obstfeld, M. (1982) 'Aggregate Spending and the Terms of Trade: Is there a Laursen–Metzler Effect?', *Quarterly Journal of Economics*, vol. 97, pp. 251–70.

Pesaran, H. M. and R. Smith (1995) 'Estimating Long-run Relationships from Dynamic Heterogeneous Panels', *Journal of Econometrics*, vol. 68, pp. 79–113.

Robertson, D. and J. Symons (1992) 'Some Strange Properties of Panel Data Estimators', *Journal of Applied Econometrics*, vol. 7, pp. 175–89.

Sachs, J. D. and F. B. Larrain (1993) *Macroeconomics in the Global Economy* (New Jersey: Prentice-Hall).

Stockman, A. and L. L. Tesar (1995) 'Tastes and Technology in a Two-country Model of the Business Cycle: Explaining International Comovements', *American Economic Review*, vol. 85, pp. 168–85.

Svensson, L. E. O. and A. Razin (1983) 'The Terms of Trade and the Current Account: The Harberger–Laursen–Metzler Effect', *Journal of Political Economy*, vol. 91, pp. 97–125.

Swamy, P. A. V. B. (1970) 'Efficient Inference in Random Coefficient Regression Model', *Econometrica*, vol. 38: pp. 311–23.

Ten Kate, A. and F. M. Venturini (1989) 'Apertura comercial y estructura de la proteccíon en Mexico: Estimaciones cuantitativas de los ochenta' (Commercial opportunities and the structure of protectionism in Mexico: quantity estimates in the 1980s), *Comercio Exterior*, vol. 39, pp. 312–29

Tybout, J. R. and M. D. Westbrook (1995) 'Trade Liberalization and the Dimensions of Efficiency Change in Mexican Manufacturing Industries', *Journal of International Economics*, vol. 39, pp. 53–78.

Yotopoulos, P. A. (1996) *Exchange Rate Policy for Trade and Development: Theory, Tests, and Case Studies* (Cambridge: Cambridge University Press).

11
Exchange-Rate Movements and the Export of Brazilian Manufactures

Afonso Ferreira and Andreu Sansó

1 Introduction

This chapter considers the extent to which exchange-rate movements affect the 'competitiveness' of Brazilian exports of manufactured goods. Changes in the exchange rate are normally split into changes in the destination currency prices of exported goods, and changes in the profit margins of the exporting firms.

A large body of literature has recently examined the empirical evaluation of these two competing effects for several countries. The importance of this question is quite obvious. If exchange-rate changes are not fully or substantially reflected in the selling prices of exported goods, their impact, as Menon (1995) argued, on the demand for exports will be limited, even when the price elasticity of demand is quite large. In this case, the efficacy of the exchange rate as a policy tool in programmes of export promotion and balance of payments adjustment may be reduced.

Section 2 presents the simple mark-up price model usually adopted in empirical studies of this kind; section 3 briefly describes the data, while section 4 reviews the econometric methodology used. Estimates of the pass-through coefficient, derived from cointegration tests based on the Engle–Granger, Shin and Johansen procedures are reported for the Brazilian case in section 5. Section 6 offers some conclusions,

2 The model

The starting point for the analysis is a mark-up price model of the type:

$$PX = (1 + \lambda) \, (CP / ER) \qquad (1)$$

187

where PX = foreign currency price of manufactured exports, CP = the production cost in domestic currency, ER = the nominal exchange rate, CP/ER = the production cost in foreign currency, and λ = mark up.

Considering that manufactured goods are typically differentiated and traded in markets characterized by imperfect competition, the adoption of the traditional mark-up model in equation (1), as a first approximation seems justified. Presuming that the mark-up may vary, according to the competitive pressures in the world market, we would have:

$$\lambda = \lambda' \frac{(PW)}{(CP/ER)} \tag{2}$$

where $\frac{(PW)}{CP/ER}$ is the gap between the price of world exports and the exporter's production cost measured in foreign currency, and $\lambda' > 0$ (Athukorala and Menon, 1994).

Combining equation (1) and (2) gives:

$$\ln PX = \delta_0 + \delta_1 \ln (CP/ER) + \delta_2 \ln PW \tag{3}$$

or, allowing the coefficients on CP and ER to differ not only in sign, but also in magnitude:

$$\ln PX = \phi_0 + \phi_1 \ln CP + \phi_2 \ln ER + \phi_3 \ln PW \tag{4}$$

The parameter ϕ_2 in equation (4) is the pass-through coefficient. When $\phi_2 = 0$, the exchange rate has no influence on the foreign currency price of manufactured exports and, therefore, exchange-rate changes affect only the exporters' profit margins, with no impact on the 'competitiveness' of the country's exports. Conversely, when $\phi_2 = -1$, that is when pass-through is complete, any changes in the exchange rate are fully transmitted to the price of exports in foreign currency, thereby affecting the 'competitiveness' of domestic production in the world market. Obviously, for values of ϕ_2 in the interval $-1 < \phi_2 < 0$, pass-through will be incomplete.

3   The data

In the empirical implementation of the model proposed in the previous section, PX was given by the price series for the Brazilian manufactured exports calculated by Guimarães *et al.* (1997), while the domestic cost variable (*CP*) was proxied by the wholesale price index, and the exchange rate *ER* was given by the ratio *real*/US$ (since most Brazilian exports are invoiced in US$, the use of this exchange rate is appropriate, in the present context). Finally, *PW* was proxied by the IFS–IMF export price series for industrial countries.

Quarterly data for the period 1977 (1st quarter) to 1996 (4th quarter) were used in all tests. Since the variables entered several test equations in lagged first differences, some observations were, however, 'lost', with the period of estimation being, for that reason, reduced to the interval 1978 (3rd quarter) to 1996 (4th quarter). The series *PX*, (*CP/ER*) and *PW* are plotted, in log form, in Figures 11.1 and 11.2.

4 Econometric methodology

We adopted cointegration analysis to determine whether equation (1), in logarithmic form, as well as equations (3) and (4), represent long-run equilibrium relationships. A preliminary step in this sort of analysis consists in examining whether the time series involved are stationary. This was done by combining unit-root DF/ADF and stationarity KPSS (Kwiatkowski, Phillips, Schmidt and Shin, 1992) tests.

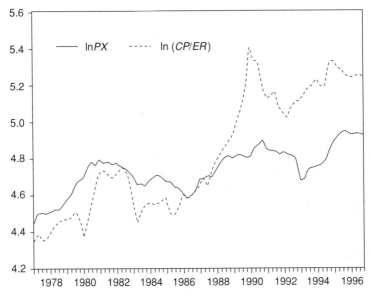

Figure 11.1   The series *PX*, (*CP/ER*) plotted in log form

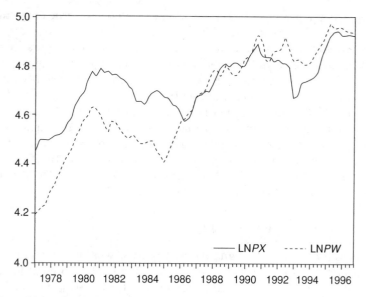

Figure 11.2   The series *PX*, *PW* plotted in log form

The DF/ADF procedure tests the null H_0: $y_t \sim I(1)$ against the alternative H_a: $y_t \sim I(0)$. In what follows, the critical values adopted for the DF/ADF tests are those derived by MacKinnon (1991) and available in Micro TSP 7.0 and EVIEWS 2.0. Unlike the DF/ADF test, the KPSS test establishes the null as H_0 : $y_t \sim I(0)$. Results of three different versions of the KPSS test for the series considered in this chapter are reported in section 5, one adopting a spectral quadratic window and the other two a Bartlett window (with automatic and manual lag selection). In performing these tests, a Gauss routine written by Andreu Sansó was used.[1]

Amano and Van Norden (1992) examine the consequences of using the KPSS stationarity test in conjunction with a standard unit-root test, such as the DF/ADF test.Their results suggest that, when this procedure is adopted, 'the frequency of incorrect conclusions may be decreased relative to the application of only standard unit-root tests. Also, such a joint testing procedure may in some cases permit researchers to be more confident about their tests results'. We have, therefore, chosen to report the results derived from both tests.

The tests for cointegration among the variables in equations (1), (3) and (4), which are also presented in section 5, were based on the Engle–Granger (1987) Shin (1994) and Johansen (1988, 1991) procedures. The Engle–Granger (1987) procedure consists in testing the OLS residuals of the cointegrating equation (in the present context, equations (1), (3) or (4) above) for the presence of a unit root, using the DF/ADF statistic. Under the null of non-stationarity of the residuals, the series involved are not cointegrated.

The procedure proposed by Shin (1994), on the other hand, makes use of the KPSS test to evaluate the null of cointegration. Similarly to the Engle–Granger method, the cointegrating equation is first estimated by OLS, with the residual series then being subjected to the KPSS test for stationarity. If the null of stationarity cannot be rejected, the series in question are said to be cointegrated. Again, following Amano and Van Norden (1992), if the diagnostic obtained from the Shin test (H_0: cointegration) does not contradict the diagnostic derived from the Engle–Granger test (H_0: no cointegration), we have strong evidence in favour of one of the hypotheses.

Finally, the Johansen (1988, 1991) procedure is based on the following vector error-correction model:

$$\Delta Z_t = \Sigma_1^p \, \Gamma_i \, \Delta Z_{t-1} + \Pi \, Z_{t-1} + v_t \tag{5}$$

where the vector Z_t contains the n variables in the model.

If the variables in Z_t are $I(1)$, the rank of matrix Π is $\rho < n$ and there exists a representation of Π such that $\Pi = \alpha\beta'$, where α and β are both $n \times \rho$ matrices. Matrix β is called the cointegrating matrix and has the property that $\beta' Z_t$ is $I(0)$, while Z_t is $I(1)$. The columns of the matrix have an economic interpretation as cointegrating vectors, that is, after normalization they may be interpreted as giving estimates of the long-run parameters of the model. In empirical applications, the main concerns consist in determining ρ, which gives the number of cointegrating vectors, and in estimating the cointegrating matrix. This is done by means of an ML procedure described in Johansen (1988, 1991).[2]

5 Results

Table 11.1 shows the DF/ADF test statistics for the presence of a unit root in the series under analysis. The DF/ADF tests suggest that all series are $I(1)$, a diagnostic confirmed by the KPSS tests reported in Table 11.2.[3]

According to the Shin test, equations (1), (3) and (4) all constitute cointegrating relationships, a result which departs from that derived

Table 11.1   DF/ADF tests (3rd qtr 1978 to 4th qtr 1996)

Variable	DF/ADF statistic		k
	without trend	*with trend*	
Levels			
ln *PX*	−1.9709	−2.5566	1
In (*CP/ER*)	−1.1045	−2.4994	1
ln *CP*	−0.1332	−2.2067	1
In *ER*	0.3009	−2.0358	2
ln *PW*	−1.5650	−2.4650	1
First differences			
In *PX*	−6.0339***		0
ln (*CP / ER*)	−6.3211***		0
In *CP*	−2.8288*		0
	−3.1300**		1
In *ER*	−3.2820**		1
In PW	−6.1387***		0

Notes: (1) The value of *k* corresponds to the lag length on the lagged dependent variable in the RHS of the ADF test equation that was required to produce approximately white-noise residuals. (2) An intercept term was included in all DF/ADF test equations. (3) The critical values,which were taken from MacKinnon (1991), are: (a) without trend: −2.5874 (10%); −2.9006 (5%); −3.5200 (1%); (b) with trend: −3.1620 (10%); −3.4704 (5%); −4.0853 (1%). * = significant at the 10% level; ** = significant at the 5% level; *** = significant at the 1% level.

Table 11.2   KPSS tests (3rd qtr 1978 to 4th qtr 1996)

Variable	Spectral quadratic window (automatic lag selection)	Barlett window (automatic lag selection)	Barlett window (manual lag selection)
Without trend			
In *PX*	0.700**	0.705**	1.059***
In (*CP/ER*)	1.022***	1.005***	1.663***
ln *CP*	1.140***	1.116***	1.881***
ln *ER*	1.139***	1.116***	1.880***
ln *PW*	1.059***	1.038***	1.708***
With trend Δ			
ln *PX*	0.074	0.077	0.110
ln (*CP/ER*)	0.110	0.111	0.165**
ln *CP*	0.266***	0.263***	0.430***
ln *ER*	0.267***	0.264***	0.432***
In PW	0.103	0.103	0.156**

Notes: The critical values, which were taken from Sephton (1995), are: (a) without trend: 0.350 (10%); 0.467 (5%); 0.730 (1%); (b) with trend: 0.121 (10%); 0.153 (5%); 0.215 (1%). * = significant at the 10% level; ** = significant at the 5% level; *** = significant at the 1% level.

from the Engle–Granger procedure, which rejects the null of no cointegration only for equation (1). The estimated cointegrating equations point to a pass-through coefficient between 11 per cent and 26 per cent, suggesting that only a small proportion of change in the exchange rate is transmitted to the export prices of Brazilian manufactured goods, in the long run. The measured impact of changes in the price of world exports on the other hand is larger, with 30–40 per cent of a variation in those prices being reflected in the price of the Brazilian exports, according to the test results presented in Table 11.3.

Table 11.3 Cointegration tests (LHS variable is ln *PX*; 3rd qtr 1978 to 4th qtr 1996)

Variable	Equation (1)	Equation (3)	Equation (4)
Cointegrating equations			
ln *CP/ER*	0.263	0.108	
ln *CP*			0.186
ln *ER*			−0.191
ln *PW*		0.295	0.392
Cointegration tests			
Engle–Granger (null hypothesis: no cointegration)			
$k = 0$	−2.516	−2.230	−2.235
$k = 1$	−3.318*	−2.720	−2.644
$k = 2$	−3.548**	−2.896	−2.912
critical values			
10%	−3.10	−3.54	−3.93
5%	−3.42	−3.86	−4.26
1%	−4.05	−4.50	−4.90
Shin (null hypothesis: cointegration)			
Spectral quadratic			
window (automatic lag			
selection)	0.069	0.110	0.106
Bartlett window			
(automatic lag selection)	0.076	0.115	0.111
Bartlett window			
(manual lag selection)	0.093	0.157	0.148*
critical values			
10%	0.228	0.164	0.119
5%	0.308	0.219	0.156
1%	0.557	0.389	0.282

Notes: The value of *k*, in the Engle–Granger test, corresponds to the lag length on the lagged dependent variable in the RHS of the DF/ADF test equation. * = significant at the 10% level; ** = significant at the 5% level; *** = significant at the 1% level.

Table 11.4 shows the results obtained when the Johansen method is applied to equation (4). The Akaike and Schwarz statistics, as well as the log-likelihood ratio test, all pointed out to an optimal VAR lag length (the value of p, in equation (5)) of 4. For this VAR lag length, the null of only one cointegrating vector was rejected in favour of the alternative hypothesis of two cointegrating vectors. Only one of the two cointegrating vectors, however, displayed the theoretically expected signs. Following what is the established practice in such situations, this is the only result taken into account here, providing the cointegrating equation:

$$\ln PX = 0.259 \ln CP - 0.267 \ln ER + 0.490 \ln PW$$

Given the evidence of non-normality of the residuals, the Johansen procedure was also applied to equation (4), with the addition of dummy variables controlling for a variety of shocks that affected the Brazilian economy during the period under analysis.[4] Again a VAR lag length of 4 was adopted. In this version of the Johansen test, also reported in Table 11.4, the LR statistic suggested the existence of only one cointegration vector, with the cointegrationg equation corresponding to:

$$\ln PX = 0.102 \ln CP - 0.104 \ln ER + 0.448 \ln PW$$

Reassuringly, the coefficients on $\ln CP$, $\ln ER$ and $\ln PW$ given by the Johansen exercise are similar to those derived from the Engle–Granger and Shin tests, suggesting a low pass-through coefficient in the range of 10 to 27 per cent.

6   Conclusions

The pass-through relationship between exchange-rate changes and prices of traded goods determines the degree of 'competitiveness' achieved from variations in the exchange rate. The efficacy of the exchange rate as a policy tool in programmes of export promotion and current-account adjustment depends critically on the coefficient of pass-through.

Newly-industrializing countries such as Brazil are generally considered to have little control over prices at which they sell. The implication is that exchange-rate changes may be of little relevance in determining the prices of their exports in international markets; that

Table 11.4   Cointegration tests: Johansen procedure (equation (4); 3rd qtr
1978 to 4th qtr 1996)

Null hypothesis	Alternative hypothesis	LR statistic	Critical values 5%	1%
Without dummies				
$\rho = 0$	$\rho = 1$	63.785**	47.21	54.46
$\rho \leq 1$	$\rho = 2$	33.577*	29.68	35.56
$\rho \leq 2$	$\rho = 3$	10.101	15.41	20.04
CV = [1, −0.259, 0.267, −0.490]				
With dummies				
$\rho \leq 0$	$\rho = 1$	62.986**	47.21	54.46
$\rho \leq 1$	$\rho = 2$	26.137	29.68	35.65
$\rho \leq 2$	$\rho = 3$	7.155	15.41	20.04
CV = [1, −0.102, 0.104, −0.448]				

Notes: (1) An intercept term was included in the cointegrating equation and in the VAR,
which corresponds to assuming a linear trend in the levels of the series. A VAR lag length
of 4 was adopted, in both exercises. Dummy variables were included in the second version
of the exercise, corresponding to: 2nd qtr 1980; 2nd qtr 1986; 3rd qtr 1989; 1st qtr 1990;
2nd qtr 1990; 1st qtr 1993 and 3rd qtr 1994. (2) ± is the cointegrating rank and gives the
number of cointegrating vectors; LR is the Likelihood Ratio test statistic for the
corresponding null hypothesis about the cointegrating rank; CV is the normalized
cointegrating vector. (3) *significant at the 5% level; **significant at the 1% level. (4) Only
cointegrating vectors with economically meaningful signs are reported. (5) The variables
entered the tests in the order (ln *PX*, ln *CP*, ln *ER*, ln *PW*). The cointegrating vectors
reported above were normalized in ln *PX*.

is, as Athukorala (1991) concludes, the pass-through coefficient is close
to zero. Our objective was to estimate the pass-through coefficient for
Brazilian export of manufactures. The point estimates derived from the
cointegration analysis conducted in our study suggest that the pass-
through of exchange-rate changes to the destination currency price of
manufactured exports does not exceed 27 per cent, and may be as low
as 10 per cent in the Brazilian case.

The adjustment of prices in foreign currency that tends to follow any
exchange-rate movement is, therefore, very limited, with variations in
the exchange rate clearly being reflected mainly in variations in the
price in domestic currency and, therefore, in the profit margins of
exporters. This means that in periods of currency depreciation,
Brazilian exporters enjoy increases in profit margins approximately
equal to the depreciation, while in periods of currency appreciation
they are forced to squeeze their margins or to drop out of the international market altogether.

As pointed out by Athukorala and Menon (1994), the coefficient ϕ_2 in equation (4) measures the direct effect of an exchange-rate change on the price of exports, for a given level of domestic costs, what they call the 'pricing to market (PTM) effect', related to strategic pricing behaviour on the part of exporting firms, 'which aims to protect market share during currency appreciation or to augment profit margins during currency depreciation'. Exchange-rate movements, however, also affect the cost of production measured in domestic currency, via their effect on the domestic price of imported inputs. The coefficient ϕ_2 therefore overestimates the *total impact* of a variation in the exchange rate on the price of exports, since that impact is equal to the *direct effect* (given by ϕ_2) *less the indirect effect* related to the change in input costs. In view of the low degree of openness and the limited reliance on imported inputs that characterized the Brazilian economy during the years 1977 to 1990, it is, however, reasonable to expect the direct effect captured by ϕ_2 to have been, by far, the most important influence in determining how exchange-rate changes affected the price of manufactured exports during the period under analysis here.

A low pass-through coefficient implies that a devaluation has a limited effect on the demand for exports, irrespective of the value of the price elasticity of demand. A devaluation, however, may still have a significant impact on the volume of exports through its supply effect: with a low pass-through, the price of exports in domestic currency, and thus the profit margins of exporting firms, increase, raising the supply of exports.

This was certainly the main channel through which exchange-rate changes until recently affected the volume of exports, in the Brazilian case. This supply effect, however, has probably become less relevant during the 1990s, as a consequence of trade liberalization. The increased dependence on imported inputs that has been brought about by the programme of trade liberalization means that the effect of a devaluation on input costs, mentioned above, may now be quite significant. As a result, the positive impact of a devaluation on the profit margins of exporting firms and on the supply of exports may have been weakened.

To summarize our argument, a devaluation has a limited impact on the foreign price of Brazilian manufactured exports and, thus, limited impact on the demand for exports. At the same time, a devaluation tends to increase production costs, measured in terms of the domestic currency, far more than it did in the past, which, in turn, tends to reduce its beneficial effect on the supply of exports. As a result, the volume of Brazilian manufactured exports may now be relatively insensitive to exchange-rate changes.

Notes

1 A more detailed description of these tests is obtainable from the authors.
2 Since the computational details of this test are well-known, they will not be reviewed here. For a description of the test procedure, the interested reader may consult Johansen (1995) and Phillips and Perron (1988) or introductory presentations such as those in Charemza and Deadman (1992) and Cuthbertson, Hall and Taylor (1992).
3 Similar results were also obtained from the stationarity test proposed by Leybourne and McCabe (1994).
4 Dummy variables corresponding to the following quarters were considered: 2nd qtr 1980; 2nd qtr 1986; 3rd qtr 1989; 1st qtr 1990; 2nd qtr 1990; 1st qtr 1993 and 3rd qtr 1994.

References

Amano, R. and S. Van Norden (1992) 'Unit Root Tests and the Burden of Proof', http://wueconb.wustl.edu/eprints/em/papers/9502/9502005.abs

Athukorala, P. (1991) 'Exchange Rate Pass-through: The Case of Korean Exports of Manufactures', *Economics Letters*, 35, pp. 79–84.

Athukorala, P. and J. Menon (1994). 'Pricing to Market Behaviour and Exchange Rate Pass-through in Japanese Exports', *Economic Journal*, vol. 104 (March), pp. 271–81.

Charemza, W. and D. Deadman (1992) *New Directions in Econometric Practice: General to Specific Modelling, Cointegration and Vector Autoregression* (Cheltenham, Glos.: Edward Elgar).

Cuthbertson, K., S. Hall and M. Taylor (1992) *Applied Econometric Techniques* (Ann Arbor, MI: The University of Michigan Press).

Engle, R. and C. Granger (1987) 'Co-integration and Error Correction: Representation, Estimation and Testing, *Econometrica*, vol. 55, pp. 251–76.

Guimarães, E *et al.* (1997) 'Indices de Preço e Quantum das Exportações Brasileiras' (Brazilian Export Price and Volume Indices), Fundação Centro de Comercio Exterior (mimeo).

Johansen, S. (1988) 'Statistical Analysis of Cointegrating Vectors', *Journal of Economic Dynamics and Control*, vol. 12, pp. 231–54.

Johansen, S. (1991) 'Estimation and Hypothesis Testing of Cointegration Vectors in Gaussian Vector Autoregressive Models', *Econometrica*, vol. 59, pp. 1551–80.

Johansen, S. (1995) *Likelihood-Based Inference in Cointegrated Vector Auto-Regressive Models* (Oxford: Oxford University Press).

Kwiatkowski, D., P. Phillips, P. Schmidt and Y. Shin (1992) 'Testing the Null Hypothesis of Stationarity against the Alternative of a Unit Root: How Sure Are We that Economic Time Series Have a Unit Root?', *Journal of Econometrics*, vol. 54, pp. 159–78.

Leybourne, S. J. and B. P. M. McCabe (1994) 'A Consistent Test for a Unit Root', *Journal of Business and Economic Statistics*, vol. 12, no. 2, pp. 157–66.

MacKinnon, J. (1991) 'Critical Values for Cointegration Tests', in R. Engle and C. Granger (eds), *Long Run Economic Relationships* (Oxford: Oxford University Press).

Menon, J. (1995) 'Exchange Rate and Import Prices for a Small Open Economy', *Applied Economics*, vol. 27, pp. 297–301.

Phillips, P. and P. Perron (1988) 'Testing for a Unit Root in Time Series Regression', *Biometrica*, vol. 75, pp. 335–46.

Sansó, A. (1998) 'Contrastes de Estacionariedad: Una Sintesis' (Testing Stationarity: A Synthesis), Departament d'Econometria, Estadistica i Economia Espanyola, Universitat de Barcelona (mimeo).

Sephton, P. (1995) 'Response Surface Estimates of the KPSS Stationarity Test', *Economics Letters*, vol. 47, pp. 255–61.

Shin, Y. (1994) 'A Residual-based Test of the Null of Cointegration against the Alternative of No Cointegration', *Econometric Theory*, vol. 10, pp. 91–115.

Part III
Labour and Income Distribution

12

The Impact of Firing Costs on Turnover and Unemployment: Evidence from Colombia

Adriana D. Kugler*

I Introduction

Job-security regulations may impose substantial rigidities on the ability of firms to adjust employment levels over the business cycle. The effects of dismissal costs on employment and unemployment are difficult to estimate, and empirical evidence on their net effects is ambiguous. Using cross-sections, Grubb and Wells (1993) argued that stricter provisions are negatively correlated with employment, while Bertola (1990) found no relation between job-security provisions and medium- and long-run employment. These mixed results are not surprising, given that cross-section studies are subject to omitted variable bias, simultaneity problems and possible endogeneity of the regulations.

Several studies relied on pooled time-series and cross-section data and panel data, with mixed results. Lazear (1990) using pooled time-series and cross-section data for 22 OECD countries over 29 years found that severance payments and advance notice requirements reduced employment. Dertouzos and Karoly (1993) used US pooled time-series and cross-section data and found a reduction in employment in states that introduced exceptions to the 'employment-at-will' doctrine. Using a panel of 8,000 US retail firms, Anderson (1993) found employment levels were higher in firms with higher adjustment costs. All these studies were subject to selection biases.

* I am grateful to George Akerlof, Antonio Cabrales, Guillermo Calvo, Albert Fishlow, Reuben Gronau, Hugo Hopenhayn, Bernardo Kugler, Ricardo Paes de Barros, Carmen Pagés-Serra, Ron Oaxaca, Richard Blundell, Dan Hamermesh, Jim Heckman, David Levine and Derek Leslie for helpful comments, and Manuel Badénes for research assistance. Fedesarrollo provided financial support.

To illustrate how job-security provisions induce self-selection, I developed a simple model of labour demand. The model highlights the selection bias that may be present in estimates of the net impact of firing costs, and shows how compositional changes may bias standard grouping estimators downwards.

I examined a major policy change in Latin America, namely the impact of the 1990 Colombian Labour Market Reform – which substantially reduced firing costs – on worker turnover; that is, exit rates into and out of unemployment. The identification strategy analysed the temporal change in labour-market legislation together with the variability in coverage across groups. To obtain consistent grouping estimators, an additional identifying assumption was required.[1]

The empirical analysis used cross-sections from the Colombian National Household Survey (NHS). These data provide information on tenure, last period of unemployment, demographic characteristics, industry, city, and indicators of whether the employee is covered by labour-market legislation. The empirical analysis showed that after controlling for composition change, the reduction in dismissal costs increased the 'hazard rate' out of employment of covered workers by up to 1.1 per cent, and the hazard rate out of unemployment of covered workers by up to 1.7 per cent relative to uncovered workers.

Section 2 describes the legislative changes introduced by the Colombian labour market reform of 1990, and section 3 presents an abbreviated model to explain the compositional change induced by a reduction in firing costs. For the full version refer to Kugler (1999). Section 4 describes the conditions required on grouping estimators for the identification and estimation of dismissal costs; section 5 describes the data and presents estimates of the incidence of firing costs on the exit rates into and out of unemployment; and section 6 examines the implied net effect of the reform on unemployment.

2   The 1990 Colombian labour market reform

The view that job-security regulations hamper the flexibility of labour markets persuaded several European countries to introduce labour-market reforms to reduce unemployment. European legislation introduced temporary contracts, whereas US legislation concentrated on exceptions to the 'employment-at-will' doctrine.

Several Latin American countries amended labour legislation to promote greater flexibility. These changes, particularly the 1990 Colombian Labour Market Reform which reduced the cost of dismissing workers, provided good data. The major policy change was a uniform reduction in severance payments.[2] The self-employed, family workers, and domestic workers were exempt and should have been unaffected, as should workers in the informal sector not protected by labour legislation.

Prior to reform, employers paid severance of one month per year worked based on the terminal salary (9.3 per cent). Any nominal withdrawals previously made by a worker from his severance pay were subtracted,[3] but the employer paid for those withdrawals in real terms. These firing costs induced inaction over hiring and firing, which reduced employment adjustment during the business cycle.[4] The 1990 reform reduced dismissal costs; employers were required to make a monthly contribution of 9.3 per cent of salary into a capitalized fund, available to the worker on severance. This legislation reduced severance payments for three reasons. First, it eliminated the additional cost of severance pay calculated on salary at the time of dismissal instead of ongoing monthly salary. Second, the new legislation reduced severance payments by stopping employees withdrawing funds for investment in education and housing.[5] Third, the replacement of severance payments by monthly contributions turned severance payments into a deferred compensation scheme; this should have stimulated dismissals and increased labour turnover for all workers covered by the legislation.[6]

The reduction in dismissal costs decreased the propensity of firms to hire from the informal sector. Prior to reform, 45 per cent of workers were employed in the formal sector, compared to 51 per cent after reform.[7] Another effect was to increase expected formal profits, inducing firms to hire formally. Moreover, with heterogeneous firms, the reduction in firing costs caused a change in the composition of the two sectors, which affected turnover.

3 A model for selection into formal and informal-sector activity

In the model of formal and informal-sector activity, the size and composition of the two sectors are endogenously determined. In particular, the model shows how both are affected by change in job-security legislation. The formal and informal sectors are distinguished by two characteristics: first, only formal-sector firms comply with labour-market regulations, such as severance pay or indemnities for unjust dismissal, and consequently formal-sector firms face higher adjustment costs; and second, this means that formal-sector firms must accumulate sufficient evidence before firing to avoid paying indemnities for unfair dismissal. The presence of unjust dismissal legislation increases monitoring costs for formal-sector firms which prefer paying 'efficiency' wages to monitoring costs,[8] whereas informal-sector firms pay 'reservation' wages. The payment of efficiency wages adds an additional adjustment cost. Formal-sector firms prefer not to adjust employment levels because the expectation of being sacked increases the efficiency wage needed to motivate workers.

Assumptions

Firms and workers are risk-neutral, infinitely lived, and face a discount factor β.

Firms (F)

F1: the revenue of firm j is $R_{jt} = \theta_t f\ (e_t l_{jt})$, where the price, θ_t, is an i.i.d. (independently and identically distributed) random variable drawn from a density $G(\theta)$; e_t are the efficiency units; and l_{jt} is employment at firm j at time t.

F2: formal firms pay legislated firing costs C while informal firms do not.

F3: firms can obtain a monitoring technology at cost s to monitor workers.[8] Without this technology, firms monitor imperfectly, as each firm j has a probability of catching a shirker q_j where q_j is uniformly distributed between $\underline{q}$ and $\bar{q}$.

Workers

W1: workers can exert effort $e = 1$, or shirk $e = 0$.

W2: workers employed in sector $S = F,I$ and firm j at time t face a separation rate x_{Sjt}.

Solution of the model

Firms determine the wage to be paid in each sector; given these wages, firms then make hiring and firing decisions; finally, given the wages and turnover patterns in each sector, each firm decides whether to produce in the formal or informal sector.[9]

Wage determination

Since the cost of the monitoring technology is excessive for formal firms, these firms pay efficiency wages. That is, a firm j producing in the formal sector pays a wage to satisfy the no-shirking condition:

$$V_{Et}^{Fj} = w_{Fjt} - 1 + \beta[\ (1-x_{Fjt})\ E_t V_{Et}+1^{Fj} + x_{Fjt} E_t U_{t+1}] \geq$$
$$V_{St}^{Fj} = w_{Fjt} + \beta[\ (1-x_{Fjt})(1-q_j)\ E_t V_{St}+1^{Fj} + ((1-x_{Fjt})q_j + x_{Fjt})\ E_t U_{t+1}]$$

where $(1-x_{Fjt})(1-q_j)$ is the probability that a worker does not get fired for shirking or any exogenous reasons, and $(1-x_{Fjt})q_j$ is the probability that a worker gets fired only for shirking. The wage that satisfies the no-shirking condition with equality is

$$w_{Fjt} = a_{Fj} + b_{Fj}/(1-x_{Fjt-1})$$

where $a_{Fj} = (E_t-1U_t - \beta E_t-1\ U_t+1) + (1-1/q_j)$ and $b_{Fj} = 1/\beta q_j$

The informal sector can perfectly monitor workers, and hence informal-sector firms pay workers their opportunity cost:

$$w_I = a_I = (E_{t-1}U_t - \beta E_{t-1}\ U_{t+1}) + 1$$

The probability of being fired by firm j in the formal sector, x_{Fjt}, is

$$x_{Fjt} = \max\{(l_t^{Fj} - l_{t+1}{}^{Fj})/\ l_t^{Fj},\ 0\}$$

and the probability of being fired in the informal sector, x_{It}, is

$$x_{It} = \max\{(l_t^I - l_{t+1}{}^I)\ /\ l^I{}_t,\ 0\}$$

Given the firing probabilities, the total cost of hiring formal workers is

$$c(l_t^{Fj},\ l_{t-1}{}^{Fj}) = w_{Fjt}\ l_t^{Fj} = a_{Fj}\ l_t^{Fj} + b_{Fj}\max\{l_{t-1}{}^{Fj},\ l_t^{Fj}\}$$

and the total cost of hiring informal workers includes the cost of monitoring, s, and is

$$c(l_t^I) = (w_I + s)l_t^I = (a_I + s)l_t^I$$

Hiring and firing decisions

At the end of time t, formal firms choose their employment at time $t + 1$ to maximize their expected discounted profits:

$$V(l_t^{Fj},\ \theta_{t+1}) = \max\ \theta_{t+1}f(e_t l_{t+1}{}^{Fj}) - c(l_{t+1}{}^{Fj},\ l_t^{Fj}) + \beta E_t\ V(l_{t+1}{}^{Fj}, \theta_{t+2})$$

where $e_t = 1$. Thus, hiring and firing decisions are determined as follows:

Case 1 formal: If $\theta_{t+1}f'(l_t^{Fj}) + \beta E_t\ \partial V(l_t^{Fj}, \theta_{t+2})/\partial l_t^{Fj} > a_{Fj} + b_{Fj}\Leftrightarrow$ $l_{t+1}{}^{Fj} > l_t^{Fj}$, firm j hires new workers at time $t + 1$. In particular the firm hires if,

$$\theta_{t+1} > \bar{\theta}^{Fj} = \{a_{Fj} + b_{Fj} - \beta E_t \partial V(l_t^{Fj}, \theta_{t+2})/\partial l_t^{Fj}\}/f'(l_t^{Fj})$$

Case 2 formal: If $\theta_{t+1}f'(l_t^{Fj}) + \beta E_t \partial V(l_t^{Fj}), \theta_{t+2})/\partial l_t^{Fj} + C < a_{Fj} \Leftrightarrow l_{t+1}^{Fj} < l_t^{Fj}$, firm j fires workers at time $t+1$. In particular, firm j fires iff,

$$\theta_{t+1} < \theta^{Fj} = \{a_{Fj} - C - \beta E_t \partial V(l_t^{Fj}, \theta_{t+2})/\partial l_t^{Fj}\} / f'(l_t^{Fj})$$

Case 3 formal: If $a_{Fj} + b_{Fj} > \theta_{t+1}f'(l_t^{Fj}) + \beta E_t \partial V(l_t^{Fj}, \theta_{t+2}) /\partial l_t^{Fj} > a_{Fj} - C \Leftrightarrow l_{t+1}^{Fj} = l_t^{Fj}$, then at time $t+1$, firm j does not hire or fire. In particular, firm j does not hire or fire iff:

$$\bar{\theta}^{Fj} > \theta_{t+1} > \theta^{Fj}$$

and the probability that firm j remains inactive is $G(\bar{\theta}^{Fj}) - G(\theta^{Fj})$

Result 1: A reduction in firing costs decreases the probability of inaction of formal firms, $G(\bar{\theta}^{Fj}) - G(\theta^{Fj})$.

Informal firms' hiring and firing decisions can be determined similarly. The present discounted profits of informal firms are:

$$V(l_t^I, \theta_{t+1}) = \max \theta_{t+1} f(e_t l_{t+1}^I) - c(l_{t+1}^I, l_t^I) + \beta E_t V (l_{t+1}^I, \theta_{t+2})$$

where $e_t = 1$. Hiring and firing is determined as before by the following cases:

Case 1 informal: If $\theta_{t+1}f'(l_t^I) + \beta E_t \partial V(l_t^I, \theta_{t+2})/\partial l_t^I > a_I + s \Leftrightarrow l_{t+1}^I > l_t^I$, informal firms hire new workers at time $t + 1$. In particular, informal firms hire iff,

$$\theta_{t+1} > \bar{\theta}^I = \{ a_I + s - \beta E_t \partial V(l_t^I, \theta_{t+2})/\partial l_t^I \}/f'(l_t^I)$$

Case 2 informal: If $\theta_t + 1 f'(l_t^I) + \beta E_t \partial V(l_t^I, \theta_{t+2})/\partial l_t^I < a_I s \Leftrightarrow l_{t+1}^I < l_t^I$, informal firms lay off workers at time $t+1$. In particular, informal firms fire iff,

$$\theta_t + 1 < \theta^I = \{ a_I + s - \beta E_t \partial V(l_t^I, \theta_{t+2})/\partial l_t^I \}/f'(l_t^I)$$

Case 3 informal: If $a_I + s > \theta_{t+1}f'(l_t^I) + \beta E_t \partial V(l_t^I, \theta_{t+2}) / \partial l_t^I > a_I + s \Leftrightarrow l_{t+1}^I = l_t^I$. However, since the LHS and the the RHS of the inequality are the same, informal firms *always* adjust their employment in response to shocks.

Choice of sector

Each firm j can choose whether to produce in the formal or informal sector. Firms producing in the formal sector pay firing costs and efficiency wages. Firms in the informal sector do not comply with labour legislation, but pay a constant cost, s, to monitor workers. Since firms differ in terms of the increase in difficulty of firing shirkers, some firms find it more profitable to hire formally and others informally.

A firm j produces in the sector that maximizes its present discounted profits. The present discounted profits of formal firms depend on whether they are hiring or firing:

$$V^e(l_t^{Fj}, \theta_{t+1}) = \int_{\theta \in \theta(\text{hire})} V^{\text{hire}}(l_t^{Fj}, \theta_{t+1}) + \int_{\theta \in \theta(\text{inactive})} V^{\text{inactive}}(l_t^{Fj}, \theta_{t+1}) + \int_{\theta \in \theta(\text{fire})} V^{\text{fire}}(l_t^{Fj}, \theta_{t+1})$$

where,

$$V^{\text{hire}}(l_t^{Fj}, \theta_{t+1}) = V^{\text{inactive}}(l_t^{Fj}, \theta_{t+1}) = \max \{ \theta_{t+1} f(l_{t+1}^{Fj}) - (a_{Fj} + b_{Fj}) l_{t+1}^{Fj} + \beta E_t V^e(l_{t+1}^{Fj}, \theta_{t+2}) \}, \text{ and}$$
$$V^{\text{fire}}(l_t^{Fj}, \theta_{t+1}) = \max \{ \theta_{t+1} f(l_{t+1}^{Fj}) - a_{Fj} l_{t+1}^{Fj} + \beta E_t V^e(l_{t+1}^{Fj}, \theta_{t+2}) \}$$

The probability of catching a shirker for firm j that is just indifferent between producing in the formal or the informal sector is, q^{crit}, and is determined by the following condition:

$$\int_{\theta \in \theta(\text{hire})} V^{\text{hire}}(l_t^{Fj}, \theta_{t+1}) + \int_{\theta \in \theta(\text{inactive})} V^{\text{inactive}}(l_t^{Fj}, \theta_{t+1}) + \int_{\theta \in \theta(\text{fire})} V^{\text{fire}}(l_t^{Fj}, \theta_{t+1}) = V^e(l_t^I, \theta_{t+1})$$

where

$$V^e(l_t^I, \theta_{t+1}) = \int_{\theta \in \theta(\text{hire})} V^{\text{hire}}(l_t^{Fj}, \theta_{t+1}) + \int_{\theta \in \theta(\text{fire})} V^{\text{fire}}(l_t^{Fj}, \theta_{t+1}) \text{ and}$$
$$V^{\text{hire}}(l_t^{Fj}, \theta_{t+1}) = V^{\text{fire}}(l_t^{Fj}, \theta_{t+1}) = \max \{ \theta_{t+1} f(e_t l_{t+1}^I) - (a_I + s) l_{t-1}^I + \beta E_t V(l_{t+1}^I, \theta_{t+2}) \}$$

Result 2: Firms with $q_j \in [q^{crit}, \bar{q}]$ produce formally, while firms with $q_j \in [\underline{q}, q^{crit}]$ produce informally.

Figure 12.1 shows the expected present discounted profits of formal and informal firms as a function of an inverse measure of the difficulty of firing shirkers. The figure shows the cut-off value that makes firm j indifferent between producing formally and informally. Moreover, Result 3 shows how this cut-off value changes in response to changes in firing costs.

Result 3: A decrease in the firing costs, C, decreases the cut-off probability of catching a shirker, q^{crit}. As the cut-off probability decreases, the size of the formal sector increases and the average probability of inaction in the formal sector increases.

Result 3 is illustrated in Figure 12.2. The reduction in firing costs shifts the expected profits of formal firms. This shift increases the number of firms producing in the formal sector and decreases the number producing informally. The shift generates a compositional change that decreases the average probability of firing and hiring. The net effect of this compositional change is to reduce the average probability of inaction of formal firms, without changing the response of informal firms to demand shocks. The model shows that a reduction in firing costs increases firing and hiring and the exit rates into and out of unemployment. However, in the model, a reduction in firing costs induces a sectoral reallocation that reduces turnover in the formal sector. Thus, this model suggests that the impact of firing costs on turnover is likely to be smaller when this reduction also induces compositional changes.

4 Identification strategy

A grouping estimator

According to the theory above, the reduction in firing costs introduced by the Colombian Labour Market Reform of 1990 should have affected a firm's decisions to fire and hire and, thus, exit rates into and out of unemployment. To examine this, an exponential hazard model is used to estimate exit rates out of employment and out of unemployment:

$$h(s_{it} \mid X_{it}, \theta_{it}) = \exp \{ \beta X_{it} + \gamma \, \mathrm{reform}_{it} + \theta_{it} \}$$

where s_{it} is the employment or unemployment spell of person i in period t, X_{it} is a vector of observed characteristics of person i in period t and θ_{it} is a vector of unobservable factors affecting turnover behaviour of person i in period t. The unobservable factors may capture either

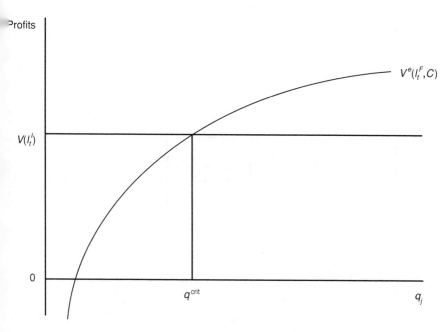

Figure 12.1   Critical value of the probability of catching a shirker

common aggregate shocks or unobservable heterogeneity across groups
of workers. Failing to account for both common shocks and unobservable heterogeneity would in general introduce bias. In order to control
for the presence of aggregate shocks, I exploit the cross-section variation between covered and uncovered workers. That is, the estimation
relies on comparing otherwise similar groups of workers affected by the
same aggregate shocks but affected differently by the labour-market
reform.

To estimate the effect of the reforms on turnover one must control
for (1) the presence of common aggregate shocks; (2) the correlation
between unobserved heterogeneity and firing costs; and (3) selection
into the covered and uncovered sectors.

Suppose workers can be categorized into two groups $g=\{F, I\}$ (that is,
formal and informal, or covered and uncovered), each sampled for at
least two periods. The following identifying assumptions allow controlling for (1) and (2):

Assumption A.1 $\theta_{it} = \theta_g + \theta_t$
Assumption A.2 $[\Delta h^{gt} \mid \theta_{it}]^2 \neq 0$

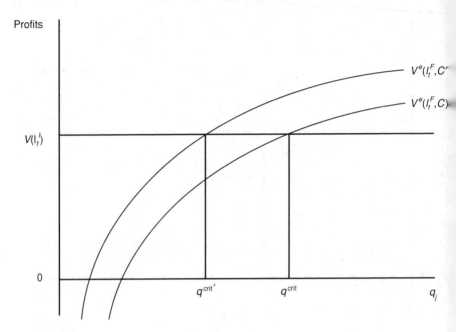

Figure 12.2 Effects of a change in firing costs on q^{crit}

where

$[\Delta h^{gt} \mid \theta_{it}] = h(s_{it} \mid X_{it}, g_i \times t, g_i, t) - h(s_{it} \mid X_{it}, g_i, t)$
and $h(s_{it} \mid X_{it}, g_i \times t, g_i, t) = h(s_{it} \mid X_{it}, g_i \times t, g_i, t, \theta_{it})$ and $h(s_{it} \mid X_{it}, g_i, t)$
$= h(s_{it} \mid X_{it}, g_i, t, \theta_{it})$

Assumption A.1 states that a group component and an additive time component can capture the unobservable factors. This assumption says that, given the observables, the difference in the average turnover between the two groups remains unchanged over time. Consequently, this assumption does not require the two groups to respond similarly to aggregate shocks, but rather for the response to be similar over time. The second assumption states that after controlling for unobservables, turnover must change differentially over time across groups. A labour-market reform between the two periods, which reduces firing-costs and affects the two groups differently, would guarantee identification of the firing-cost effect.

Considering the case with two groups and two time periods yields the following difference of differences estimator of the effect of firing costs on turnover:

$$\Delta h^{\text{formal} \times \text{post90}} = h(s_{it} \mid X_{it}, \text{formal}_i \times \text{post90}_t, \text{formal}_i, \text{post90}_t, \gamma_2 = \gamma_2^{\,\circ})$$
$$- h(s_{it} \mid X, \text{formal}_i, \text{post90}_t, \gamma_2 = 0)$$
$$= \exp\{\beta^\circ\, X_{it} + \gamma_0^{\,\circ}\text{formal}_i + \gamma_1^{\,\circ}\text{post90}_t + \gamma_2^{\,\circ}\,\text{formal}_i \times \text{post90}_t\} -$$
$$\exp\{\beta^\circ X_{it} + \gamma_0^{\,\circ}\text{formal}_i + \gamma_1^{\,\circ}\text{post90}_t\}$$

where β° and γ° are the estimates of the parameters of the model. Because the exponential hazard is a non-linear model, the estimated coefficient $\gamma2^\circ$ cannot be interpreted as a marginal effect. Instead, since the reform variable (formal$_i \times$ post90$_t$) is discrete, the marginal effect of the reduction in firing costs is estimated by predicting two hazards, one with the interaction term set equal to one and the other with the interaction term set equal to zero. The firing-cost effect on turnover is, then, estimated as the average difference in the two hazards over the sample of post-1990 workers in the formal sector. Moreover, with exponential hazards the sample counterpart of the firing cost effect can be obtained using the inverse of the firing cost effect on employment and unemployment spells:

$$\Delta \bar{h}^{gt} = \Delta[\bar{h}^{\text{post90}} - \bar{h}^{\text{pre90}}]^{\text{formal}} - \Delta[\bar{h}^{\text{post90}} - \bar{h}^{\text{pre90}}]^{\text{informal}}$$

where, $\bar{h}^{gt} = 1/\bar{s}^{gt}$ and $\Delta \bar{s}^{gt} = \Delta[\bar{s}^{\text{post90}} - \bar{s}^{\text{pre90}}]^{\text{formal}} - \Delta[\bar{s}^{\text{post90}} - \bar{s}^{\text{pre90}}]^{\text{informal}}$

Possible selection biases

A potential problem with the approach above is that it assumes that selection into the formal and informal sectors is constant over time, and selection effects can be fully accounted for by the group effect. Nonetheless, as shown by the model in section 3, changes in firing costs after reform are likely to induce sector reallocation. In particular, sector reallocation is likely to cause firms with higher adjustment costs to self-select into the formal sector – reducing average turnover. This means sectoral reallocation would introduce a downward bias in the firing-cost effect, and the grouping estimator considered above would provide a lower bound of the effects of firing costs on turnover.

The presence of selection effects that change over time would imply that unobservables are a more general function of time and group. To control for the possibility that unobservables may change over time across groups, the identifying assumptions above were modified:

Modified assumption A.1 $\theta_{it} = \theta_g + \theta_t + \theta_{gt}$
Modified assumption A.2 $[\Delta h^{gt} \mid \theta_{it}]^2 \neq 0$

where

$$[\Delta h^{gt} \mid \theta_{it}] = h(s_{it} \mid X_{it}, p(g_i) \times t, p(g_i), t) - h(s_{it} \mid X_{it}, p(g_i), t) = h(s_{it} \mid X_{it}, p(g_i) \times t, p(g_i), t, \theta_{it}) - h(s_{it} \mid X_{it}, p(g_i), t, \theta_{it})$$

and $p(g_i = \text{formal}_i) = \text{Prob} \ (g^* > 0) = \text{Prob} \ (\delta Z_{it} + \varepsilon > 0) = \Phi(\delta Z_{it})$ and Cov $(\theta_{it}, Z_{it}) = 0$

Modified assumption A.1 states that unobservables are a function of a group effect, a time effect, and a joint time-group effect. The time-group effect implies the presence of changes in the composition of groups over time. Thus, one can no longer use the approach above to capture the effect of firing costs on turnover, because the difference in the hazards would now capture both the direct effect of the reform from a reduction in firing costs as well as an indirect composition effect. Modified assumption A.2 states that turnover must vary differentially across groups over time, over and above any turnover variation induced by changes in the composition of the two groups. An extra 'reform' is required to control for the composition effect. This assumption requires the use of an exogenous source of variation that affects selection into the formal and informal sectors but that is independent of the unobservables. The estimator that imposes these assumptions is implemented, as before, by estimating the average difference in the hazards, but instrumenting for selection into the formal and informal sectors.

5 Empirical analysis

This section examines the impact of the 1990 Colombian Labour Market Reform on the hazard rates of formal workers out of employment and out of unemployment.

Data

The data are drawn from the NHS for June of 1988, 1992 and 1996 undertaken in seven Colombian metropolitan areas. The benefit of using the June NHS is that it includes special modules on informality that allow formal workers (covered by the reform) to be distinguished from informal workers (uncovered). As discussed in section 4, the possibility of separating workers into these two groups helps to control for common shocks that may have affected the turnover of all workers. The June waves contain information on whether a worker's employer pays social security taxes or not. This information provides a good proxy of formal and informal sector employment, as it indicates whether the employer complies with labour legislation.[10] The June data include information on whether the worker is permanent or temporary, as well as on gender, age, marital status, educational attainment, number of dependants, city and sector of employment.

Table 12.1 presents summary statistics of formal and informal workers, before and after the reform; columns 1 and 2 give the characteristics of formal workers, and columns 3 and 4 of informal workers. The two groups are similar both before and after the reform with regards to gender and age composition, marital status and household size. They differ, however, on educational composition. The formal sector has a greater share of workers with university education, and this difference increased slightly after the reform.

These summary statistics suggest that the raw differences in the turnover patterns of covered and uncovered workers may reflect, in

Table 12.1 Basic characteristics of formal and informal workers (according to affiliation to the social security system) before and after reform

Variable	Formal		Informal	
	Pre-reform	*Post-reform*	*Pre-reform*	*Post-reform*
Share of total employment (%)	44.84	51.05	55.16	48.95
% of men	68.69	64.95	69.60	67.56
% of married workers	69.79	73.38	68.10	72.17
Average no. of dependants	0.81	0.72	0.80	0.78
Average age (years)	35.52	35.87	36.01	36.54
% aged < 25 yrs.	15.37	12.36	22.90	19.19
% aged 25–54 yrs.	77.16	81.20	65.58	69.79
% aged > 55 yrs.	7.46	6.44	11.52	11.03
Average education (years)	8.97	9.74	6.09	6.67
% with 0–5 years education	29.46	22.35	56.24	49.17
% with 6–10 years education	27.52	25.00	27.45	29.26
% with high school degree	21.65	27.02	10.28	14.36
% with 12–15 years education	8.77	10.11	3.06	3.57
% with > 16 years education	12.59	15.51	2.97	3.64
% of permanent workforce	90.66	88.84	77.64	74.50

part, differential turnover behaviour btween the two groups due to differences in composition. For this reason, the use of formal hazard models in the analysis below, which allows for controlling of individual characteristics, will be crucial in identifying the effect of the labour-market reform. Moreover, Table 12.1 shows an increase in the share of formal workers after 1990, from 45 to 51 per cent, indicating that the reform could have induced changes in the composition of the two sectors suggesting the potential presence of selection biases.

Tenure and unemployment spells, before and after the reform

Average tenure

The framework above suggests that, if compositional changes were unimportant, the reform should have encouraged more firings and increased the hazard rate out of employment and reduced the average tenure of formal workers (covered by the reform) relative to informal workers (uncovered).[11]

Table 12.2 shows the average tenure of the covered and uncovered groups, before and after the 1990 Colombian Labour Market Reform. The first line corresponds to the average tenure prior to reform and the second after reform; the third line corresponds to the differences. The last line provides the sample difference of the differences estimate of the effect of the reform on tenure, $\Delta \bar{s}^{gt}$. As expected, average tenure of formal workers decreased relative to the average tenure of informal workers by 14.9 and 15.8 weeks after reform. Moreover, the sample difference of differences estimates of the effect of the reform on the hazards out of employment indicate that this increased between 7.2 and 7.5 per cent for formal workers relative to informal workers.

Table 12.2 Sample difference of differences estimates of the effect of the reform on average tenure

Period	Definition 1*		Definition 2**	
	Formal	Informal	Formal	Informal
Pre-reform	5.60	4.52	4.82	4.28
Post-reform	5.31	4.54	4.55	4.34
Differences	−0.29	0.02	−0.27	0.06
Differences-in-difference	−0.31 years (= −3.72 months = −14.88 weeks)		−0.33 years (= −3.96 months = −15.84 weeks)	

Unemployment duration

The theory above also suggests that if compositional changes were unimportant, the reform should have encouraged more hirings, increased the hazard rate out of unemployment and reduced average unemployment spells of formal workers (covered by the reform) relative to informal workers (uncovered).[12] Table 12.3 presents the sample difference of differences estimates for unemployment spells, $\Delta \bar{s}^{gt}$.[13] The results show that the average unemployment spell of workers whose spell ended with a formal-sector job decreased between 3.08 and 4.12 weeks relative to those whose unemployment spell ended in an informal-sector job. In addition, the sample estimates of the effect of reform on the hazard rate out of unemployment increased between 7.4 per cent and 10.7 per cent for formal workers relative to informal workers.

Hazard models

As it is possible that tenure and unemployment spells, as well as hazard rates, changed after the reform resulting from changes in the characteristics of workers and firms, we now consider formal duration models. As described earlier in this section, the following exponential hazard model is considered:

$$h(s_{it} \mid X_{it}, \theta_{it}) = \exp \{\beta X_{it} + \gamma_0 \, \text{formal}_i + \gamma_1 \, \text{post90}_t + \gamma_2 \, \text{formal}_i \times \text{post90}_t\}$$

Table 12.3   Sample difference of differences estimates of the effect of the reform on average unemployment duration

Period	Definition 1*		Definition 2**	
	Formal	Informal	Formal	Informal
Pre-reform	7.33	8.73	7.35	8.63
Post-reform	7.60	9.77	7.38	9.72
Differences	0.27	1.04	0.03	1.09
Differences-in-difference	−0.77 months		−1.03 months	
	(= −3.08 weeks)		(= −4.12 weeks)	

Notes: *Definition 1: formal workers are defined as those whose employer pays social security taxes; informal workers are defined as those whose employer does not pay social security contributions. **Definition 2: this is the standard definition of informality. Formal workers are defined as wage-earners employed by firms with more than 10 employees; informal workers are wage-earners employed by firms with less than 10 employees, family workers, domestic workers and self-employed workers. In Colombia, the last three categories of informal workers are exempt from severance-pay legislation.

where X_{it} is a $1 \times k$ vector of regressors, and β is a $k \times 1$ vector of parameters. In the specifications considered below, the vector X_{it} includes: age, education, sex, marital status, number of dependants, the city where the person lives, and industry of employment. These variables help to control for observable differences between formal and informal workers that affect their turnover behaviour.

The specification also includes the following variables to estimate the effect of job-security legislation on the exit rates out of employment and out of unemployment. A variable is included that takes the value of 1 if worker i is formal (covered by the legislation), and zero if worker i is informal (uncovered). This variable controls for constant differences between these two groups. One would expect γ_0 to be negative since the dismissal of formal workers is more costly, both before and after reform. In addition, the specification includes a variable post90 that takes the value of 1 for post-1990 observations and the value of zero for pre-1990 observations. The coefficient on the post90 dummy controls for non-treatment shocks affecting the turnover behaviour of all workers after 1990.

More importantly, an interaction term of the post90 and the formal variables is included in the estimation. A test of the impact of the labour-market reform is a test that the coefficient on the interaction term, γ_2, is different from zero. This test considers whether workers covered by the legislation changed their turnover behaviour relative to uncovered workers after 1990. In particular, if one expects the reduction in firing costs to have increased turnover, then one would expect γ_2 to be positive. However, as the exponential hazard is a non-linear function, the coefficient γ_2 cannot be interpreted as the marginal effect of reform. Instead, the marginal effect of reform is the average of the difference between the hazard with the interaction variable set equal to 1, and the hazard with the interaction set equal to zero, $\Delta h^{formal \times post90}$, over the sample of workers affected.

The results of the estimation of the exit hazard rates out of employment (not shown here), show that, after controlling for observables, the coefficient on the interaction term falls to 0.0582 and continues to be significant at the 1 per cent significance level. Estimating the marginal effect indicates that the reduction in firing costs introduced by the reform increased the exit rates out of employment for formal workers by 0.85 per cent relative to informal workers.[14] To control for the possibility that formal-sector jobs were affected more by shocks after reform, because these jobs were in industries receiving different shocks after 1990, we included industry dummies as additional covariates in the estimation. The results do not change substantially and the predicted turnover response for the covered group increases to 0.9 per cent and continues to be significant at the 1 per cent level.[15] We also examined whether it is the extension in the use of temporary contracts or the reduction in severance payments that accounts for increased turnover. The results show that while the hazard out of employment increased by 1.2 per cent for temporary formal workers relative to informal workers, the hazards out of employment also increased by 0.8 per cent for permanent formal workers relative to informal workers.[16] We considered an alternative definition of informality to check for the robustness of the results. This specification used the standard definition of informality described above, and the results are similar. The hazard out of employment increased by 1.0 per cent for formal workers relative to informal workers, and the effect is significant at the 1 per cent level. Finally, to control for time-variant groups, we used the estimator proposed in section 3, in which the formal variable is instrumented with firm size and the skill requirement of the industry of employment. The marginal effect increases to 1.1 per cent after controlling for selection bias and it remains significant.

Further study of the exponential hazards out of unemployment showed that the exit hazard out of unemployment increased for formal workers relative to informal workers after reform when no controls are included. The coefficient on the interaction term increases after controlling for observables. We found that the escape rate out of unemployment increased for both temporary and permanent workers covered by the reform, but the hazard out of unemployment was higher for those who took permanent jobs. The predicted response for the covered group increased to 1.7 per cent when using alternative groups. Finally, the hazards out of unemployment increased to 1.6 per cent after controlling for selection bias.

6 Conclusion

The Colombian Labour Market Reform of 1990 provides an interesting quasi-experiment to analyse the effects of a reduction in firing costs. This study exploited the temporal change in the 1990 Colombian labour legislation, together with the variability in coverage between formal and informal-sector workers, to identify the effects of firing costs on turnover. Using Colombian micro data, we found that after controlling for changes in composition the hazard rate out of employment increased 1.1 per cent and the hazard rate out of unemployment increased 1.6 per cent for formal workers relative to informal workers.

The steady-state conditions of the model, together with these estimates, indicate that the reform caused a decrease in the unemployment rate of a third of a percentage point, or a quarter of the total drop in unemployment between the late 1980s and mid-1990s.[17] Reform contributed to reducing unemployment both because it generated greater flows out of than into unemployment, and because it induced a reallocation towards the formal sector. The importance of this reallocation effect indicates that welfare considerations of labour market reform should not only recognize the efficiency gains from greater mobility and the benefits from lower unemployment that reform might induce, but also the welfare gains of compositional change towards better jobs.

Notes

1   An alternative approach would consist of choosing groups that are affected differently by the reform, but whose composition cannot change in response to the reform. This is the ingenious approach taken in Blundell, Duncan and Meghir (1998). However, there are no natural groups that fulfill these conditions in the context considered here.

2   Moreover, the reform introduced other changes in the legislation that also contributed to lowering firing costs. First, while prior to 1990 the legislation allowed the use of fixed-term contracts for a minimum duration of a year, the reform extended the use of fixed-term contracts for less than a year. Second, the 1990 reform widened the legal definition of 'just-cause' dismissals to include economic conditions. Third, while the reform increased the cost of 'unjustly' dismissing workers with more than ten years of tenure, it also eliminated the ability for these workers to sue for backpay and reinstatement.

3   Prior to the 1990 Labour Market Reform, workers could withdraw money out of their severance payment before job break-up to use for investments in education and housing Lora and Henao (1995).

4   This can be seen in a simple two-period model, where firms maximize their expected present discounted profits:

$$f(l_1) - wl_1 + E\{ \theta f(l_2) - wl_2 - C \max (l_1 - l_2, 0)\}$$

and where θ is a demand shock in the second period, which is distributed uniformly between $[\theta, \bar{\theta}]$. Firms hire if $\theta f'(l_1) > w$, they fire if $w > \theta f'(l_1) + C$, and thus they do not adjust their employment if the demand shock $\theta \in [\theta_{min}, \theta_{max}]$, where $\theta_{min} \equiv (w - C)/f'(l_1)$ and $\theta_{max} \equiv w/f'(l_1)$. Hence, it is easy to show that the probability of remaining inactive, $G(\theta_{max}) - G(\theta_{min})$, increases as firing costs increase.

5 Previous studies have estimated that the additional cost from paying severance based on the salary at the time of separation, together with the real cost of withdrawals to the employers, implied an additional 35 per cent of the average cost of severance payments in the manufacturing sector before 1990 (Ocampo, 1987). In the context of the two-period model change implied an increase in both θ_{max} and θ_{min}, but a greater increase in θ_{min}, since $\theta_{max} \equiv 1.093*w/f'(l_1)$ and $\theta_{min} \equiv [1.093*w - (C-SP)]/f'(l_1)$ after the reform. Thus, this change should had decreased the corridor of inaction, $G(\theta_{max}) - G(\theta_{min})$.

6 The NHS provides information about whether one's employer pays social security contributions. This information is a good proxy of formality, as it provides an indication of whether the employer complies or not with labour legislation.

7 Formal firms may also prefer paying efficiency wages rather than monitoring costs if they are subject to minimum wage legislation.

8 The cost of purchasing this technology for formal sector firms is $s = \infty$.

9 For simplicity, it is assumed that workers are allocated randomly to the formal and informal sectors.

10 Below, I also use the standard definition of informality to separate the sample into covered and uncovered groups and to check the robustness of the results to the definition of informality being used. According to this definition, formal workers are wage-earners employed in firms with more than ten employees, and informal workers are wage-earners employed in firms with less than ten employees, family workers, domestic workers and self-employed workers (except for professionals). The benefit from using this definition is that the last three categories of informal workers (family, domestic and self-employed workers) are exempt from severance payments.

11 In addition, the reform should have increased hirings, the hazard out of unemployment and the fraction of workers with short tenures (those just hired) and, thus, should have decreased the average tenure among formal workers after the reform.

12 As indicated above, the reform should have also increased the hazard out of employment, thus, increasing the fraction of unemployed workers with short spells (those just fired) and decreasing the average unemployment spells among unemployed formal workers after the reform.

13 Unemployed workers are defined as formal if the job subsequent to their spell was in the formal sector and as informal if the job subsequent to their spell was in the informal sector.

14 Exit hazards out of employment are likely to have increased after the reform both because of increased layoffs and quits. Quits are likely to increase after the reform because of the increased availability of alternative job opportunities. Unfortunately, however, the data do not allow one to distinguish between layoff and quit hazard rates.

15 In addition, another specification was estimated which included an interaction of the formal × post90 interaction with the various industry dummies and the results did not change substantially. Moreover, while one would have expected tradable industries to have been affected differently by shocks after 1990 due to trade liberalization, this is not confirmed by the data.

16 The possibility of hiring temporary workers would be expected to generate a dual labour market within the firm, in which temporary workers are used as a margin of adjustment to demand fluctuations and allow firms to insulate permanent workers, Saint Paul (1996). Thus, if the extension in the use of temporary contracts allowed by the reform was alone responsible for the increased turnover in the formal sector, then we would have expected a decrease in the hazards of formal permanent workers and not an increase as it was observed.

17 The steady-state conditions of the model with separate formal and informal markets imply that the flows into unemployment must equal the flows out of unemployment in each sector, that is $\cap_{\forall j \in s} X_{sj} e_s = \cap_{\forall j \in es} a_{sj} U_s$ and $e_s + u_s = 1$ for $s = F,I$, where x_{sj} is the hazard out of employment and a_{sj} is the hazard out of unemployment of firm j in sector s. The aggregate unemployment rate is $u = p_F \cdot u_F + (1-p_F)^* u_I$, where p_F is the proportion of formal workers.

References

Anderson, P. (1993) 'Linear Adjustment Costs and Seasonal Labour Demand: Evidence from Retail Trade Firms', *Quarterly Journal of Economics*, vol. 108, no. 4, pp. 1015–42.

Bertola, G. (1990) 'Job Security, Employment, and Wages', *European Economic Review*, vol. 54, no. 4, pp. 851–79.

Blundell, R., A. Duncan and C. Meghir (1998) 'Estimating Labour Supply Responses using Tax Reforms', *Econometrica*, vol. 56, no. 4, pp. 827–61.

Dertouzos, J. and L. Karoly (1993) 'Employment Effects of Worker Protection: Evidence from the U.S.', in C. Buechtermann (ed.), *Employment Security and Labour Market Behaviour* (Ithaca, NY: ILR Press).

Grubb, D. and W. Wells (1993) 'Employment Regulations and Pattern of Work in EC Countries', *OECD Economic Studies*, vol. 21, pp. 7–39.

Hopenhayn, H. and R. Rogerson (1993) 'Job Turnover and Policy Evaluation: A General Equilibrium Analysis', *Journal of Political Economy*, vol. 101, no. 5, pp. 915–38.

Krueger, A. (1991) 'The Evolution of Unjust Dismissal Legislation in the U.S.', *Industrial and Labour Relations Review*, pp. 644–60.

Kugler, A. D. (1999) 'The Impact of Firing Costs on Turnover and Unemployment. Evidence from the Colombian Labour Market', *Reform and International Tax and Public Finance Journal*, vol. 6, no. 3, pp. 389–410.

Lazear, E. (1990) 'Job Security Provisions and Employment', *Quarterly Journal of Economics*, vol. 105, no. 3, pp. 699–726.

Lora, E. and M. L. Henao (1995) 'Efectos Económicos y Sociales de la Legislación Laboral' (The Economic and Social Effects of Labour Legislation), *Coyuntura Social*, vol. 13, pp. 47–68.

Ocampo, J. A. (1987) 'El Régimen Prestacional del Sector Privado' (Private Sector Loan System), in J. A. Ocampo and M. Ramírez (eds), *El Problema Laboral Colombiano* (Colombian Labour Problems) (Bogotá: Departamento Nacional de Planeación).

OECD (1990) *Employment Outlook* (Paris: OECD Publications).

Saint-Paul, G. (1996) *Dual Labour Markets: A Macroeconomic Perspective* (Cambridge, MA: MIT Press).

13
Structural Reform and the Distributional Effects of Price Changes in Argentina 1988–98

Fernando H. Navajas*

1 Introduction

This chapter considers the distribution effects of price changes in Argentina following a decade of structural reform. During the 1990s, Argentina introduced price stabilization policies, changed its tax and expenditure systems, privatized public services and industries, eliminated international trade barriers through sharp reductions in tariffs, and, finally, deregulated many goods and services markets.

There have been few attempts at measuring the economy-wide distribution impact of these economic reforms; public opinion in Argentina has been influenced by too much speculation and too little measurement. Generally, structural reform was considered to increase efficiency but with negative effects on distribution. Part of this bias is explained by a lack of data; for example, there was a gap of over ten years between the last two household expenditure surveys (HESs). We used the most recent HES to measure change in the distribution of expenditure, and to evaluate the welfare effects of price changes over the past decade. We assessed the distributional impact of economic and structural reform.

Little has been published on the macroeconomic impact on distribution of incomes. The effects of privatization have traditionally been assessed using partial equilibrium models, where the key trade-off is between allocative and productive efficiency, with economy-wide distribution impact being of a second order of magnitude, as in Vickers and Yarrow (1988). Other papers on privatization, such as Boycko, Schleifer and Vishny (1996) also considered efficiency rather than distribution.

* I am grateful to E. Bour and L. Gasparini for useful comments, to J. Pantano for his assistance and to R. Martinez for the detailed price data-set.

Distribution aspects were not neglected within that framework, but the analysis focused on evaluating alternative regulatory regimes.

On the empirical side, for example, a variant of the applied welfare analysis of privatization in a partial equilibrium context concerned surplus accounting for various groups, such as consumers, workers, suppliers, government or shareholders. However this type of analysis is restricted to firms or sectors. Other empirical analyses have used a general equilibrium model to evaluate the distributive consequences of privatization. Chisari, Estache and Romero (1997), in the only general equilibrium model applied to Argentina on this topic, computed the aggregate effects of the privatization of network utilities (water and sanitation, electricity, natural gas and telecommunications) on the personal distribution of income. This was a simulation exercise of the consequences of efficiency gains under different assumptions associated with the 'effectiveness' of post-privatization regulation. The effects arose mainly through changes in the prices and quantities of privatized goods and services.[1] Their results suggested a gain to society equivalent to 41 per cent of household income, with a further 16 per cent achievable through effective regulation. When these gains were measured by household quintile (on a per capita income basis) the gains (as a percentage of household income for each quintile) rose from 29 per cent (an additional 20 per cent with effective regulation) for the first quintile to 59 per cent (with an additional 17 per cent with effective regulation) for the fifth. The gains were greater, absolutely and in percentage terms, for the higher income groups, but effective regulation was more beneficial to the lower-income households.

The other major reform undertaken by Argentina during the 1990s was the opening up of the economy. This implied important changes in relative prices. In fact, the major deregulation brought about by trade reform had different effects from privatization. While the benefits of the latter depended on the effectiveness of the regulatory regime to control or mitigate monopoly power until such time as competition became effective, the former brought immediate potential welfare improvements. Its distributional impact, as with most structural reform, depended on changes in the price and quantity of goods and services, as well as the primary factors of production. Other effects – such as the changes in the distribution of assets and the impact on public sector finance – may also be important in the evaluation of privatization and deregulation in a developing economy such as Argentina.

We adopted a simple methodology to quantify one aspect of the distributional impact of structural reform, focusing on the distribution of household consumption and evaluating the distribution impact of relative price changes. This approach derives from the marginal tax-reform theory of Feldstein (1972), Guesnerie (1977), Amhad and Stern (1984), as proposed and implemented by Newbery (1995). It relies on the concept of the 'distributional characteristics of goods', also discussed in Navajas and Porto (1994), which can be measured from household expenditure data. The main advantage of using this approach is that it measures the impact of the relative prices of goods and services, together with an evaluation of changes in the distribution of consumption. The major drawback in the Argentine case is the lack of adequate data. In Argentina only two HESs were available, one from the mid-1980s, a useful pre-reform benchmark, and the more complete survey carried out in 1996/7.

Changes in consumer prices were only one consequence of structural reform, but Chisari, Estache and Romero (1997) found evidence that in Argentina other effects (changes in employment and wages, for instance) were less relevant. Besides, when evaluating price changes there were other factors, such as the quality of goods or services, that had welfare consequences even though their (differential) distributive effects were, perhaps, less significant. We contend that privatization in an economy such as Argentina's, where infrastructure for many services was limited, the question of access had important distributive consequences. For this reason we have provided some evidence on the improvement in access to, and coverage of, services after privatization.

The chapter is organized as follows. In section 2 we discuss our approach, and present the basic formulae. Section 3 measures the distributional characteristics of goods and provides measures for consumption inequality using the recent HES. These results are compared with data provided and estimated by Newbery (1995) for Hungary and Britain; we then compared the changes between HES 1985/6 and 1996/7. Section 4 measures the welfare impact of relative price changes, describing changes for different types of goods (from non-durables to public services) in order to ascertain the pattern of relative price changes. We performed sensitivity tests before presenting our main findings on the distributive changes of relative prices and the role of structural reforms. Section 5 evaluates the changes in access or coverage of infrastructure services and extends the concept of distribution characteristics. Finally, section 6 summarizes the conclusions and results.

2 Welfare impact of relative price changes

We followed the methodology of welfare economics to evaluate aggregate welfare from final outcomes on individual utility assuming some aggregation (social-welfare) function. Each agent h ($h = 1, \ldots, H$) has an indirect utility function $V^h = V^h(q, m^h)$ that depends on a vector of n consumer prices q, of goods and services, and on the monetary income (m^h, which includes all forms of income including government transfers). Social welfare is represented by an aggregation of individual utilities, that is, $W = W(V^1, \ldots, V^H)$. Usual assumptions behind this framework are for example: a market clearing economy (no rationing in labour markets for instance), and the evaluation is at the level of consumer prices. This basic framework is simple, not because other complexities could not be introduced, but rather because these might hinder progress towards measurement.

Suppose a reform gives rise to a change in price q_i that in turn has a welfare impact given by the partial derivative:

$$\partial W/\partial q_i = \sum_h (\partial W/\partial V_h).(\partial V_h/\partial q_i) = -\sum_h \beta^h . x_i^h \qquad (1)$$

where $\beta = (\partial W/\partial V^h).(\partial V^h/\partial m^h)$ is the marginal social utility of income of h; x_i^h is the quantity of good i consumed by agent h, and Roy's identity has been used.

Defining the distributional caracteristic of good i as:

$$d_i = \sum_h (\beta^h/\bar{\beta}) . (x_i^h/X_i) \qquad (2)$$

where $X_i = \sum_h x_i^h$ is total consumption of i and $\bar{\beta} = \sum_h \beta^h/H$ is the mean of the β, then the impact of q_i change can be stated as:

$$\partial W/\partial q_i = -\bar{\beta} . d_i . X_i \qquad (3)$$

The concept of the 'distributional characteristics of a good', developed by Feldstein (1972) and others, has been largely used in the theory of optimal indirect taxation. It can be seen as the socially weighted sum of the participation of agent h in the total consumption of good i, where social weights depend on the marginal social utility of income (in turn affected by the distributive weights in the social-welfare function).

This approach overcomes difficulties with evaluations based on an econometric estimation of demand systems. Given the data limitations, no such system of estimation was available for Argentina. On the other hand, this approach requires some auxiliary assumptions on the form of the social welfare and individual utility functions for the estimation of parameters β^h. The most simple parametrization adopted in the literature (Newbery, 1995; Navajas and Porto, 1990, 1994; Porto and Gasparini, 1992, for examples relating to Argentina) assumed that the social welfare function was additive in utility levels U, that is $W = \Sigma U^h/H$ and that individual agents have iso-elastic utilities defined on consumption or real expenditure of the type $U^h \equiv (g^h)^{1 -}$ $^v/(1 - v)$ for $v \neq 1$ and $U^h \equiv \log g^h$ for $v = 1$, where g^h is household expenditure (per equivalent adult) and v is interpreted as a coefficient of inequality aversion. Under these assumptions, the social marginal utility of income of h can be computed by the expression $\beta^h = (g^h)^{-v}$, that is, the inverse of expenditure per equivalent adult raised to the coefficient v. Under this specification, social welfare can be approximated by the (socially) weighted sum of expenditures per equivalent adult.[2]

Newbery (1995) developed the above to obtain a simple formula to evaluate the distributional impact of the relative price changes of goods, assuming that real income remains constant. This is set out below for illustrative purposes, with minor adaptations to his notation, and extending the formula to the limit case of maximum inequality aversion ($v \to \infty$). We have also extended the presentation to include a simple and intuitive graphical representation of the welfare impact of the change in relative prices.

Let us assume all agents face the same price for goods and services, and define a consumer price index for time t as $P_t = \Sigma \alpha_i . q_{it}$, resulting from the weighted sum of prices of the n existing goods (with the weights given by budget shares obtained from a HES in a base period 0) dividing each of the n prices by this index gives a vector of relative prices, relative to the general price level $\pi_t = (\pi_{1t}, \ldots, \pi_{nt})$. Due to the condition of zero degree homogeneity (in prices and incomes) of the indirect utility function, we get $V^h = V^h (q_t, m_t^h) = V^h(\pi_t, y_t^h)$ where $y_t^h = m_t^h/P_t$. In the following, it is assumed that the real income of each agent y^h is constant.

Assuming a small change in relative prices, the change in welfare can be approximated[3] using equation (3) but defined for the transformation of the utility function:

$$\Delta W \approx \sum_i \sum_h (\partial W/\partial V^h) . (\partial V^h/\partial \pi_i) . \Delta \pi_i = -\Sigma_i \Sigma_h \beta^h . x_i^h . \Delta \pi_i = -\bar{\beta}\Sigma_i d_i . X_i . \Delta \pi_i \quad (4)$$

If prices in the base period are all normalized to 1, then $P_0 = 1$ with all $\pi_{i0} = 1$ and given that social welfare can be approximated by the weighted (by β^h) sum of expenditure per equivalent adult g^h,[4] it follows from expression (4) that the percentage change in welfare can be approximated by:[5]

$$\Delta W / W \approx \frac{-\bar{\beta} \sum_j d_i \cdot \alpha_i \cdot (\sum_j \pi_{j0} \cdot X_{j0}) \cdot \Delta \pi_i}{\sum_h \beta^h \sum_i \pi_{i0} \cdot x_{i0}^h} = -\frac{\sum_i d_i \cdot \alpha_i \cdot \Delta \pi_i}{\sum_i d_i \alpha_i} \tag{5}$$

The limiting case of maximum consumption inequality aversion ($v \to \infty$) corresponds to the case where only the utility of the agent with the lower consumption or expenditure matters. If this agent is denoted by the supra-index 1, then we get $\beta^h/\beta^1 = (g^1/g^h)^v$ for all $h \neq 1$ tending to zero (given that $g^1 < g^h$). In this case, it can easily be shown that normalizing the distributional characteristic in expression (2) by β^1 (and taking this equal to 1, without loss of generality) instead of the average β, we get t, the distributional characteristic of a good given by the share of agent 1 in the total consumption of the good (cf. Navajas and Porto, 1994). We define it as $\theta_i^1 = x_i^1/X_i$. Expression (5) can then be approximated by:

$$(\Delta W / W)_{v \to \infty} = -\frac{\sum_i \theta_i^1 \cdot \alpha_i \cdot \Delta \pi_i}{\sum_i \theta_i^1 \cdot \alpha_i} \tag{5'}$$

A simple illustration of the welfare impact of relative price changes is shown below assuming that the relative price for any to goods, denoted by k and l, change in the opposite direction, with all the other relative prices and the general price level remaining constant. From the definition of the index $P_t = \sum \alpha_i . q_{it}$ and dividing each side by P_t we get:

$$1 = \alpha_k \cdot \pi_k + \alpha_l \cdot \pi_l + \sum_{i \neq k, l} \alpha_i \pi_i \tag{6}$$

Variations in the relative prices of goods k and l satisfy this condition giving rise to variations such that:

$$(\partial \pi_k / \partial \pi_l)_{\bar{P}} = -\alpha_l / \alpha_k \tag{7}$$

On the other hand, from expression (5) and in the case that only k and l change, we get:

$$\Delta W / W = \frac{d_k \cdot \alpha_k}{\sum_i d_i \cdot \alpha_i} \cdot \Delta \pi_k + \frac{d_l \cdot \alpha_l}{\sum_i d_i \cdot \alpha_i} \cdot \Delta \pi_l \tag{8}$$

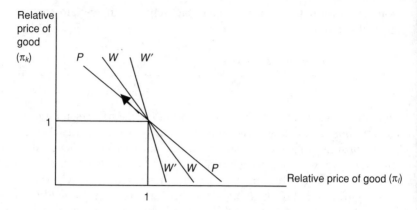

Figure 13.1 Welfare changes following relative price changes

From this expression, it follows that changes in relative prices of k and l that keep welfare constant are such that (assuming infinitesimal changes):

$$(\partial \pi_k / \partial \pi_l)_{\Delta W / W = 0} = -\frac{d_l \cdot \alpha_l}{d_k \cdot \alpha_k} \tag{9}$$

Figure 13.1 above shows the direction of the relative price changes that can give rise to increases or decreases in welfare. The line segment PP represents changes in relative prices that satisfy expression (6), while the line segment WW represents changes that keep welfare constant. Points above and to the right of line WW show a decrease in welfare while points below and to the left show an increase. If the distributional characteristic of good l is greater than that of the good k, then the slope of WW (given by expression (9)) is greater in absolute terms than the slope of PP (given by expression (7)), as shown in Figure 13.1. While the slope of PP is given by the ratio of shares α (relative shares in the basket that defines the price index), the slope of WW (relative to the slope of PP) is determined by the ratio of distributional characteristics and therefore by the degree of inequality aversion (v). Line WW rotates clockwise for greater values of parameter v. In the extreme case that $v \to \infty$, line $W'W'$ has a slope relative to PP that depends on the ratio of consumption shares of the 'poor', θ_i^l.

Changes in relative prices that satisfy condition (6) are movements along PP. Thus a reduction of π_l and a corresponding increase in π_k, as indicated in Figure 13.1 by the arrow, improves welfare. The magnitude of the welfare gain depends on the position of *WW* which in turn depends on the distributional characteristics and, by extension, on the distributive weights or the degree of inequality aversion. In the case illustrated in Figure 13.1, and given the change of relative prices denoted by the arrow, the greater the aversion to consumption inequality in social judgements the greater the welfare gain from the change in relative prices. This simple representation seems to fit intuitively as an explanation of the direction of relative price changes in Argentina in the last decade and of the welfare gains reported in section 4. Relative prices of goods with (relatively) higher and lower distributional characteristics showed decreases and inceases, respectively. The higher the weights for lower consumption households, the greater the welfare gain of the observed pattern of relative price changes. Thus, given the pattern of changes, the effects are as much pro-poor as possible.

3 The distribution of consumption in Argentina 1985/6–1996/7

Distributional characteristics and consumption inequality measures for 1996/97: household data

The 1996/7 HES for the metropolitan region (INDEC, 1999) allowed us to work at household level and to compute the distributional characteristics of goods and consumption inequality measures with micro data. In line with Newbery (1995) we examined the distributional characteristics of 92 goods based on a sample of 4,907 households. We were then able to compare performance across countries and periods, such as those performed by Newbery for Hungary pre and post-reform, and for the UK. Figure 13.2 illustrates this. The y-axis show the distributional characteristics for each good ordered (decreasingly) for the case where the inequality aversion parameter is unity ($v = 1$), while the x-axis shows cumulative aggregate expenditure. Lines for lower ($v = 0.5$) and higher ($v = 2$) inequality aversion parameters are included in the Figure.[4] The steeper the slope of the distributional characteristic line (for a given v) the more unequal the distribution of consumption for a given year.

The distributional characteristics line for Argentina 1996/97 shows clear inequality of consumption. Comparing Figure 13.2 with Newbery's for Hungary (1987–91) and the UK (1991), it is clear that

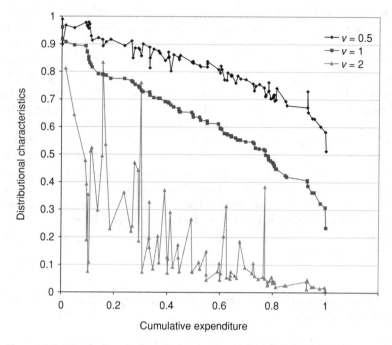

Figure 13.2 Distributional characteristics of goods from HES 1996/7

Argentina has a more unequal distribution of consumption, as the distributional characteristic line is steeper.[5] Another feature of the Argentine data is the sensitivity of the distributional characteristic line to changes in the degree of inequality aversion (with some goods jumping in rank as v increased from 1 to 2). Table 13.1 illustrates this for different inequality measures of consumption or expenditure per equivalent adult and the Atkinson Index (for $v = 0.5$, 1 and 2). We also included Gini coefficients of income distribution as reported by other studies, showing, as expected, that income inequality is more pronounced than consumption inequality.[6]

The Atkinson Index is obtained from an iso-elastic social welfare function similar to the (reduced-form) one used for computing distributive weights β^h that enter into the estimation of distributional characteristics. In notation, the Atkinson Index is written as follows (see also Champernowne and Cowell, 1998, chapter 4) where coefficient w_h is the weight of 'agent' h in the total number of agents:

$$A = 1 - [\sum_h w_h \cdot \left(\frac{g^h}{\overline{g}}\right)^{1-v}]^{\frac{1}{1-v}} \quad \text{for } v \neq 1$$

$$= 1 - \exp\left\{\frac{1}{n}\sum_h \log\left(\frac{g^h}{\overline{g}}\right)\right\} \quad \text{for } v = 1 \qquad (10)$$

Table 13.1 confirms Argentina's greater consumption inequality. For example, using the Atkinson index with $v = 1$, while social welfare in the UK in 1991 was calculated at 82 per cent (1 − 0.18), the hypothetical value for Argentina was 71 per cent (1 − 0.29) in 1996/7. In Hungary in 1991 the value was 92 per cent (1 − 0.08).

Distributional characteristics and consumption inequality measures: 1985/6 and 1996/7

An analysis of changes in the distribution of consumption across years could in principle be obtained by observing changes in the distributional characteristic line and Table 13.1. While this exercise required panel information not available for Argentina, we have, nevertheless, attempted to compare the distributional characteristics and inequality measures using both HESs.

The earlier HES, INDEC (1988), covered the Metropolitan Region of Buenos Aires from mid-1985 to mid-1986, and gave a quintile grouping by income per capita for 47 groups of goods and services. Unfortunately, the original data were no longer available. We therefore regrouped the (micro) 1996/7 HES data to conform to the published information in the 1985/6 HES. This gave a classification of expenditure per quintile of income (ordered by per capita income) for 46 goods and services. Although this was less than half the number of goods

Table 13.1 Consumption inequality measures

	Argentina 1996/97	UK[1] 1991	Hungary[1] 1991
Gini	0.451	0.346	0.229
Atkinson ($v = 0.5$)	0.154	0.097	0.042
Atkinson ($v = 1$)	0.289	0.181	0.081
Atkinson ($v = 2$)	0.562	0.323	0.151
Gini Income	0.548[2]	0.260[3]	0.246[3]

Sources: INDEC (1999) and [1] Newbery (1995); [2] Gasparini (1998); [3] Deninger and Squire (1996)

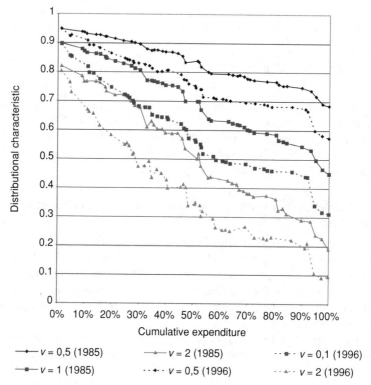

Figure 13.3 Comparison of distributional characteristics for 46 goods

compared in the previous section,[7] it allowed us to estimate the distributional characteristics of these 46 goods and compare the two HESs.

The results are illustrated in Figure 13.3, showing both HES distributional characteristics lines for different values of the coefficient v. It will be seen that the HES 1996/7 lines are below the HES 1985/6 lines, and the 'fall' in the lines is sensitive to the coefficient v. Thus, the comparison between both HESs shows a distinct increase in consumption inequality during the decade. Table 13.2 shows the inequality measures computed from the available data. The Gini coefficient moves from 0.33 to 0.38, while the Atkinson index rises from 0.17 to 0.23 for the case that $v = 1$. Further, the loss of information from working with more aggregated data lowers the values of inequality measures. This is observed not only for the Gini coefficient (0.38 against 0.45 from

Table 13.2   Consumption inequality measures 1985/86–1996/97

| | Household Expenditure Survey | |
	1985/86	1996/97
Gini	0.33	0.38
Atkinson (v = 0.5)	0.09	0.12
Atkinson (v = 1)	0.17	0.23
Atkinson (v = 2)	0.31	0.41

Sources: Computed from INDEC (1988) and INDEC (1999)

Table 13.1), but also for the Atkinson index for $v = 1$ (0.23 against 0.29 from Table 13.1).[8]

4   Distributional impact of relative price changes, 1988–98

The approximation to the welfare impact of relative price changes reported in expressions (5) and (5′) needs more disaggregated data than that available in Argentina. Newbery (1995), for example, partially overcame these difficulties for Hungary and the UK by using panels and taking year-on-year change for some 100 goods. Our calculations, though less robust or exact, are nevertheless considered useful and relevant to current discussion on Argentina. First, an approximation can be obtained using existing data of the likely direction of the distributive impact of relative price changes. While the results reported using more disaggregated data might change the magnitude, we are confident the direction of change is correct. Second, we tried to clarify the interplay between structural reform, the resulting pattern of relative prices and the welfare implications. In Newbery (1995) only aggregate results are reported and there is no reference to specific goods and services.[9] As we considered it important to analyse the pattern of relative price changes in Argentina after structural reform, we attempted to break down these aggregate results.

In order to compare the two Argentinian HESs, we classified the 46 goods and our results into 8 groups. These groups are defined as: non-durable goods (NDG) – chiefly food; clothing (CLO) – including shoes; housing (HOU); durable goods (DG); education (EDUC); health (HEA); private services (PRS); and public services (PUS). This classification enabled us to prepare a simple description of the pattern of relative price changes, a pattern based on three probable facts. First, that unilateral trade liberalization and integration within Mercosur, together with major changes in distribution and retailing, should have created important gains for consumers. Second, that private and social services moved in opposite directions, partly the result of the correction of non-tradable goods prices, partly the inefficiencies and absence of competition in some services, such as the health sector. Third, that the effects of the privatization of public utilities was probably neutral, as productive efficiency and cost effectiveness would in part be neutralized – at the level of consumer prices – by the elimination of cross-subsidies (gas and electricity just before privatization and telecommunications later) or by a weak regulatory policy that allowed price increases (in water, transport, roads).[10]

Table 13.3 summarizes – at the 8-goods group level – the information relevant to the distributional impact of relative price changes; that is, the distributional characteristics d_i (for different values of coefficient v), the shares in the price index basket α_i, and the relative prices between 1988 (base year of the current CPI which is based on the HES 1985/6) and 1998.[11] In Table 13.3 we show only three intermediate years, 1991, 1994 and 1995, because they separate three periods (up to the convertibility plan, to the tequila crisis, and since then) where the results differ markedly.

The data presented in Table 13.3 appear consistent with the likely pattern of relative price changes described above. Goods subject to complete deregulation through the liberalization of trade, such as non-durables (NDG), durables (DG) and clothing (CLO) showed a drop in relative prices, as did public services (PUS), but only between extremes and not for all sub-periods. The relative prices of social services (education EDU and health HEA), private services (PRS) and housing (HOU) increased considerably. Table 13.3 shows this pattern with the relative price of goods with higher distributional characteristics (and a greater weight in the CPI) such as NDG decreasing, while other goods such as social and private services increased. There is a clear negative correlation between distributional characteristics (or distributional characteristics weighted by the shares α) and relative price changes.[12]

Table 13.4 reports the results of computing expressions (5) and (5′) on the data summarized in Table 13.3 for the 46 goods[13] The upper panel of Table 13.4 shows the welfare impact of relative price changes for the four periods and for different coefficients of inequality aversion ($v = 0.5, 1, 2$ and $\to \infty$) decomposing the changes for each of the 8 groups of goods, using HES 1985/6 data. The lower panel shows the same calculations using HES 1996/7 data. The results reported here and in Tables 13.5 and 13.6 can be read (1) across types of goods; (2) across time periods; (3) for different distributive weights and (4) for different HESs.

Table 13.3 Basic data for evaluating the distributional impact of relative price changes

Goods Groups	Distributional characteristics 1985/86				Distributional characteristics 1996/97				Basket shares %		Relative prices				
	$v=0.5$	$v=1$	$v=2$	$v=\infty$	$v=0.5$	$v=1$	$v=2$	$v=\infty$	1985/86	1996/97	1988	1991	1994	1995	1998
Non-durable consumer (NDCG)	0.90	0.81	0.68	0.10	0.85	0.73	0.58	0.09	43	33	100	79.4	76.4	76.1	76.0
Clothing (CLO)	0.81	0.65	0.46	0.05	0.75	0.57	0.37	0.05	9	6	100	83.5	61.9	58.7	52.6
Housing (HOU)	0.78	0.61	0.39	0.04	0.70	0.48	0.25	0.02	4	9	100	99.6	132.3	133.3	126.4
Durable consumer goods (DCG)	0.76	0.58	0.35	0.03	0.69	0.48	0.25	0.02	8	8	100	116.7	88.0	88.2	84.3
Education (EDU)	0.81	0.66	0.46	0.06	0.72	0.51	0.29	0.03	3	4	100	213.2	249.7	251.7	253.3
Health (HEA)	0.79	0.62	0.40	0.04	0.74	0.54	0.32	0.04	7	10	100	131.2	152.0	153.6	153.3
Private services (PRS)	0.74	0.54	0.31	0.03	0.68	0.45	0.23	0.02	14	17	100	153.2	167.6	166.8	164.6
Public Services (PUS)	0.84	0.70	0.53	0.07	0.82	0.67	0.50	0.07	12	14	100	67.8	64.8	67.6	80.5
									100	100					

Source: Estimates from INDEC (1988 and 1999)

One result was that the welfare impact of relative price changes for 1988–98 using the 1985/6 HES showed positive changes. The gain is almost 4 per cent for $v = 1$, and increases with the distributional weight of the poor, reaching 12 per cent for the extreme case. This result does not hold for the HES 1996/7: a welfare loss of 3.6 per cent is observed with $v = 1$. However, this negative result is reversed at higher values of v, reaching 8 per cent for the extreme case. Table 13.4 helps to identify the pattern of relative price changes and confirms that, regardless of the HES data used, there is an intrinsic bias in favour of the poor, when the distributional weights used favour lower consumption groups.

Welfare gains were not evenly distibuted during the decade 1988–98. They were greatest between 1988 and 1991, when prices stabilized and trade was liberalized, and 1991 to1994, the period of intense privatization.

The positive impact was unevenly distributed across goods and services, as noted in Table 13.3. Goods affected by world or regional competition (NDG, DG and CLO) contributed most to the welfare gain, regardless of the time period or HES used. On the other hand, goods and services such as EDU, HEA and PRS contributed to welfare losses and negative distributive effects that accrued at the end of the 1980s and early 1990s, again irrespective of the HES used.

The major privatized sectors (water and sanitation, natural gas, electricity, telecommunications and fuels) contributed welfare gains between 1988 and 1998, regardless of the HES used. However, these were concentrated between 1988 and 1991 before the major privatizations, and continued to 1994. After 1994 there is evidence of some welfare loss. The contribution of public services to the aggregate welfare loss regarding relative price changes in the second half of the 1990s appears undeniable as can be seen from Table 13.4.

Table 13.5 merely tests sensitivity by varying the weights over time. 1980s weights were applied to 1988–91; 1990s weights to 1994–98; and an average of the two for 1991–94 and the whole period 1988–98. The effects of these weights changed the estimates as follows: for period 1988–98, the welfare impact was reduced to zero where $v = 1$, negative at lower values and positive and increasing at higher values of v.

Finally Table 13.6 repeats the exercise using the whole sample of 46 goods and services and, where the 1996/7 HES weights were used, applied the measurement to decile groups of households. The results were, first, greater welfare gains (4.4 per cent with $v = 1$) between 1988 and 1998 using the 1985/6 HES; the same conclusions apply regarding

Table 13.4 Welfare Effects of Relative Price Changes 1988–1998

Welfare impact (%) using distributional characteristics and shares from HES 1985/86

Goods	1988-91				1991-94				1994-98				1988-98			
	$v=0.5$	$v=1$	$v=2$	$v=\infty$	$v=0.5$	$v=1$	$v=2$	$v=\infty$	$v=0.5$	$v=1$	$v=2$	$v=\infty$	$v=0.5$	$v=1$	$v=2$	$v=\infty$
Non-durable consumer goods (NDCG)	9.4	10.1	11.3	13.0	1.7	1.9	2.1	2.4	0.3	0.3	0.3	0.4	11.0	11.8	13.3	15.2
Clothing (CLO)	1.5	1.5	1.4	1.2	2.4	2.3	2.1	1.9	1.4	1.3	1.2	1.1	4.3	4.2	3.9	3.4
Housing (HOU)	0.0	0.0	0.0	0.0	-1.3	-1.2	-1.1	-0.8	0.2	0.2	0.1	0.1	-1.1	-1.0	-0.9	-0.7
Durables goods (CDG)	-1.2	-1.1	-0.9	-0.6	1.7	1.6	1.3	0.9	0.3	0.3	0.2	0.2	1.1	1.0	0.8	0.6
Education (EDU)	-3.0	-2.9	-2.7	-2.4	-0.5	-0.4	-0.4	-0.4	0.0	0.0	0.0	0.0	-4.1	-3.9	-3.7	-3.3
Health (HEA)	-2.1	-2.0	-1.7	-1.2	-1.1	-1.0	-0.9	-0.6	-0.1	-0.1	0.0	0.0	-3.6	-3.4	-2.9	-2.1
Private services (PRS)	-6.7	-5.8	-4.5	-2.9	-1.2	-1.0	-0.8	-0.5	-0.2	0.2	0.1	0.1	-8.1	-7.1	-5.4	-3.5
Public services (PUS)	3.8	3.8	3.8	3.9	0.5	0.5	0.5	0.5	-2.8	-2.9	-2.9	-2.9	2.3	2.3	2.3	2.3
Total	1.8	3.6	6.8	10.9	2.3	2.5	2.9	3.4	-0.6	-0.7	-0.9	-1.1	1.9	3.9	7.4	12.0

Table 13.4 Welfare Effects of Relative Price Changes 1988-1998 – Continued

Goods	Welfare impact (%) using distributional characteristics and shares from HES 1996/97															
	1988-91				1991-94				1994-98				1988-98			
	$v=0.5$	$v=1$	$v=2$	$v=\infty$	$v=0.5$	$v=1$	$v=2$	$v=\infty$	$v=0.5$	$v=1$	$v=2$	$v=\infty$	$v=0.5$	$v=1$	$v=2$	$v=\infty$
Non-durable consumer goods (NDCG)	7.6	8.4	9.7	11.2	1.4	1.6	1.8	2.1	0.2	0.2	0.3	0.3	8.9	9.8	11.4	13.1
Clothing (CLO)	0.9	0.9	0.9	0.8	1.5	1.4	1.4	1.3	0.9	0.8	0.8	0.8	2.7	2.6	2.5	2.4
Housing (HOU)	0.0	0.0	0.0	0.0	-2.6	-2.3	-1.8	-1.2	0.4	0.3	0.2	0.2	-2.1	-1.9	-1.4	-1.0
Durable goods (CDG)	-1.1	-1.0	-0.8	-0.6	1.7	1.5	1.2	0.8	0.3	0.3	0.2	0.1	1.1	0.9	0.7	0.5
Education (EDU)	-4.5	-4.1	-3.4	-2.4	-0.7	-0.6	-0.5	-0.4	-0.1	-0.1	0.0	0.0	-6.0	-5.5	-4.6	-3.3
Health (HEA)	-2.9	-2.7	-2.4	-2.0	-1.5	-1.4	-1.2	-1.0	-0.1	-0.1	-0.1	-0.1	-5.0	-4.7	-4.1	-3.5
Private services (PRS)	-7.7	-6.6	-4.9	-3.3	-1.4	-1.2	-0.9	-0.6	0.3	0.2	0.2	0.1	-9.4	-8.0	-5.9	-4.0
Public services (PUS)	4.8	5.1	5.6	6.0	0.6	0.7	0.8	0.8	-3.6	-3.8	-4.2	-4.5	2.9	3.1	3.4	3.6
Total	-2.9	0.0	4.8	9.7	-0.9	-0.3	0.7	1.9	-1.8	-2.1	-2.6	-3.1	-6.9	-3.6	2.0	8.0

Source: Estimation from INDEC (1988, 1999 and 'INDEC Informa')

Table 13.5 Welfare Effects of Relative Price Changes 1998–1998 (using average weights)

| Goods | Welfare impact using distributional characteristics and shares (%) HES 1985/86 (1988–91), HES 1996/97 (1994–98) and an average of both (1991–94 and 1988–98) | | | | | | | | | | | | | | | |
| | 1988–91 | | | | 1991–94 | | | | 1994–98 | | | | 1988–98 | | | |
	$v=0.5$	$v=1$	$v=2$	$v=\infty$	$v=0.5$	$v=1$	$v=2$	$v=\infty$	$v=0.5$	$v=1$	$v=2$	$v=\infty$	$v=0.5$	$v=1$	$v=2$	$v=\infty$
Non-durable consumer goods (NDCG)	9.4	10.1	11.3	13.0	1.6	1.7	2.0	2.2	0.2	0.2	0.3	0.3	9.9	10.8	12.3	14.2
Clothing (CLO)	1.5	1.5	1.4	1.2	1.9	1.9	1.8	1.6	0.9	0.8	0.8	0.8	3.5	3.4	3.2	2.9
Housing (HOU)	0.0	0.0	0.0	0.0	−2.0	−1.8	−1.5	−1.1	0.4	0.3	0.2	0.2	−1.6	−1.4	−1.2	−0.9
Durable goods (CDG)	−1.2	−1.1	−0.9	−0.6	1.7	1.5	1.2	0.9	0.3	0.3	0.2	0.1	1.1	1.0	0.8	0.5
Education (EDU)	−3.0	−2.9	−2.7	−2.4	−0.6	−0.5	−0.5	−0.4	−0.1	−0.1	0.0	0.0	−5.1	−4.8	−4.3	−3.6
Health (HEA)	−2.1	−2.0	−1.7	−1.2	−1.3	−1.2	−1.0	−0.8	−0.1	−0.1	−0.1	−0.1	−4.3	−4.0	−3.5	−2.7
Private services (PRS)	−6.7	−5.8	−4.5	−2.9	−1.3	−1.1	−0.8	−0.5	0.3	0.2	0.2	0.1	−8.7	−7.6	−5.7	−3.7
Public services (PUS)	3.8	3.8	3.8	3.9	0.6	0.6	0.6	0.6	−3.6	−3.8	−4.2	−4.5	2.6	2.7	2.8	2.9
Total	1.8	3.6	6.8	10.9	0.7	1.1	1.7	2.5	−1.8	−2.1	−2.6	−3.1	−2.5	0.0	4.4	9.7

Source: Estimation from INDEC (1988, 1999 and 'INDEC Informa')

Table 13.6 Welfare Effects of Relative Price Changes 1988–1998 (46 goods and for quintile and decile groups)

Period	HES 1985/86 Quintile groups (%)				Households 1996/97 Quintile groups (%)				Decile groups (%)			
	v=0.5	v=1	v=2	v=∞	v=0.5	v=1	v=2	v=∞	v=0.5	v=1	v=2	v=∞
1988–91	2.09	4.26	7.99	12.83	-3.29	-0.06	5.57	11.54	-3.12	0.24	6.23	14.10
1991–92	1.14	1.00	0.72	0.21	-0.59	-0.53	-0.45	-0.46	-0.61	-0.55	-0.44	-0.22
1992–93	1.03	1.00	0.93	0.78	-0.67	-0.54	-0.34	-0.19	-0.67	-0.54	-0.31	0.01
1993–94	0.68	0.73	0.83	0.99	-0.71	-0.61	-0.40	-0.15	-0.71	-0.60	-0.37	0.04
1994–95	-0.01	-0.06	-0.14	-0.26	-0.37	-0.49	-0.69	-0.92	-0.39	-0.51	-0.73	-1.07
1995–96	-0.11	-0.14	-0.20	-0.29	-0.33	-0.43	-0.62	-0.85	-0.34	-0.45	-0.66	-1.03
1996–97	-0.02	0.00	0.03	0.07	-1.11	-1.20	-1.30	-1.28	-1.12	-1.21	-1.30	-1.27
1997–98	-0.15	-0.33	-0.66	-1.17	-0.26	-0.50	-0.90	-1.32	-0.28	-0.52	-0.94	-1.38
1988–91	2.09	4.26	7.99	12.83	-3.29	-0.06	5.57	11.54	-3.12	0.24	6.23	14.10
1991–94	2.18	2.14	2.01	1.68	-3.11	-2.66	-1.91	-1.25	-3.11	-2.64	-1.79	-0.47
1995–98	-0.49	-0.70	-1.06	-1.64	-2.02	-2.46	-3.18	-3.80	-2.05	-2.51	-3.25	-4.04
1988–98	2.15	4.37	8.16	12.87	-10.19	-6.57	-0.24	6.44	-10.04	-6.30	0.47	9.74

Source: Estimates using information from INDEC (1988, 1999)

periods. On the other hand, the welfare loss was greater using the 1996/7 HES, but the same qualitative results on the sensitivity to distributive weights apply. The exercise on decile groups yielded the same results; actually, welfare losses were reduced (and gains increased). That is, the data were not sensitive to measurement by decile instead of quintile.

5 The distribution characteristics of access to public service infrastructure 1985/6–96/7

Navajas (1999) demonstrates that the U-shaped behaviour of public service relative prices cannot be attributed to errors in the measurement of prices of privatized utilities. However, there is another dimension to public services concealed by the above estimates, which might help an assessment of performance after privatization. Since public services are provided through a network infrastructure, access to these services is of paramount importance, particularly where coverage falls below the population's needs.[14]

Recent studies on the regulation of public utilities in Argentina (FIEL, 1999) concluded that privatization generally increased the coverage of services. Assuming this increased the participation of lower-income groups – given that medium and higher income groups already enjoyed access – the results suggest a positive distributive effect. However, given the lack of data, it has been impossible until now to substantiate this claim. Table 13.7 shows access to utilities by quintile groups (classified by income per capita) using the HESs. Access increased in most sectors, with the exception of sanitation,[15] and the lower quintile groups benefited most from these improvements.

This observation suggested further work on distribution. Using the literature on optimal pricing in public services (Navajas and Porto, 1990 for an application to Argentina),[16] the distributional characteristic of access to the good or service i was defined as the weighted sum (with the social distributive weights β^h) across income groups (h) of the access of group h to the good i. In notation:

$$d_i^N = \sum_h \beta^h (N_i^h/N^h) \tag{11}$$

where N_i^h/N^h is the proportion of households of group h with access to service i. When we applied this expression to the 1985/86 and 1996/97 HESs data for different values of parameter v, the results showed an increase in distribution and access for all services except sanitation.[17]

Table 13.7 Access to public services 1985/86–1996/97 (% of households by quintile)

| | HES 1985/86 | | | | | | HES 1996/97 | | | | | |
| | Quintile group | | | | | | Quintile group | | | | | |
Service	*1*	*2*	*3*	*4*	*5*	*Total*	*1*	*2*	*3*	*4*	*5*	*Total*
Sanitation	30.0	54.2	61.1	73.2	88.4	61.4	27.0	45.5	58.1	72.5	87.4	58.1
Natural gas	41.4	68.3	77.0	89.1	95.0	74.2	53.7	79.5	89.3	94.9	98.9	83.3
Electricity	72.2	87.5	92.4	91.1	98.8	88.2	99.6	99.7	99.9	100.0	100.0	99.8
Telephone	9.5	27.6	36.0	54.5	68.8	39.3	31.7	55.7	74.5	84.0	91.7	67.5
Water	44.8	67.0	72.6	83.7	92.7	72.2	51.9	70.5	78.4	85.3	94.9	76.2

Source: Estimated from INDEC (1988, 1999)

These results show that irrespective of the welfare effects of relative price changes, privatization increased the distribution of the network. Although this chapter has provided convincing evidence on the direction of the change in access to public services, we were unable, due inadequate data, to provide quantitative measures of the welfare impact.

6 Conclusions

This chapter has focused on the distribution of consumption in Argentina using a simple methodology to assess the distributional impact of relative price changes, following a decade of structural reform. The measurement of distribution characteristics and consumption inequality indices revealed a degree of inequality that increased during the 1990s. Recent studies on income distribution in Argentina by Gasparini (1998, 1999) suggested that long- and short-term movements in the inequality of incomes were associated with gaps in education and skills-training, restricted access to labour markets, and rising unemployment following severe macroeconomic shocks. We addressed one aspect of the likely effect of structural reform, namely, the impact of relative price changes. Despite data limitations, we have obtained some useful results that help identify a possible pattern of the welfare effects of relative price changes for Argentina between 1988 and 1998.

First, the results were robust enough to contradict the idea that relative price changes following structural reform in Argentina decreased welfare or contained a negative or distributive bias. The opposite seems more likely. Welfare appeared to improve most the more relative price changes were biased towards the poor, irrespective of HES used.

Second, the welfare impact was not uniformly distributed, either across time or across goods and services irrespective of the HES used for computation. Welfare gains were concentrated on the years 1988–94, when most reform took place, followed by losses in later years. Across the spectrum of goods and services, we noted relative price reductions in goods with (relatively) high distributional characteristics, and increases in the rest, as shown in Figure 13.1. The relative price reduction of goods exposed (direct or indirectly) to intense foreign competition and to deregulation (such as non-durables, durables, clothing) contributed greatly to aggregate welfare gains and to positive distributive effects. Others, such as housing, social (education, health) and private services moved in the opposite direction. The relative prices of privatized public services were U-shaped, with gains between the extremes; this group was mainly responsible for the negative welfare impact recorded in the last years.

Third, we have argued that to complete the assessment of the distributive impact of privatization, due care needs to be taken of the changes in access to public service infrastructure. The extension of the concept of distributional characteristics to access showed a positive welfare and distributive impact in the last decade.

Fourth, further work seemed to yield useful results, depending on the quality of the data-set, when reexamining earlier results using the HES 1985/6 micro data-set and a breakdown of HES 1996/7 by region.

Notes

1   Other effects seem less important. For instance the effect of privatization on the labour market and the rise in unemployment.

2   Substituting the iso-elastic utility function in the welfare function and using the definition of β^h we obtain $W = (1/H.(1 - v)) \Sigma\beta^h g^h$. Thus, the percentage variation in welfare is given $\Delta W/W = \Sigma\beta^h . \Delta g^h / . \Sigma\beta^h . g^h$

3   It is assumed that there exists enough disagregation in goods, agents and time periods (that is, changes are small enough) such that the approximation be as less inexact as possible. This is particularly important in the case where the utility function is normalized and defined over prices relative to the general price level. In this case – unlike equation (3) – a change in a relative price due for example to a change in the price of one good, can affect the general price level and other relative prices, unless the change and the share of the good in total expenditure are small enough. This condition does not arise in empirical exercises (because HESs have a finite number of goods), and for this reason they are necessarily inexact

4   The loss of monotonicity in the lines for $v = 0.5$ and $v = 2$ is due to the fact that the goods are ordered according to the distributional characteristics for $v = 1$.

5   In Figure 13.2 we see that, for example, at a 50 per cent cumulative expenditure, the distributional characteristics line for $v = 1$ has a value of 0.62, while for Britain in 1991 it is almost 0.7 and for Hungary (starting from a more equal distribution) it is around 0.85.

6   The ranking of income and consumption inequalities in the three countries should be the same, and that happens despite some differences due to the non-homogeneity of data sources.

7   The loss of one good is due to different classifications between both HES. However, working with the goods and services defined for the HESs 1996/7 in INDEC (1999) it is possible to find a fairly good approximation to conform both HESs to the HES 1985/86 as published in INDEC (1988).

8   The bias is for the level of the indices and for a given year, but they do not necessarily imply a bias in the reported increase in inequality.

9   In the case of Hungary examined by Newbery it seems that the emphasis is on an exercise of indirect tax reform in a closed economy, since references are made to a move from a very complicated structure of subsidies to a

more uniform tax system. Thus, it becomes difficult to describe a pattern of relative price changes.

10 According to FIEL's (1999) book on regulatory reform in Argentina, there is no pattern of price changes after privatization, and case-by-case results suggest that preexisting distortions, competition and regulatory control explain different results.

11 Prices come from a data-set (originally obtained from the HES and published by INDEC with base period 1988 = 100 when reporting price changes) which is much more disaggregated – at the goods level – than the data in INDEC (1988) – which reports on the distribution of expenditure per household. This information was reclassified to match the data in INDEC (1988). The structure of shares α for 1985/86 reported in Table 13.3 comes from this latter classification since it is more accurate and consistent with price changes as reported by INDEC. For 1996/97 the structure of shares α has been constructed from the HES.

12 This is so regardless of the HES being used to compute the former. See Navajas (1999) for an illustration of these correlations.

13 All numerical estimations use the information for the 46 goods but aggregate them in a different mode. Tables 13.4 and 13.5 measure impact at the eight-group level. Table 13.6 measures the same effects from a single impact and is therefore more accurate.

14 Access and coverage have different meanings depending on whether they are seen as objectives (for instance in the 'universal service obligation' understood as an objective regardless of economic evaluation), or as the outcome of an economic evaluation (in the extreme case, equal access to all willing to pay for the service). The distinction is less relevant for water and sanitation where for efficiency and distributive reasons almost full coverage is desirable and would also be justified on economic grounds. It is no accident that some basic needs indicators of poverty in Argentina (and elsewhere) depend on access to water and sanitation. See Chisari and Estache (1997) for detailed discussion.

15 The fact that access to sanitation has decreased for all quintile groups suggests problems in the measurement of both HESs that makes the comparison unreliable.

16 In this chapter we extended a two-part tariff model (see for example Brown and Sibley, 1987) to include distributional concerns and proceeded to measure its implications for many public services in Argentina. It is important to notice that the parameter of distributional characteristics of access as defined above arises from the solution of that pricing model

17 Another way to represent these results is by drawing the corresponding distributional characteristics lines to show how they moved upwards between surveys; see Navajas (1999).

References

Ahmad, E. and N. Stern (1984) 'The Theory of Reform and Indian Indirect Taxes', *Journal of Public Economics*, vol. 25, pp. 259–98.

Atkinson, A. (1970) 'On the Measurement of Inequality', *Journal of Economic Theory*, vol. 2, pp. 244–63.

Boycko, M., A. Schleifer and R. Vishny (1996) 'A Theory of Privatisation', *Economic Journal*, vol. 106, pp. 309–19.

Brown, D. and D. Sibley (1987) *The Theory of Public Utility Pricing* (Cambridge: Cambridge University Press).

Champernowne, D. and F. Cowell (1998) *Economic Inequality and Income Distribution* (Cambridge: Cambridge University Press).

Chisari, O. and A. Estache (1997) 'The Needs of the Poor in Infrastructure Privatization: The Role of Universal Service Obligations. The Case of Argentina', World Bank working paper (mimeo).

Chisari, O., A. Estache and C. Romero (1997) *Winners and Losers from Utility Privatization in Argentina. Lessons from a General Equilibrium Model*, Policy Research Working Paper, no. 1824 (Washington: The World Bank).

Deninger, K. and L. Squire (1996) 'A New Data Set Measuring Income Inequality', *World Bank Economic Review*, vol. 10, no. 3, pp. 565–91.

Feldstein, M. (1972) 'Distributional Equity and the Optimal Structure of Public Sector Prices', *American Economic Review*, vol. 62, pp. 32–6.

FIEL (1999) *Regulation of Competition and Public Services: Theory and Recent Experience in Argentina* (in Spanish) (Buenos Aires: Fundación de investigaciones económicas latinoamericanas).

Gasparini, L. (1998) 'Income and Welfare Distribution Inequality: Estimates for Argentina' (in Spanish), mimeo, FIEL.

Gasparini, L. (1999) 'An Analysis of Income Distribution based on Decompositions' (in Spanish), mimeo, FIEL.

Guesnerie, R. (1977) 'On the Direction of Tax Reform', *Journal of Public Economics*, vol. 7, pp. 179–202.

INDEC (1988) *Expenditure and Household Income Survey* (in Spanish) Estudios 11 (Buenos Aires: Instituto Nacional de Estadística y Censos).

INDEC (1999) *National Survey of Household Expenditure: Metropolitan Region of Greater Buenos Aires* (in Spanish) (Buenos Aires: Instituto Nacional de Estadística y Censos).

Navajas, F. (1999) 'The Distributional Impact of Relative Price Changes in Argentina 1988–1998 and the Effects of Privatization and Economic Deregulation' (in Spanish), Serie Seminarios no. 9, 1999, Universidad Torcuato Di Tella.

Navajas, F. and A. Porto (1990) 'The Quasi-Optimal Two Part Tariff: Efficiency, Equity and Finance' (in Spanish), *El Trimestre Económico*, vol. 57(4), no. 228, pp. 863–87.

Navajas, F. and A. Porto (1994) 'Budget Shares, Distributional Characteristics and the Direction of Tax Reforms', *Economics Letters*, vol. 45, pp. 475–79.

Newbery, D. (1995) 'The Distributional Impact of Price Changes in Hungary and the United Kingdom', *Economic Journal*, vol. 105, pp. 847–63.

Porto, A. and L. Gasparini (1992) 'The Distributional Impact of Social Expenditure' (in Spanish) *Desarrollo Económico*, vol. 31, no. 124, pp. 487–502.

Vickers, J. and G. Yarrow (1988) *Privatization: An Economic Analysis* (Cambridge, Mass.: MIT Press).

14
Endogenous Child Mortality, the Price of Child-specific Goods and Fertility Decisions: Evidence from Argentina

Alessandro Cigno and Graciela Pinal

1 Introduction

A theoretical paper, Cigno (1998), modelled fertility and infant mortality as the joint outcome of fertility and expenditure decisions under conditions of uncertainty as to the number of children who might survive to adulthood. The model predicted that if parents were aware that the amount of resources spent on each child improved that child's chances of survival, then an increase in the observed (aggregate) survival rate might induce parents to spend more on each child born, and reduce the number of births. This implies that public expenditure on, say, sanitation or mass immunization might discourage births, and that its direct mortality-reducing effects may be reinforced by induced private action. However, if parents were not aware of the effects of their actions on the survival chances of their own offspring, all that is likely to be achieved by such a policy is an increase in the number of births. It is thus of some importance to establish empirically whether parents regard the survival chances of their own children as dependent on their actions or not.

If it is true that an increase in the aggregate survival rate is unlikely to discourage births unless parents regard the survival probabilty of their own children as independent of their own actions, the usual finding of a positive correlation between fertility and premature mortality as discussed by Rosenzweig and Wolpin (1982) or Cochrane and Zachariah (1983), but consider also Chowdhury (1988) for a cautionary note, then it may be taken as symptomatic that parents regard such a probability as endogenous. But this would not rule out the competing hypothesis. In this chapter we derive a stronger implication of the endogenous survival probability hypothesis, and test it against time-series data from the Andine Province of Salta, in north-western Argentina. The results are consistent with the hypothesis of endogeneity, and suggest some additional policy considerations.

2 The model

The model is a reelaboration of Cigno (1998), with a small extension to allow for changes in the price of child-specific goods. Parents are expected-utility maximizers; they control fertility but are uncertain as to how many of their children will survive to adulthood. Their *ex post* utility is $U = u(a) + v(n)$, where a denotes parental consumption, and n the number of children who survive to adulthood. We are assuming, therefore, that parents derive utility from children who survive long enough to become adults, not from their birth *per se*. The functions $u(.)$ and $v(.)$ are increasing and strictly concave.[1] The budget constraint is $a + bpq = y$, where y denotes income, b the number of births, q the quantity and p the price of goods (including healthcare, as well as food, and so on) consumed by each child. The probability of n children surviving out of b that are born is positively conditioned by q. If parents are not aware of this effect, their expectation of n is equal to bs, where s is the observed (aggregate) survival rate. If they are, their expectation of n will still be conditioned by s, but may be higher or lower than bs depending on their choice of q.

Writing $f(n, .)$ for the probability density of n, the expected utility of the parents will then be:

$$E(U) = u(y - bpq) + g(b, q, s) \equiv u(y - bpq) + \int_0^b v(n)f(n, b, q, s)dn \quad (1)$$

if they are aware of the effect of q on the survival chances of their offspring:

$$E(U) = u(y - bpq) + g(b, s) \equiv u(y - bpq) + \int_0^b v(n)f(n, b, s)dn \quad (1')$$

if they are not.

Consider, first, the case shown in equation (1) where parents regard the survival probability of their children as independent of their actions, and thus treat q as a parameter in choosing b. Assuming an interior solution, the comparative-statics effects of y, p and s on b are

$$(\partial b/\partial y) = (-ru'/D) \tag{2}$$

$$(\partial b/\partial p) = (I + bpqr)u'(q/D) \tag{3}$$

and

$$(\partial b/\partial s) = -(g_{bs}/D) \tag{4}$$

where $D \equiv p^2 q^2 u'' + g_{bb}$ and $r \equiv -u''u'$. Since D is negative for the second-order condition, and r positive for concavity of $u(.)$, fertility is clearly increasing in income, and decreasing in the price of child-specific goods. That is true, notice, irrespective of the properties of the probability law, described by $f(n,.)$, and of the parents' degree of risk-aversion, reflected in the curvature of $v(.)$. The effect of the aggregate survival rate takes the sign of g_{bs}, which cannot plausibly be negative (a negative g_{bs} would mean that a rise in the probability of survival *reduces* the expected utility of an extra birth!).[2] Therefore, the observed positive correlation between fertility (b) and child mortality $(1 - s)$ cannot be explained by a decision model which takes the survival rate as exogenous.

Next, consider the case of equation (1') where parents are aware of the effect of q on $f(n,.)$, and choose that quantity optimally together with b. Now:

$$(\partial b/\partial y) = -bp^2 r (u')^2 (G/H) \tag{5}$$

$$(\partial b/\partial p) = \{[(bpqr - \gamma_{qq}) + u'rK]bpq + u'G\}(g_q/H) \tag{6}$$

and

$$(\partial b/\partial s) = [(bpqr - \gamma_{qq}) g_q g_{bs} - g_b g_{qs} K]/qH \tag{7}$$

where H is the Hessian determinant, γ_{ij} the elasticity of g_i to j $(i,j = b,q)$, $G \equiv 1 - \gamma_{qb} + \gamma_{qq}$, $J \equiv 1 - \gamma_{bq} + \gamma_{bb}$, and $K \equiv 1 - \gamma_{bq} + bpqr$. Since H must be positive, and γ_{qq} negative, for second-order conditions, but G, J and K can have any sign, the comparative effects are now ambiguous. It is thus clear that endogenizing the probability of survival makes the model compatible with the observation of a positive correlation between fertility and child mortality. Let us see what that implies.

If one were to find empirically that fertility is negatively correlated with the price of child-specific goods, or positively correlated with the aggregate survival rate, that could mean either that parents regard the probability of survival of their own children as dependent on how well they feed and care for them, or that they regard it as an act of God. By contrast, if one were to find that fertility is positively correlated with the price of child-specific goods, or negatively correlated with the observed survival rate, that would rule out the hypothesis that parents are not aware of the consequences of their actions for the probability that their own children will live to be adults.[3] That is a testable proposition. But, how would parents change their actions in response to external stimuli, in particular to public policy? To answer this question, we need an extra assumption.

Assume that K is positive (for that to be true, it is enough that γ_{bq} is less than one, or that total household expenditure on children, bpq, is 'large'). The effect of s will then be positive if γ_{qs} is negative, ambiguous if γ_{qs} is positive. Since a rise in s, holding q constant, could be the result of an increase in public expenditures for health, sanitation and so forth, a negative value of γ_{qs} would indicate that public and private expenditures are *complements* in the production of child health, while a positive value of γ_{qs} would indicate that public and private expenditures are *substitutes*. If, empirically, it were found that the aggregate survival rate has a negative effect on fertility, that could then be taken as an indication that private and public expenditures are likely to be complementary and, therefore, that greater public effort on this front is likely to induce parents to spend more for each child.[4] By contrast, the finding of a positive effect on fertility could mean that parents respond to increased public expenditure by spending less per child, and use some of the saving to finance extra births.

3 Evidence from Argentina

We looked at time-series data relating to the Andine Province (federated state) of Salta, in the north-west of Argentina. One of the poorest provinces in the country, this border area shares some of the characteristics, including ethnic mix, of neighbouring Bolivia. Our interest in it arises from the considerable variation displayed by fertility and child mortality rates in this province over the last quarter of a century, and from privileged access to data which allowed us to construct a sub-index for prices of child-specific goods. The longest period for which we could get information on all the relevant variables was 1970–94.

Fertility and mortality data are shown in Figure 14.1. Since estimates of the total fertility rate were not available on a year-by-year basis, we

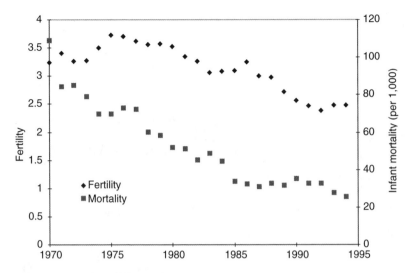

Figure 14.1 Fertility and mortality

used the crude birth rate, adjusted for the proportion of women aged
15–49. Our fertility measure may be interpreted as the number of live
births per woman of fertile age. It fell substantially, from 6.5 to 4.8
between 1970 and 1992, but then rose to nearly 5 in 1993 and 1994.
Mortality (right-hand scale) is defined as the number of children who
die before reaching their first birthday per thousand live births. That is
what is generally called infant mortality. However, since mortality
rates at higher ages (not available for all years) are highly correlated
with infant mortality, we took the latter as a proxy for premature mortality in general. And, since the mortality rate is the complement of the
survival rate, we also use our mortality index as a negative proxy for
the observed (aggregate) survival rate that, according to the model outlined in the last section, is among the determinants of individual birth
decisions. Mortality falls from 109 in 1970, to less than 26 in 1994.
That is a very sharp drop, but there are fluctuations (for example, mortality rises from 31 in 1987 to 35 in 1990, before starting to fall again). The
scatter diagram in Figure 14.2 shows the customary positive association
between aggregate fertility and aggregate mortality (lagged one year),
implying a negative association between fertility and survival rates.

Income and price data are shown in Figure 14.3 based on GDP per
head at 1970 prices; household disposable income which would have
been more appropriate was not available at the provincial level. Prices

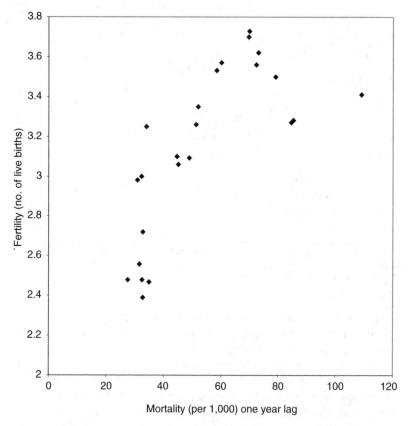

Figure 14.2 Fertility and mortality correlation with a one-year lag

were measured as the ratio of a sub-index of child-specific goods to the
general retail price index. We included in the sub-index all the relevant
items relating specifically to child needs that we could find; this
included baby milk, children's clothing and primary school materials.
It will be seen that real per capita income fluctuates around a rising
trend, while the relative price of child-specific goods fluctuates around
a declining one.

   Since the unit-root test[5] revealed that the fertility series in first differences was stationary, we fitted an error-correction model of the general
form:

$$\Delta Y(t) = \alpha + \beta Y(t-1) + \Sigma_i \beta_i \Delta Y(t-1) + \gamma X(t-1) + \Sigma_i \gamma_i \Delta X(t-i) \quad (8)$$

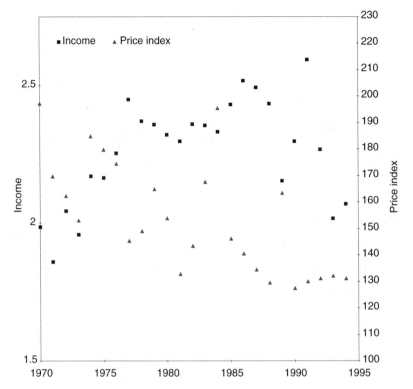

Figure 14.3 Income and price index of child-specific goods

where Y is the dependent variable (our measure of fertility), and X the vector of explanatory variables (our measures of household income, price of child-specific goods, and aggregate mortality). All variables are expressed in logarithms. The long-term elasticity of fertility to the jth explanatory variable ($j = 1,2,3$) is given by ($-\gamma_j/\beta$), where γ_j denotes the jth element of the vector of coefficients γ.

OLS estimates are reported in Table 14.1. By the adjusted R^2, F, and Amemiya-prediction criteria, the model performs quite well. Since the Durbin–Watson h-statistic falls in the area of indeterminacy, however, we reestimated the model using the Beach–Makinnon maximum-likelihood method for auto-correlated data. These results, shown in Table 14.2, are almost identical to the OLS estimates. Income is not significant in either level or first differences. The price of child-specific goods is significant in level, but not in first differences. Mortality is significant in level, and in first differences lagged by one

Table 14.1 OLS estimate of model

Variable	Coefficient	Standard error	Mean of X
Constant	−0.180202	0.5672	
Fertility (−1)	−0.551054	0.1506	3.44346
Change in fertility (−1)	0.045282	0.1815	−0.01448
Change in fertility (−2)	0.201248	0.1987	−0.01383
Income (−1)	0.115609	0.1916	0.82777
Change in income (−1)	−0.047507	0.1462	0.00605
Change in income (−2)	0.108483	0.06087	45.45243
Price (−1)	0.241708	0.1291	5.02639
Change in price (−1)	−0.086334	0.0925	−0.01859
Change in price (−2)	−0.108104	0.0606	45.63034
Mortality (−1)	0.192531	0.06712	3.9004
Change in mortality (−1)	−0.131691	0.1099	−0.05463
Change in mortality (−2)	−0.011153	0.07866	−0.05107

Notes: All variables are in logs. Dependent variable is change in fertility. Number of observations = 22; mean dependent variable = −0.0126; h statistic (lagged y) = 0.7973; estimated autocorrelation = 0.8924; R squared = 0.81732; adjusted R-squared = 0.57376; F (12 9) = 3.3556; probability value for F = 0.03864; Akaike information = −6.8773; Amemiya prediction = 0.00123

Table 14.2 Beach–Mackinnon maximum likehood estimates

Variable	Coefficient	Standard error	Mean of X
Constant	0.219989	0.6034	
Fertility (−1)	−0.585617	0.163	3.44346
Change in fertility (−1)	−0.00323017	0.174	−0.01448
Change in fertility (−2)	0.37049	0.1561	−0.01383
Income (−1)	0.081595	0.2294	0.82777
Change in income (−1)	−0.084451	0.0554	0.00605
Change in income (−2)	0.0952353	0.1229	45.45243
Price (−1)	0.167765	0.08694	5.02639
Change in price (−1)	−0.0697404	0.05514	−0.01859
Change in price (−2)	−0.0949486	0.07967	45.63034
Mortality (−1)	0.22546	0.1018	3.9004
Change in mortality (−1)	−0.0800986	0.06774	−0.05463
Change in mortality (−2)	0.0653794	0.07866	−0.05107

Notes: All variables are in logs. Dependent variable is change in fertility. Number of observations = 22; mean dependent variable = −0.0126; Durbin–Watson measure = 0.7133

year. Not surprisingly, since it picks up the effects of accidental events such as epidemics, as well as of the realizations of past parental and government policy decisions, aggregate child mortality affects both the long-term trend and the short-term dynamics of birth decisions. The price of child-specific goods, on the other hand, appears to affect only the long-term trend – suggesting that household spending patterns are insensitive to temporary fluctuations in relative prices.

The estimated long-term effect of the price variable is positive, with an elasticity of nearly 0.5; mortality is also positive, with an elasticity of about 0.3 (the positive fertility–mortality association thus survives even after controlling for income and price). The first of these findings rejects the hypothesis that parents take the probability of survival of their own children as independent of their own actions. The second reinforces this conclusion, and adds the information that death-reducing public intervention is likely to be complementary, rather than a substitute for the amount of food, medical care and so on provided by parents to each of their children.

4 Conclusion

Our finding that decisions on births are affected positively by the price of child-specific goods, and negatively by the observed child survival rate, is consistent with the theoretical predictions of a model in which parents are aware that the survival probability of their own childen is positively conditioned by how much food and medical care is bought for each child. Under rather weak conditions, the second of these findings can be taken as evidence that public and private mortality-reducing expenditures are complementary rather than substitutes.

In the light of the model in question, our empirical results have two important policy implications. One is that mortality-reducing public action, such as expenditure on sanitation or preventative medicine, is likely to induce parents to reduce the number of children born to each family, but induce greater expenditure on each of their own children. Induced private action thus reinforces the direct death-preventing effect of public action. No such reinforcement would take place if the survival probability of children were seen by parents as totally exogenous, or if public intervention were considered a substitute for private action. Another policy implication is that price subsidies on items which enter into the cost of raising a child have a positive effect on child survival probability and a negative one on fertility, and may thus be seen as alternative to, or additional to direct death-preventing public expenditure.[6]

Notes

1 If we think of the life-cycle of each individual as consisting of three periods, childhood, middle age (the active period when decisions, including fertility decisions, are taken) and old age, we can interpret $u(a)$ as the decision-maker's direct utility from middle-age consumption, and $v(n)$ as the utility in old age, given that n of the children survived to middle age, where today's middle-aged are interested in their children surviving to the next period because they expect some transfer T from each of them, as discussed in Cigno (1993), then $v(n) \equiv z(Y + Tn)$, where Y is old-age income, and $z(.)$ the old-age period utility function. However, if parents derive direct utility from having children, as in Becker's models, then $v(n) \equiv z(Y, n)$. Which is the case makes no difference to the arguments here.

2 Representing the effect of a rise in the expected number of survivors (out of any given number of births) on the expected marginal utility of an extra birth, g_{bs} is the sum of two partial effects. The first, positive, is the increase in the number of survivors, holding their marginal utility constant. The second, negative, is the decrease in the marginal utility of survivors, holding their number constant. The curvature of $v(.)$ would have to be very pronounced indeed (parents would have to be extremely risk-averse), or n be very 'lumpy' (if the couple had only one grown-up child, for example, an extra suvivor would represent a 100 per cent increase), for the latter, a second-order effect, to dominate over the former. Cigno (1998) tabulates g_{bs} for the case in which $f(n,.)$ is gamma-shaped, and parents display constant relative risk-aversion. For plausible parameter values, g_{bs} is positive (and decreasing in s).

3 That would be true even if parents believed (against the evidence) that children survive to adulthood with probability one ($n = b$). If that were the case, the model would reduce to the one originally formulated by Becker, where parents deterministically choose the quantity (number) and quality (consumption) of children. In that model, an increase in the price of an item entering into the cost of raising a child may raise the quality, but never the quantity of children (Becker and Lewis, 1973).

4 The effect of s on q is given by

$$(\partial q/\partial s) = [\gamma_{bb} - bq^4 r)qg_{qs} + bpg_{bs}K](u'/bH)$$

clearly positive if g_{qs} is negative.

5 Results available on request from the second author.

6 That is consistent with the finding of Rosenzweig and Wolpin (1982), based on Indian household survey data, that subsidizing items of parental expenditure such as schooling or medical care would discourage fertility and encourage expenditure per child, and that such a policy could be a useful adjunct of direct death-reducing forms of public intervention such as the improvement of water sources.

References

Becker, G. S. and H. G. Lewis (1973) 'On the Interaction between the Quantity and Quality of Children', *Journal of Political Economy*, vol. 81, pp. 279–88.

Chowdhury, A. R. (1988) 'The Infant Mortality–Fertility Debate: Some International Evidence', *Southern Economic Journal*, vol. 33, pp. 666–74.

Cigno, A. (1993) 'Intergenerational Transfers Without Altruism: Family, Market and State', *European Journal of Political Economy*, vol. 9, pp. 505–18.

Cigno, A. (1998) 'Fertility Decisions when Infant Survival is Endogenous', *Journal of Population Economics*, vol. 11, pp. 21–8.

Cochrane, S. H. and K.C. Zachariah (1983) 'Infant and Child Mortality as a Determinant of Fertility', World Bank Staff Working Papers no. 556.

Rosenzweig, M. R. and K. I. Wolpin (1982) 'Governmental Interventions and Household Behavior in a Developing Country', *Journal of Development Economics*, vol. 10, pp. 209–25.

15
Child Labour in Peru: An Empirical Analysis and its Modelling implications

*Ranjan Ray**

1 Introduction

There has been growing interest in the subject of child labour among academics, professionals and the media. Notwithstanding almost universal agreement that child labour is undesirable, there is wide disagreement on how to tackle this problem. The formulation of policies that are effective in curbing child labour requires an analysis of its key determinants, and such an analysis of Peruvian child labour is the motivation of the present study. There has been, in recent years, a rapidly expanding literature on child labour – see Grootaert and Kanbur (1995), Basu (1999) for surveys. While certain studies, for example Knight (1980) and Horn (1995), mainly discussed the qualitative features of child labour, the recent literature has focused attention on the quantitative aspects taking advantage, as in Patrinos and Psacharopoulos (1997), of the increasing availability of good quality data on child employment. The present study is in line with this recent literature. Keeping in mind the close connection between education and employment, we prepared regression estimates of child participation in schooling and in the labour market, paying special attention to the interaction between the two. Our study also included tobit estimates of child labour hours in Peru regressed on a selection of personal, family and community characteristics, and compares them with those of Ghanaian child labour hours.[1]

This study has the following features:

---

* I am grateful to the seminar participants, especially Bina Agarwal, Kaushik Basu and Subrata Ghatak, for useful remarks, and to Adrian Breen and Geoffrey Lancaster for their research assistance. This research was supported by a grant from the Australian Research Council.

1   We seek to answer, using Peruvian data, the question of whether poverty is the key determinant of child labour, as is widely believed. Such a view underlines, for example, the 'luxury axiom' of Basu and Van (1998, p. 416) and reflects the belief that, in developing economies and in the absence of a satisfactory credit market, households, especially in rural areas, react to temporary income shortfalls by increasing their dependence on child-labour earnings. The present study proposes to test this association, applying it to Peruvian data. The empirical exercise also investigates the link, if any, between household poverty and child schooling.

2   Special attention is paid in our empirical investigation to the interaction between the adult and child labour markets. Unlike the analytical literature on child labour (see Basu and Van, 1998; Bardhan and Udry, 1999), we distinguish between adult male and adult female wages in studying their impact on child labour. A key empirical result, discussed later, is that the nature of interaction between adult male and child labour markets is different from that between adult female and child labour markets.

3   This study also contains an analysis of the determinants of wages paid to child labour in Peru, using detailed household records in Peru to construct the child wage data required for the analysis.

The rest of the chapter is organized as follows. Section 2 describes the data-set. Section 3 is divided into three subsections that (a) report and discuss the probit regression estimates of child participation in the labour market and in schooling; (b) analyse the determinants of child wages; and (c) present and compare the tobit regression estimates of Peruvian and Ghanian child-labour hours. Section 4 discusses the analytical implication of these results by distinguishing between adult male and adult female effects in a model of child labour. Section 5 summarizes the principal findings, discusses the possible implications and suggests directions for further research.

2 Data-set and its principal features

The child labour data for this study came from the Peru Living Standards Measurement Survey (PLSS) (1994). This survey was conducted as part of the Living Standards Measurement Study (LSMS)[2] households surveys in a number of developing countries. The PLSS covered 3,623 households containing information on child labour and child schooling of 5,231 children aged 6–17 years. Child labour refers to

Table 15.1   Participation rates of Peruvian children in employment and in schooling (%)

Age	Employment			Schooling		
	Boys	*Girls*	*Overall*	*Boys*	*Girls*	*Overall*
6	7.9	11.6	9.6	90.5	89.3	89.9
7	12.9	11.8	12.4	93.1	94.6	93.8
8	17.6	11.6	14.3	95.5	95.9	95.7
9	18.5	17.1	17.8	98.1	99.5	98.8
10	29.4	22.1	25.8	97.2	97.1	97.2
11	31.8	21.7	27.0	98.3	96.7	97.5
12	37.7	27.0	32.2	95.5	94.8	95.1
13	32.0	27.3	29.5	96.1	88.1	91.9
14	48.7	32.4	40.6	89.3	90.1	89.7
15	51.8	32.7	42.2	88.2	83.2	85.7
16	46.1	34.9	40.4	82.7	74.4	78.5
17	57.1	27.9	42.6	63.9	58.7	61.3
Total	31.8	22.7	27.3	90.9	89.0	90.0

Source: PLSS (1994)

children in full-time paid employment. Note that although on the International Labour Organization (ILO)-based definition a working child aged 15 years or over does not constitute child labour, we follow conventional practice in extending the age limit to 17 years in order to better capture the interaction between child schooling and child labour.

Table 15.1 presents the age-specific participation rates of Peruvian children in the labour market and in schooling. The following remarks apply. First, the child participation rate in the labour market increases with child age. In the case of child schooling, the participation rate peaks around 9 years, and then falls. Second, the gender imbalance in child employment with boys registering higher participation rates, contrasts with a more even gender balance in child schooling. Third, the labour-force participation rates of Peruvian children are sharply higher than the figure of 11 per cent reported by ILO (1996) for Latin America. Fourth, the figures suggest that in the age group 10–14 years, Peruvian children tend to combine schooling with employment.

The construction of child wage data involved the combination of income and work information from a number of sources. The wage figures relate only to children involved in labour pursuits outside the home, and receiving cash payments for their labour. The Peruvian sample provided wage information on 274 working children.

3 Econometric estimates

The probit estimates of child participation

Table 15.2. presents estimates of the coefficients in the probit regression[3] of the child labour participation rate on its various determinants. Child age exhibits nonlinearity in its effect on child employment via significance of the 'age-square' coefficient. Consistent with the results of previous studies, we find that an increase in female education reduces the likelihood of children entering the labour market.

The estimated regression coefficient of the expenditure variable suggests some support for the 'luxury axiom', which implies an inverse relationship between the household's economic circumstances and the likelihood of its children entering the labour market. However, the insignificance of the estimated coefficient of the 'poverty' variable is inconsistent with this axiom. The poverty line was set at 50 per cent of the sample median expenditure.

A rise in the adult male wage exerts a significantly negative impact on a household's propensity to put its children into employment. The insignificance of the female wage coefficient shows that this is not the case with respect to adult female labour. This confirms that the nature of interaction between child labour and adult male labour is quite different from that between child and adult female labour. Of the remaining determinants, the community variables are of particular interest. Improved sewerage disposal reduces the likelihood of child labour, though somewhat paradoxically a worsening water storage system also reduces child labour.

We also calculated the coefficient estimates in the Probit regression of child schooling participation. The gender-coefficient estimate showed that a gender differential exists in favour of boys' schooling. Improving adult female education in the household leads to increased probability of schooling for its children. Family size and composition do not have much of an impact on child schooling. The insignificance of the poverty and expenditure variables suggest that a household's economic circumstance has little impact on the child's schooling enrolment.

Determinants of child wages

Next we examined the key determinants of wages paid to child labour using the 2-step procedure developed by Heckman (1979) to correct for 'sample selectivity'. The negative estimate of the coefficient of the 'child-gender' variable suggests gender bias against working girls in the wage

Table 15.2 Probit regression estimates[a] of child labour participation[b] equation in Peru

Variable	Coefficient estimate[c]
Constant	−254.45[e]
	(35.38)
Child characteristics	
Age of child	39.92[e]
	(5.57)
(Age of child)^2	−1.06[e]
	(.23)
Child gender	−41.29[e]
(0 = boy; 1 = girl)	(4.41)
Years of schooling	15.76[e]
	(4.45)
Currently enrolled in school	−30.61[e]
(0 = no, 1 = yes)	(7.59)
Ability to write (0 = no, 1 = yes)	−28.72[e]
	(7.81)
Family characteristics	
Poverty status (1 = below poverty line; 0 = above)	.026
	(6.96)
Expenditure per equivalent adult	−.0053[e]
	(.0017)
Region of residence (1 = urban, 0 = rural)	−95.77[e]
	(6.26)
No. of children	2.78[d]
	(1.32)
No. of adults	−5.50[e]
	(1.90)
Gender of household head	2.39
(0 = male, 1 = female)	(7.22)
Age of household head	−.072
	(.223)
Maximum female education	−9.92[e]
	(2.26)
Maximum male wage	−.684[e]
	(.139)
Maximum female wage	.259
	(.388)
(Maximum female wage)^2	.001
	(.006)

Table 15.2   Probit regression estimates[a] of child labour participation[b] equation in Peru – Continued

Variable	Coefficient estimate[c]
Community characteristics	
Water storage (1 = best, 6 = worst)	−3.46[e]
	(1.38)
Disposal of sewerage (1 = best, 6 worst)	10.32[e]
	(1.59)
Electricity (1 = yes, 0 = no)	−.528
	(3.55)
Quality of water supply (1 = good, 0 = contaminated)	−2.91
	(4.48)
Cragg–Uhler R^2	.417
Log likelihood	−2176.3
χ^2_{21}	1776.48

Notes: [a] Standard errors in brackets;   [b] The dependent variable takes the value 0 if the child does not work and 1 if the child does work;   [c] All the coefficient estimates and their standard errors have been multiplied by 100;   [d] Significant at 5 per cent level;   [e] Significant at 1 per cent level
Source: Author's calculations

payment for their labour. Neither the child's school enrolment status nor the community variables have any significant impact on child wages.

The tobit regression estimates of child labour hours: comparison of Peru and Ghana

Let us now move from child labour-force participation rates to the labour hours spent by children in full-time, economically gainful activities. To put the Peruvian results in a wider perspective, we compared the Peruvian estimates with those of Ghanaian child labour. The data on the labour hours of Ghanaian children came from the Ghana Living Standards Measurement Surveys (GLSS) in 1988–89.[4]

Taking the comparable child characteristics, at sample mean, between Ghana and Peru, we noted first that a typical Peruvian household contains more children than the Ghanian family. However, the percentage rate of Peruvian child labour-force participation is no higher than the Ghanaian figure. Second, Peru's record on child schooling is superior to Ghana's. Third, in relation to the adult, the child works similar hours in both countries.

Next we prepared estimates of the selectivity-corrected tobit regressions of boys' and girls' labour hours, respectively, in Ghana and Peru on the various determinants. The following features are worth noting:

264 Labour and Income Distribution

1 Both countries agree that, regardless of gender, the poverty
coefficient is insignificant, thereby providing (somewhat surprisingly) little support for the hypothesis that household poverty is a
significant determinant of child labour.

2 In both countries, older children work longer hours than younger
children. However, in Ghana, but not in Peru, the significance of
the negative coefficient estimate of the squared age variable suggests
that the positive effect of age on Ghanaian child labour hours
weakens in the later age categories.

3 Both countries agree that rising education levels of parents contribute significantly to the reduction of child labour. Both countries,
also, agree on the general responsiveness of child labour hours to a
deteriorating community infrastructure, though the effects are not
always in the expected direction.

4 The results confirm that child labour hours respond positively to
child wage in both countries. The nature of responsiveness of child
labour hours to adult wages is dependent on the gender of the child
and of the adult. The two countries differ on the magnitude and
direction of such responsiveness.

4 Some analytical implications

One of the main empirical results of this study is the differential
response of child labour participation rates to male and female wage
changes. To model this behaviour, we took a variant of the Basu and
Van (1998) utility function as follows:

$$U = (c - s)(1 - e + \delta) \tag{1}$$

where c is the household's total consumption, $e\varepsilon$ [0,1] is the child's
labour supply (or effort), so that $(1 - e)$ is the child's leisure, and s,
$\delta > 0$ are parameters. While s may be thought of as 'subsistence consumption', $\delta(> 0)$ ensures a positive marginal utility of consumption of
the household whether or not the child works, that is for $e = 1$ and 0.

The household's budget constraint is now given by:

$$c \leq ew_c + d(e)w_f + w_m \tag{2}$$

where w_c, w_f and w_m are child, female and male wages, respectively,
and $d(e)$ is a dummy variable which takes a value of 1 if $e = 1$, that is if
the child works, 0 otherwise.

The household's problem is to maximize U subject to equation (2). Note now that if the household chooses *not* to let its child work, that is $e = 0$, then $U = (w_m - s)(1 + \delta)$ since neither the mother nor the child will work. Alternatively, if $e = 1$, then $U = (w_c + w_f + w_m - s)\delta$. Hence, the child will be sent to work if:

$$(w_c + w_f + w_m - s)\delta \geq (w_m - s)(1 + \delta)$$
$$\text{or } (w_c + w_f)\delta \geq w_m - s \tag{3}$$

Hence, as the female wage w_f increases, the child increases her labour supply[5] since equation (3) is more likely to hold. Alternatively, as w_m increases, the child is less likely to work, as the Peruvian evidence presented earlier, and also Ray (2000a), suggests.

Let us now turn to the objective function itself. We consider the following CES generalization of the Stone–Geary utility function used by Basu and Van (1998, equation 13).

$$U(c_m, c_f, c_c, e_m, e_f, e_c)$$
$$= \left[\sum_{k=1}^{3} \beta_k^1 (c_k - s_k)^{\rho_c} \right]^{1/\rho_c} + \left[\sum_{k=1}^{3} \beta_k^2 (T_k - t_k - e_k)^{\rho_c} \right]^{1/\rho_c} \tag{4}$$

where c_k, s_k, T_k and t_k are, respectively, actual consumption, subsistence consumption, maximum time available, minimum time required for leisure and non-labour activities, and e_k denotes labour hours for the male, female and the child ($k = m, f, c$).

The corresponding household budget constraint is given by:

$$p_m c_m + p_f c_f + p_c c_c = w_m e_m + w_f e_f + w_c e_c \tag{5}$$

where p_k is the unit price of consumption of household member $k(= m, f, c)$ and w_k is the corresponding wage rate. Maximizing equation (4) with respect to $\{c_k, e_k\}$ subject to equation (5) yields, on rearranging, the following consumption and earnings equations:

$$p_i c_i = p_i s_i + \phi_i^1 \left(X - \sum_k p_k s_k \right) \tag{6}$$
$$i = m, f, c$$
$$w_i e_i = w_i T_i - w_i t_i - \phi_i^2 \left(\sum_k w_k T_k - \sum_k w_k t_k - X \right) \tag{7}$$

where

$$\phi_i^1 = \frac{\beta_i^1 (c_i - s_i)^{\rho_e}}{\sum_k \beta_k^1 (c_k - s_k)^{\rho_e}}$$

$$\phi_i^2 = \frac{\beta_i^2 (T_i - t_i - e_i)^{\rho_e}}{\sum_k \beta_k^2 (T_k - t_k - e_k)^{\rho_e}}$$

$X = \Sigma w_i e_i = \Sigma p_i c_i$ (that is, we assume that the household consumes its entire earnings)

Let us now define $\delta_i = \frac{p_i c_i}{w_i e_i}$, namely, the ratio of consumption to earnings by household member i. Hence, $\delta_i > 1$ implies a net resource transfer to i, and $\delta_i < 1$, a corresponding resource outflow from i. In case of the child, it is easily verified that $\delta_c \gtrless 1$ according as:

$$(p_c s_c - \phi_c^1 S) \gtrless (w_c T_c^* - \phi_c^2 T^*) + (\phi_c^2 - \phi_c^1)X \qquad (8)$$

where $T_k^* = T_k - t_k, T^* = \sum_k w_k T_k^*$, and $S = \sum p_i s_i$ is the aggregate subsistence consumption in the household. Equation (8), in turn, implies that if $\phi_c^2 \approx 0$, and $S \approx X$, then $\delta_c \gtrless 1$ according as $p_c s_c \gtrless w_e T_c^*$. Since the left-hand side of this last inequality (that is, the child's subsistence consumption) will almost certainly be less than the right-hand side (that is, the maximum earnings that the child can bring), $\delta_c < 1$ in this case. This leads us to the following proposition.

Proposition If the child labour supply is inelastic with respect to aggregate household income, then in a poor household living around the subsistence level of consumption, child labour is 'exploitative' in the sense that the child's earnings exceed her/his consumption; that is, it leads to a net resource outflow from the child.

The above discussion also suggests the following:
1 Because of the appearance of X on the right-hand side of equation (8), the nature of the inequality would change over the expenditure distribution. In other words, as X increases, child labour will at some point cease to be 'exploitative' in the above sense.

2 Equation (8) can be rearranged to yield the following: $\delta_c \gtrless 1$ according to:

$$X \gtrless \frac{(w_c T_c^* - p_c s_c) + (\phi_c^1 S - \phi_c^2 T^*)}{(\phi_c^1 - \phi_c^2)} \tag{9}$$

and equation (9) yields the following cut-off point for aggregate household expenditure when the resource flow from the child changes direction.

$$\begin{aligned}
X &= \frac{(w_c T_c^* - p_c s_c) + (\phi_c^1 S - \phi_c^2 T^*)}{(\phi_c^1 - \phi_c^2)} \\
&= \frac{(1 - \phi_c^2) w_c T_c^* - p_c s_c + \left(\phi_c^1 S - \phi_c^2 w_m T_m^* - \phi_c^* w_f T_f^*\right)}{(\phi_c^1 - \phi_c^2)}
\end{aligned} \tag{10}$$

Equation (10) suggests that by providing better schools, recreational facilities and/or improved child care, the authorities increase t_c, namely the minimum non-labour time required by the child, thus lowering T_c^* and, hence, reducing the cut-off point at which child labour ceases to be 'exploitative' in the sense discussed above.

5 Conclusions

This chapter has investigated the determinants of the participation rates of Peruvian children in the labour market and in schooling. We have investigated the hypothesis of a direct link between household poverty and child labour, namely that households below the poverty line are more likely to put their children into employment compared to those above the poverty line. The Peruvian evidence does not provide much support for this hypothesis although, elsewhere, using Pakistani data, we found considerable support for this idea. The absence of a strong link between household poverty and child labour is also seen in the tobit regression of child-labour hours in Peru and Ghana on a variety of child, family and community characteristics. Neither country finds the estimated poverty coefficient significant, where poverty is defined over non-child adult income. It is common in the development literature to view child-labour earnings as providing the necessary cushion for households to absorb temporary income shortfalls. In failing to find strong evidence of any link between household poverty and child labour, the Peruvian and Ghanaian results suggest that this view need not be universally valid. The Peruvian data also suggest that children, especially in the older age categories, combine schooling with employment to a much greater extent than in many other countries. The results of this study also show that the interaction between adult male and child labour is qualitatively quite different from that between adult female and child labour.

This study could usefully be extended by jointly estimating child participation in employment and in schooling using a proper simultaneous equations framework. Such an extension, besides recognizing the simultaneity in decisions on child labour and child schooling, ought to treat the poverty variable as 'endogenous', since the household's economic circumstance is itself dependent on the household's decision to send its children to the labour market.

Notes

1   Full details of our calculations are available from the author.
2   See Grosh and Glewwe (1995) for an overview and general description of the LSMS data-sets.
3   See Ray (2000a) for the corresponding coefficient estimates based on logit regression.
4   See Ray (2000c) for more details on the Ghanaian data and results.
5   This is suggested by the Pakistani evidence in Ray (2000b).

References

Bardhan, P. and C. Udry (1999) *Development Microeconomics* (Oxford: Oxford University Press).
Basu, K. (1999) 'Child Labour: Cause, Consequence and Cure with Remarks on International Labour Standards', *Journal of Economic Literature*, vol. 37, no. 3, pp. 1083–119.
Basu, K. and P. H. Van (1998) 'The Economics of Child Labour', *American Economic Review*, vol. 88, no. 3, pp. 412–27.
Grootaert, C. and R. Kanbur (1995) 'Child Labour: An Economic Perspective', *International Labour Review*, vol. 134, no. 2, pp. 187–203.
Grosh, M. and P. Glewwe (1995) 'A Guide to Living Standards Measurement Surveys and their Data Sets', LSMS working paper no. 120, World Bank, Washington, DC.
Heckman, J. (1979) 'Sample Selection Bias as a Specification Error', *Econometrica*, vol. 47, no. 1, pp. 153–61.
Horn, P. (1995) *Children's Work and Welfare, 1780–1890* (Cambridge: Cambridge University Press).
ILO (1996) *Economically Active Populations: Estimates and Projections, 1950–2010*, (Geneva: International Labour Organization).
Knight, W. J. (1980) *The World's Exploited Children: Growing Up Sadly*, US Department of Labour, Bureau of International Labour Affairs, monograph no. 4, Washington DC.

Patrinos, H. A. and G. Psacharopoulos (1997) 'Family Size, Schooling and Child Labour in Peru: An Empirical Analysis', *Journal of Population Economics*, vol. 10, no. 4, pp. 387–406.

Ray, R. (2000a) 'Analysis of Child Labour in Peru and Pakistan: A Comparative Study', *Journal of Population Economics*, vol. 13, pp. 3–19.

Ray, R. (2000b) 'Child Labour, Child Schooling and their Interaction with Adult Labour', *World Bank Economic Review*, vol. 14, no. 2, pp. 347–67.

Ray, R. (2000c) 'The Determinants of Child Labour and Child Schooling in Ghana', University of Tasmania, March (mimeo).